MODERN
SOUTH AFRICA

OTHER TITLES IN THE COMPARATIVE SOCIETIES SERIES

MODERN SOUTH AFRICA

A Volume in the Comparative Societies Series

PHILLIP T. GAY

San Diego State University—San Diego

Boston   Burr Ridge, IL   Dubuque, IA   Madison, WI   New York
San Francisco   St. Louis   Bangkok   Bogotá   Caracas   Kuala Lumpur
Lisbon   London   Madrid   Mexico City   Milan   Montreal   New Delhi
Santiago   Seoul   Singapore   Sydney   Taipei   Toronto

McGraw-Hill Higher Education

A Division of The **McGraw-Hill** Companies

MODERN SOUTH AFRICA

Published by McGraw-Hill, an imprint of The McGraw-Hill Companies, Inc., 1221 Avenue of the Americas, New York, NY, 10020. Copyright © 2001, by The McGraw-Hill Companies, Inc. All rights reserved. No part of this publication may be reproduced or distributed in any form or by any means, or stored in a data base or retrieval system, without the prior written consent of The McGraw-Hill Companies, Inc., including, but not limited to, in any network or other electronic storage or transmission, or broadcast for distance learning.

Some ancillaries, including electronic and print components, may not be available to customers outside the United States. This book is printed on acid-free paper.

1 2 3 4 5 6 7 8 9 0 DOC/DOC 0 9 8 7 6 5 4 3 2 1

ISBN 0-07-235211-6

Publisher: *Phillip A. Butcher*
Sponsoring editor: *Sally Constable*
Editorial assistant: *Alyson DeMonte*
Project manager: *Anna M. Chan*
Production supervisor: *Debra R. Sylvester*
Designer: *Artemio Ortiz*
Compositor: *Shepherd Incorporated*
Typeface: *10/12 Palatino*
Printer: *R. R. Donnelley & Sons Company*

Library of Congress Cataloging-in-Publication Data

Gay, Phillip T.
    Modern South Africa / Phillip T. Gay.
       p. cm.—(Comparative societies series)
      ISBN 0-07-235211-6 (softcover : alk. paper)
      1. South Africa—Social conditions—1994- 2. South Africa. I. Title. II. Series.

HN801.A8 G39 2001
306'.0968—dc21

00-064740

www.mhhe.com

In one of the early scenes of the movie *Reds*, the U.S. revolutionary journalist John Reed, just back from covering the beginning of World War I, is asked by a roomful of business leaders, "What is this War really about?" John Reed stands and stops all conversation with a one-word reply—"profits." Today, war between major industrial nations would disrupt profits much more than create money for a military industrial complex. Highly integrated global markets and infrastructures support the daily life of suburban families in Chicago and urban squatter settlements in Bombay. These ties produce a social and economic ecology that transcends political and cultural boundaries.

The world is a very different place than it was for our parents and grandparents. Those rare epic events of world war certainly invaded their everyday lives and futures, but we now find that daily events thousands of miles away, in countries large and small, have a greater impact on North Americans than ever before, with the speed of this impact multiplied many times in recent decades. Our standard of living, jobs, and even prospects of living in a healthy environment have never before been so dependent on outside forces.

Yet there is much evidence that North Americans have less easy access to good information about the outside world than even a few years ago. Since the end of the Cold War, newspaper and television coverage of events in other countries has dropped dramatically. It is difficult to put much blame on the mass media, however: International news seldom sells any more. There is simply less interest.

It is not surprising, then, that Americans know comparatively little about the outside world. A recent *Los Angeles Times* survey provides a good example: People in eight countries were asked five basic questions about current events of the day. Americans were dead last in their knowledge, trailing people from Canada, Mexico, England, France, Spain, Germany, and Italy.* It is also not surprising that the annual report published by the Swiss World Economic Forum always ranks American executives quite low in their international experience and understanding.

Such ignorance harms American competitiveness in the world economy in many ways. But there is much more. Seymour Martin Lipset put it nicely in one of his recent books: "Those who know only one country know no country" (Lipset 1996: 17). Considerable time spent in a foreign

---

*For example, whereas only 3 percent of Germans missed all five questions, 37 percent of the Americans did (*Los Angeles Times*, March 16, 1994).

country is one of the best stimulants for a sociological imagination: Studying or doing research in other countries makes us realize how much we really, in fact, have learned about our own society in the process. Seeing other social arrangements, ways of doing things, and foreign perspectives allows for far greater insight into the familiar, our own society. This is also to say that ignorance limits solutions to many of our own serious social problems. How many Americans, for example, are aware that levels of poverty are much lower in all other advanced nations and that the workable government services in those countries keep poverty low? Likewise, how many Americans are aware of alternative means of providing health care and quality education or reducing crime?

We can take heart in the fact that sociology in the United States has become more comparative in recent decades. A comparative approach, of course, was at the heart of classical European sociology during the 1800s. But as sociology was transported from Europe to the United States early in the 20th century, it lost much of this comparative focus. In recent years, sociology journals have published more comparative research. There are large data sets with samples from many countries around the world in research seeking general laws on issues such as the causes of social mobility or political violence, all very much in the tradition of Durkheim. But we also need much more of the old Max Weber. His was a qualitative historical and comparative perspective (Smelser 1976; Ragin and Zaret 1983). Weber's methodology provides a richer understanding of other societies, a greater recognition of the complexity of social, cultural, and historical forces shaping each society. Ahead of his time in many ways, C. Wright Mills was planning a qualitative comparative sociology of world regions just before his death in 1961 (Horowitz 1983: 324). [Too few American sociologists have yet to follow in his footsteps.]

Following these trends, sociology textbooks in the United States have also become more comparative in content in recent years. And while this tendency must be applauded, it is not enough. Typically, there is an example from Japan here, another from Germany there, and so on, haphazardly for a few countries in different subject areas as the writer's knowledge of these bits and pieces allows. What we need are the textbook equivalents of a richer Weberian comparative analysis, a qualitative comparative analysis of the social, cultural, and historical forces that have combined to make relatively unique societies around the world. It is this type of comparative material that can best help people in the United States overcome their lack of understanding about other countries and allow them to see their own society with much greater insight.

The Comparative Societies Series, of which this book is a part, has been designed as a small step in filling this need. We have currently selected 12 countries on which to focus: Japan, Thailand, Switzerland, Mexico, Eritrea, Hungary, Germany, China, India, Iran, Brazil, and Russia. We selected these countries as representatives of major world regions and cultures, and each will be examined in separate books written by talented sociologists. All of these basic sociological issues and topics will be covered: Each book will begin with a look at the important historical and geographical forces shaping the society, then turn to basic aspects of social organization and culture. From there each book will proceed to examine the political and economic institutions of the specific country, along with the social stratification, the family, religion, education, and finally urbanization, demography, social problems, and social change.

Although each volume in the Comparative Societies Series is of necessity brief to allow for use as supplementary readings in standard sociology courses, we have tried to assure that this brief coverage provides students with sufficient information to better understand each society, as well as their own. The ideal would be to transport every student to another country for a period of observation and learning. Realizing the unfortunate impracticality of this ideal, we hope to do the next best thing—to at least mentally move these students to a country very different from their own, provide something of the everyday reality of the people in these other countries, and demonstrate how the tools of sociological analysis can help them see these societies as well as their own with much greater understanding.

Harold R. Kerbo
San Luis Obispo, CA
June 1997

South Africa has long been a world supplier of fine wines, glittering gold, sparkling diamonds, and world-class golfers, surfers, and tennis and rugby players.

But until the 1990s, South Africa was most widely known as the land of Apartheid—its violently imposed, violently sustained system of racial inequalities that reduced Nonwhites to the status of noncitizens rather than merely second-class citizens, of the lands of their and and their ancestors' birth. Apartheid was especially onerous in that not only did it deprive Blacks of all the basic citizenship rights enjoyed by white South Africans, it also stripped Blacks of any basic human right that any White was obliged to respect.

Then, after decades of both violent and nonviolent opposition to the Apartheid state, things changed. The laws of Apartheid were finally no more. People of all races could vote. People of all races could hold elected offices. All the "Whites Only" signs came down. All professions, occupations, schools, beaches, hotels, motels, theaters, parks, restaurants, towns, neighborhoods—everything was now legally open to persons of all races.

The Republic of South Africa gives official recognition to four races, or **population groups:**

- **Africans**—sometimes referred to as Blacks, and much less often Natives—are South Africa's largest group, constituting approximately 77 percent of the country's current population of nearly 45 million.

- **Whites,** who constitute somewhere between 10 and 12 percent of the country's current population, are its second largest population group.

- **Coloureds**—persons of mixed racial ancestry—constitute approximately 9 percent of South Africa's current population and are its third largest group.

- **Asians** constitute approximately 3 percent of South Africa's population in the early twenty-first century.

Approximately 60 percent of South Africa's current white population call Afrikaans (a Dutch derivative) their native language. The remaining 40 percent of the white population live in homes where the primary spoken language is English. Afrikaans is also spoken by the majority (80–90 percent) of the country's officially designated Coloureds. Most black Africans speak English and, to varying degrees, a tribal language. In all, the Republic of South Africa has 11 official languages and scores of officially recognized black African tribal groups.

Though about two-thirds of its approximately 45 million citizens profess to be Christians of one sort or another, within the South African population are also significant numbers of Muslims (1.1 percent), Hindus (1.3 percent), Jews (1 percent), and adherents to a plethora of indigenous African religious beliefs (30 percent).

On April 27, 1994, the political party that gave the world Apartheid was voted out of power and replaced by a multiracial party pledged to end all vestiges of Apartheid. To make South Africa a "rainbow nation" where people of all races lived together in peace, harmony, social and political equality, and economic prosperity was the oft-stated goal of the new governing party.

The 1994 elections brought about real, concrete, substantive, revolutionary changes. Persons who just a few years ago had been in prison, in exile, under "banning orders," or otherwise prevented from engaging in political activities were suddenly the country's top political leaders. In some cases people shared power with, or directly exercised it over, some of the same state, military, police, and intelligence agency officials responsible for their decades of imprisonment, exile, or banishment.

"A miracle," some people called the new situation. Blacks in power didn't line up former Apartheid state officials against a wall and shoot them. There were no expropriations of white wealth and properties. The majority of South African Whites seemed committed to remaining in South Africa, hoping that racial peace, harmony, and equity, in concert with economic prosperity, were possible in a society in which primarily Blacks hold political power. Maybe life really would be better, or at least no worse for anyone, than before, most South Africans hoped. Maybe white South Africans had finally done something of which they could be exceedingly proud. Maybe the world had a lot to learn from South Africans. If racial peace, harmony, forgiveness, reconciliation, justice, equality, and all the rest can come to be in South Africa after Apartheid and all that went before, why can't it happen everywhere? it was asked (Gay 1997: 250).

That was then, the mid-1990s, in the immediate aftermath of South Africa's first multiracial elections. Now, during the 2000s, more and more people both inside and outside the country are beginning to see the Republic of South Africa as shaping up to be more of a big disappointment or a sad shame than a miracle. White, Black, Coloured, and Asian people didn't all suddenly come to love each other with the death of Apartheid and coming to power of a multiracial political party.

South Africa's official rates of both interpersonal and interracial crime and violence are now among the highest, if not the highest, in the world. There is widespread White, Coloured, and Asian disgruntlement over the government's affirmative action programs and taxation systems, which many see as being discriminatory against all Nonblacks.

There are Blacks who, having neither forgotten nor forgiven the inequities of the past, feel that all governmental policies and decisions should be implemented with the purpose of giving the advantage to Blacks. As an African country, their reasoning goes, South Africa should be ruled by and in the interests of indigenous black Africans. Not by and in the interests of descendants of Europeans, Coloureds, or Asians. Africa for Africans is their stated goal. Africa for *black* Africans, that is.

Growing numbers of Whites, on the other hand, have come to feel that South Africa has already become, and will forever remain, a country governed by and for black Africans, and only black Africans. Many are now seriously considering getting out of South Africa while they can, before their social, political, and economic situations worsen to the point of becoming similar to the life situations of Blacks before and during the years of Apartheid.

There also exists widespread dissatisfaction among the masses of unemployed, unskilled, undereducated South African Blacks still subsisting at the bottoms of the social, political, and economic hierarchies—many still without electricity, indoor plumbing, and the same educational opportunities available to growing numbers of other Blacks.

Having never wanted to be a part of any rainbow of colors, there are still Whites agitating for the creation—somehow, somewhere within the country's present territorial boundaries—of a separate, politically independent white homeland for themselves and their descendants.

Plus, as both cause and consequence of its present-day high rates of crime and violence and long history of violent interracial relationships, South Africa also has one of the highest rates of firearms possession by private citizens of any nation in the world. This itself could turn into a full-fledged political problem. Politically dissatisfied groups, as well as socially and economically frustrated individuals, with guns are more likely to engage in gun-violence against their perceived enemies than are those not in possession of guns. It only stands to reason. And since very few people in possession of guns are willing to surrender them, the South African government could soon be faced with more resistance than it can handle if it were to try to force them to do so.

Also, though South Africa's major political parties can all claim *some* support from persons of all races, there exists no political party in which the country's four population groups are even close to being proportionally represented. Political party affiliation, like most other things in South Africa, still tends to greatly correlate, though not perfectly, with race. It also tends to correlate to a significant extent with tribal membership.

All in all, then, the demise of judicially mandated Apartheid notwithstanding, South Africans remain sharply divided along racial lines. Not very many South Africans live in other than essentially one-race neighborhoods. Racially integrated church congregations are rare, as are racially integrated nonprofessional sports teams, social clubs, and close friendships across racial lines. In fact, outside of work situations where it is required, very few South Africans are involved in close, sustained personal contact with persons of other races, and most seem to accept it as a not particularly undesirable fact of South African life.

The Republic of South Africa. Where is it? Why is it? How did it come to be as it is today? What is the likelihood of it evolving into a nation in which interracial, interethnic, intertribal peace, harmony, justice, equity, respect, and congeniality are norms rather than goals? Can economic inequalities be reduced before they come to constitute a more serious threat to political stability than they already do? This book is an attempt to help provide answers to these and other questions.

As everyone knows, no book of this sort is the work of only person. Those to whom I am most indebted are cited in the text and the bibliography. I thank them, and all those whose names appear in their bibliographies.

I thank Harold R. Kerbo, Professor of Sociology, California Polytechnic, San Luis Obispo, and editor of this Comparative Societies series.

Thank you, Harold for allowing me to come aboard.

I thank Kate Purcell, the former McGraw-Hill editor who was so very helpful in getting this book off and running. I thank Alyson DeMonte, one of the current McGraw-Hill editors of this series, and the person with whom I worked most closely. Thank you, both Kate and Alyson, for your patience, understanding, open-mindedness, flexibility, and cool, calm, constant encouragement. I needed that.

Phillip T. Gay

CONTENTS

Chapter 12

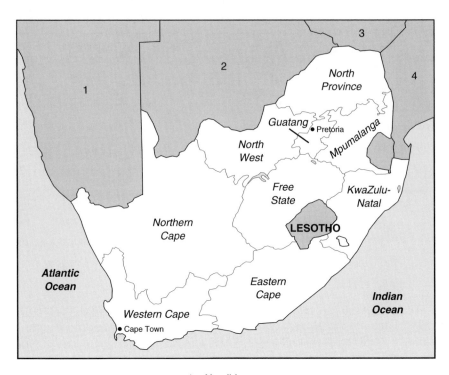

1 = Namibia
2 = Botswana
3 = Zimbabwe
4 = Mozambique

CHAPTER 1

Introduction

A TOPOGRAPHICAL OVERVIEW

The Republic of South Africa lies south of the equator at the southern-most tip of the African continent, between latitudes 23 and 45 degrees north and longitudes 19 and 33 degrees east. Its total land area is 471,445 square miles, making it less than one-eighth the size of the United States but more than twice the size of France and approximately one and four-fifths the size of Texas.

The *World Book Encyclopedia* (Fetter 1992: 616) gives its greatest extension from east to west as 1,010 miles, from north to south as 875 miles. Beyond its northern borders are the independent nations of Namibia, Botswana, Zimbabwe, Mozambique, and Swaziland. The Indian Ocean runs along its eastern shores; the Atlantic Ocean runs along its western shores. The two oceans converge at its southern tip.

South Africa is not only a land populated by diverse peoples, it is also a land of great topographical diversity. Within its borders are arid deserts, expansive plains, broad mountain ranges, and deep, verdant valleys. There are also vast stretches of fertile farmland and productive ranches of diverse sorts and sizes, ranging from tiny to huge, from cattle ranch to ostrich farm. There are world-acclaimed vineyards in South Africa's Western Cape Province. Great surf and warm sunny beaches are found along its coasts. The country has modern cities with towering sky-scrapers of glass, steel, and concrete and affluent suburbs of meticulously maintained lawns and clear, temperature-controlled backyard swimming pools. And ringing the modern cities, towns, and affluent suburbs are squalid urban slums and rural shantytowns where goats, chickens, wild dogs, and raw sewage water still run freely.

South African weather, on the other hand, is not generally as variable as its landscape and people. Snow and drought are not unknown at

1

certain times in certain areas, but daytime weather throughout most of the country is most often sunny and warm without being scorching or otherwise uncomfortably hot. Like other countries in the Southern Hemisphere, South Africa's warmest month is usually January; its coolest month is July.

THE INDIGENOUS PEOPLE

Although South Africa's white (i.e., European-ancestored) population is larger than that of any other sub-Saharan African nation, the lands that it now encompasses remained free of sustained European incursion far longer than did any of the African lands to the north. This was so for several reasons. There were relatively few hospitable harbors along its coast. There were no reports of rich gold deposits in any of its inland areas. There were no extensively navigable inland waterways, thus making incursions into the inland areas more difficult than seemed worth the trouble. There were also those formidable mountain ranges not far from the region's eastern and western edges. And there were the region's indigenous peoples, reputed to be widely scattered and fiercely resistant to being enslaved or involved in the enslavement of others.

The term **culture,** or a group's culture, refers to the means by which that group adapts to its environment in order to meet its members' needs for food, shelter, intergroup communication, intergroup solidarity, protection from enemies, recreation, and other things necessary for survival. Thus, cultures may be differentiated by their different values, beliefs, lifestyles, technology, language, cuisine, aspirations, and whatever else serves to affirm and contribute to the maintenance of their members' distinctive ways of living, thinking, and interacting with each other and with members of other groups.

Before the arrival of the first white settlers there were three culturally distinct groups of indigenous people living on the lands at the southern tip of the African continent: the Khoikhoi, the Bushmen/San, and the Xhosa.

The light-brown-complexioned **Khoikhoi** were a pastoral people; their peripatetic way of life centered around cattle and sheep tending. They had clicking, clucking sounds in their speech, which caused Europeans to called them **Hottentots,** a pejorative term.

The **Bushmen** were nonpastoral hunters and gatherers, living on the edges of Khoikhoi territory along the Atlantic coast and in and around the desert regions of what would become the Cape Colony. Though the Bushman tended to be shorter in stature than Khoikhoi, the two groups were linguistically related. Bushmen were also of lightish brown complexion and **steatopygic** (possessed of excessively large buttocks) body type. Until quite recently, sensitive scholars considered *Bushmen* to be a pejorative term and took care to refer to these people as **San** or the San people. But Bushmen is no longer a politically incorrect term; in fact, it has come to light that San originally carried a pejorative connotation.

The **Xhosa** were speakers of a variety of Bantu languages; in addition, they were physically larger and typically darker brown complexioned than the Khoikhoi and Bushmen. They lived in tribal communities of mixed farmers—settled agriculturists who also maintained herds of cattle—in and around communities located north and east of the Khoikhoi and Bushmen areas. It was the Xhosa and other equally dark Africans who would come to be referred to as Blacks, Natives, **Africans,** Bantu, or **Kaffirs.** Although Bantu, which literally means "people" is a pejorative term, *kaffir,* which in Arabic means "nonbeliever," is even more so. It has long carried the same contemptuous connotation as *nigger.*

Relations between Khoikhoi herders, Bushmen hunters-gatherers, and Xhosa mixed farmers were sometimes cordial and purposefully cooperative—as when herders and hunter-gatherers exchanged milk for meat. Or as also sometimes happened, "hunters served their herder patrons . . . by defending them against human and animal aggression and even looking after their sheep and cattle." It also sometimes even happened that "entire bands [of hunter-gatherers] were assimilated into the herding way of life and incorporated into the herders' clans" (Thompson 1995: 14).

It was also the case—as evidenced by the light-brown complexion and Asiatic eyes of former South African president Nelson Mandela and others of the Thembu and other Cape tribal groups—that herders and hunter-gatherers were sometimes both culturally and biologically assimilated into Xhosa tribal groups.

At other times, though, relations between the herder, hunter-gatherer, and mixed farmer groups were not so cordial. Violent conflicts frequently arose over sheep and cattle rustling, conflicting land usage, or the killing, by poisoned arrows, of Khoikhoi and Xhosa cattle by Bushmen, either desperate for food or sick and tired of Khoikhoi and Xhosa encroachments onto the lands over which only they had traditionally roamed.

THE FIRST EUROPEANS TO ARRIVE

The first Europeans to come to South Africa with the intention of staying for a while arrived on a ship that dropped anchor in Table Bay, which leads into what is now the port city of Cape Town, located on the lower southwestern tip of the Cape of Good Hope. The year of their arrival was 1652. Approximately 100 or so in number, they were all employees of the **Dutch East India Company,** under the command of Jan van Riebeeck.

Like van Riebeeck, most of these first Europeans to arrive were Dutch, but there were also Germans, Danes, and Englishmen among them. And though some may have arrived with slaves (Le May 1995: 15), none were of the Dutch, German, Danish, English, or any other upper-class nobility. Nor did any member of the van Riebeeck contingent belong to any national or other formal military order. In addition, few of members of this first contingent were highly skilled or educated. Nor was it their intent to establish a political, religious, or other kind of colony or to subjugate the natives and establish farms and villages all over southernmost Africa.

There were a few women among this first contingent—van Riebeeck's wife, Maria de la Quelliere, and the wives of Hendrik Boom ("the master gardener") and Willem Wylant (the contingent's lay chaplain) being the most prominent—but few members arrived in families (Welsh 1999: 27). They were mostly men from the lower social classes of their countries of birth, arrived to construct and maintain a replenishment station—replete with military fortifications—at which Dutch East India Company ships enroute to and from Asian ports could stop and take in fresh water, fresh fruit and vegetables (to be grown by Company employees), and meat (to be secured during peaceful negotiations with the Khoikhoi). The replenishment station was also to serve as a place for Dutch East India Company ships to drop off their gravely ill and seriously injured for more extensive medical treatment than they could receive at sea.

If they had something to offer in return, ships flying the flags of other nations would also be able to stop in at the Table Bay station and receive the same services as received by Dutch ships. The Dutch East India Company, after all, existed to make money for its shareholders, any way it could.

But the Dutch East India Company was much more than just your common, ordinary money-making company. Formed in 1602 by the merging of a number of small companies, the Dutch East India Company was, by 1652,

> the world's greatest trading corporation . . . a state outside the state. Operating under a charter from the States-General [the Dutch government], it had sovereign rights in and east of the Cape of Good Hope, and . . . was the dominant European maritime power in southeast Asia. Its fleet, numbering some 6,000 ships totaling at least 600,000 tons, was manned by perhaps 48,000 sailors (Thompson 1995: 33).

Primary among the Company's sovereign rights were the rights to conclude treaties, maintain military forces, issue coinage, and administer the systems of government and justice in the lands over which it held control.

The Table Bay settlement (later Cape Town), thus started out as a business enterprise, operated by an organization whose main concern was profits. This concern with making the Cape station a profitable enterprise was to be a crucial determinant of Company policies regarding European settlement of the Cape, European immigration to the Cape, and Company and European settler relations with the Cape's indigenous peoples. In the beginning, however, there were no settlers, only those 100 or so Company employees who arrived under the command of van Riebeeck.

The Company employees soon learned that the Khoikhoi were undependable trading partners. These seminomadic people moved their herds from place to place as the seasons changed, but not in accordance with any predictable schedule or timetable. As a result, the employees sent to the Cape station to provide replenishment to Company ships' crews enroute to other lands were, at first, themselves constantly at risk of being without fresh meat for relatively long periods of time. This was particularly so during winter months, as the Khoikhoi herder bands generally didn't return to the Table Bay area until the summer. During the first year, for instance, employee "rations were reduced to fish, seals, seagulls, penguins and even cormorants, an unappetizing fowl." Then during the second year, "the boy in charge of the [Company] herd [being developed to reduce dependency on the Khoikhoi] was killed and all the cattle stolen [by the Khoikhoi]" (Welsh 1999: 27–29). Under Company orders to avoid military engagement with the Khoikhoi—for warfare with indigenous peoples would be both dangerous and costly—there was nothing van Riebeeck could do to bring the cattle thieves to justice, either. It was a very difficult first few years for him and those under his command.

In 1657, wanting to decrease their dependence on the Khoikhoi, the Company released nine—six Dutch and three German—of its Cape station employees from their contracts to become "free burghers" (independent landholders) with ownership rights to as much land in the Liesbeeck valley—located on the eastern side of the hills beyond the replenishment station—as they could cultivate within three years (Patterson 1981; Welsh 1999; Thompson 1995).

These free burghers were not, however, entirely free. According to the terms of their release from Company employment, they were, among other things, bound to sell their grain, fruits, and vegetables to the Company at fixed prices determined by the Company. At the end of every year they were obliged to relinquish one-tenth of their livestock to the Company. Trade with the Khoikhoi was also severely restricted; otherwise the Khoikhoi could become serious Company competitors for settler products. Violations of any of these restrictions could result in violators losing the lands they had been given and returned to the status as Company employees obligated to work out the balance of their contracts. The first groups of burghers also had no political rights and continued to be subject to Company directives and discipline (Welsh 1999: 31).

Though slavery existed in other Dutch colonies—and a few slaves apparently did, in fact, arrive with the first contingent of Company employees (Le May 1995: 15)—the Company at first sought to avoid the widespread institution of slavery at the Cape settlement. Slavery, it was reasoned, would cause its European employees to become lazy, slothful, and unwilling to do things for themselves that they had previously done quite easily without slaves. As a result, among the 144 people at the Cape settlement in April 1657, there were "100 employees, 10 free burghers, 6 married women, 12 children, [and only] 10 slaves and 6 convicts" (Le May 1995: 35).

But due to an increasing need for labor and difficulties in enticing sufficient numbers of Europeans to the Cape, the number of slaves began to increase more rapidly in March 1658, when

> a Portuguese slaver was captured and 250 head of her cargo taken to the Cape. Many of these were too young for work, and were sent to school under the chaplain, under the eye of the Commandant himself for the first few days; they were stimulated to industry by the promise of a tot of brandy and tobacco when their lessons were satisfactorily learnt. Some of the others who were fit for employment—relatively few—were transferred on credit, to the free burghers to help on their farms (Le May 1995: 35–36).

By the end of 1658, approximately 500 more slaves had arrived. There were also, by the end of 1658, more burghers. Another 40 or so Company employees were released from their contracts to try their hands at carpentry, fishing, tailoring, and other things beside farming. During subsequent years still more Company employees would be released from their contracts to become free burghers, and slaves would be brought in from Madagascar, Indonesia, India, Ceylon, and other parts of Asia under Dutch hegemony, as well as from Portuguese-dominated Angola, Mozambique, and other parts of Africa.

At first, Company officials had good reason to question whether the use of slave labor was worth all the expense and trouble it entailed. Runaways were a large problem. Slaves cost money; each runaway represented a financial loss. So large was the runaway problem that

> On 8 September [1658] the free burghers [many in debt for runaways] handed back half of their slave stock to the Company. Fortunately the Khoikhoi were more than ready to hunt down the runaways both for reward, and since some of the fugitives, being cannibals, subsisted by eating Khoikhoi, and most of the slaves were recaptured; but reliance upon so uncertain a source of labor remained dangerous (Le May 1995: 36).

Also during 1658 Company officials began to have to absorb the loss of runaway free burghers. Some of these runaways left the lands they had been given to cultivate, without paying their debts to the Company, to try their hands at being independent artisans, tradesmen, hunters, black market cattle dealers, and the like (Le May 1995: 18).

Nor were the runaway free burghers the only ones causing problems. The free burghers who remained on the land staged a short-lived strike during which they withheld their produce. Going over the head of Commander van Riebeeck, they petitioned the Company's higher authorities off the Cape to ease some of the restrictions placed on them; in addition, the free burghers charged the Company's leading Cape officials with furthering their own economic interests to the detriment of hard-working farmers like themselves. Jan van Riebeeck himself, though not specifically mentioned in the petition, was, for instance, the owner of a farm that "was already notably the richest in the whole settlement" (Welsh 1999: 34).

Though Company officials responded to this organized protest by, among other things, raising the prices they paid for free burgher farm products—thereby increasing the costs of operating the Cape station—free burghers continued to abandon the lands the Company had allotted to them, many trekking inland, north and east, in search of fresh land farther away from close Company monitoring.

As a result of the continuous free burgher flight from Company control, settler farms began to encroach more and more on the grassy (i.e., grazing) lands north and east of the Table Bay replenishment station over which the Khoikhoi and their cattle had traditionally wandered freely. A consequence of this was an increase in conflict between the settlers and the Khoikhoi, over cattle as well as land. Khoikhoi stole settlers' cattle; settlers stole Khoikhoi cattle.

The first concentrated military campaign against the Khoikhoi was instituted in May 1659, by which time there were approximately 60 Company employees turned free burghers spread out over formerly Khoikhoi lands beyond the original Table Bay settlement (Patterson 1981: 3). The immediate precipitator of this campaign was a Khoikhoi cattle raid during which a burgher was killed.

In retaliation, the Company put together its own united military force, consisting of a 150-man assortment of burghers, employees from the replenishment station, and men from the Company ship *Honingen*. Divided into three distinct companies, each commanded by a commandant, this ad hoc military force went out to take vengeance on the offending Khoikhoi. South Africa's first white **commandos,** these men were spurred on by the offer of "a hundred guilders . . . for the capture of Doman, the Khoikhoi leader, and forty for that of a 'common Hottentot' (half that sum for a head, although an upper lip was an acceptable substitute)" (Patterson 1981: 37). By late July, the commandos had attained their objectives: Doman had been wounded in battle, and the Khoikhoi bands under his command were routed.

Still, since warfare against indigenous peoples was both expensive and dangerous, the Company continued to do its best to avoid it. It cost the Company money to maintain, deploy, and support armed troops out in the field. Plus, sending employees into battle as members of commando units took them them away from their normal duties. The Company didn't exist to engage in warfare; it existed to make money for its shareholders.

There was also the possibility of united military action by the indigenous peoples on a scale larger than that accomplished by Doman. If that happened, the entire Company settlement could be annihilated. Therefore, insofar as possible, the Company was always willing to peacefully accommodate the Khoikhoi and other indigenous peoples—who did, after all, vastly outnumber them—though often at odds with each other over land and cattle. The Company realized that the Khoikhoi and others held the potential of overcoming whatever European forces could be amassed against them.

That is why it was against Company policy to enslave Khoikhoi; instead, the Company attempted to integrate them into the economic life of the Cape Colony, as servants and sometimes as more or less social equals. For example, a Khoikhoi boy was employed to watch over the Company herd. Also, a young Khoikhoi girl, Eva, was adopted by the van Riebeeck family, lived in the family's household, adopted the Christian faith, became fluent in Dutch, and, in 1664, married the settlement's assistant surgeon, Pieter van Mierhoff, who was of Danish origin (Welsh 1999: 32). Moreover, the Eva van Mierhoff wedding was no small, furtive affair.

> It was celebrated in style: the bride was given a dowry, the bridegroom was promoted and the commander and his council were hosts at the marriage to signify their approval . . . [Eva's children by van Mierhoff] were educated at the Company's expense and one of her daughters married a successful European farmer (Le May: 1995: 15).

In 1688, the Cape Colony's mostly Dutch and German free burghers were joined by approximately 200 French Huguenot males and females of all ages. **Huguenots** being Calvinist Protestants who had fled to the Netherlands in the wake of fiercely violent persecution in France resulting in thousands being slaughtered.

Brought to the Cape at Company expense and given free land, the Huguenots—lest they come to constitute a self-consciously unassimilated minority within the white population—were deliberately scattered out among the earlier-arrived Protestant Calvinist, Dutch-speaking population.

To further assure the assimilation of the French settlers, the Company also disallowed the use of the French language in all official discourse. It was a success. Exactly what the Company wanted to happen, happened: ethnogenesis, that is, the coming together of previously distinct ethnic groups to form a new ethnic group. Within a generation or two, the descendants of the 1688 French Huguenot immigrants were Dutch-speakers, widely intermarried with the Dutch- and German-ancestored settlers, and attenders at Dutch Reformed Church services. Some even dropped their French names for Dutch equivalents. "Colberts, for instance, became Groegelaars, Villons became Viljoens, and Pinards became Pienaars" (Le May 1995: 19).

But most Huguenots and their descendants retained their French names. As a result, present-day **Afrikaners**—as Dutch-speaking, white South Africans affiliated with the Dutch Reformed Church would come to be called—are only somewhat less likely to have names such as Terreblanche, du Toit, Malan, and de Villiers than they are to have names such as Botha, Verwoerd, Vorster, van der Merwe, and Hertzog.

Dutch-speaking, white South Africans affiliated with the Dutch Reformed Church are also sometimes referred to as **Boers,** which means "farmers" in Dutch. The term came into use during the seventeenth century to differentiate the Cape's Dutch-speaking farmers from its Dutch-speaking Company employees and other urban dwellers. But during the nineteenth century, both *Boer* and *Afrikaner* came to be used by academics and nonacademics alike to refer to all Dutch-speaking South African whites. Therefore, *Boer* and *Afrikaner* will, of grammatical necessity, appear interchangeably throughout the rest of this book.

Apart from French names, the 1688 French Huguenots, who so rapidly assimilated into existent white, Dutch-speaking communities, brought something else new and lasting to the Cape: an ultimately prosperous, world-respected wine-making industry, still today concentrated in the Western Cape in and around French Hoeck, Stellenbosch, and Drakenstein.

So rapidly and prominently did the French Huguenots assimilate into the Afrikaner population that in 1707 Company officials had reason to wonder if they hadn't assimilated just a bit too rapidly and become a bit too influential within the free burgher population.

It was in 1707 that, having for years been irked by the Company's arbitrary fixing of grain prices, its ban on cattle bartering, and all the other restrictions imposed on them, the burghers were able, after an unsatisfying confrontation with the Company's local representatives—to smuggle a petition off the Cape to officials at Company headquarters. Of note is that, although Huguenots and their descendants made up decidedly less than half of the burgher population, half the petition's signees were Huguenots. The petitioners wanted the recall of the Cape governor Willem van der Stal. They were protesting that van der Stal and other Cape officials, despite Company policy prohibiting such from occuring, had acquired "one-third of the colony's farm lands, and [succeeded] in cornering the colony's meat and wine contracts" (Patterson 1981: 5).

As its signers had desired, the 1707 petition led to the recall of van der Stal. The petition also, however, gave Company officials cause to fear that an increase in white settlers would create more problems for the Company, with their demands for higher prices for their farm products and the recall of officials and their constant land and cattle conflicts with the natives, which threatened to lead to major warfare. Therefore, assisted immigration from Europe (à la all those troublemaking French Huguenot petition signers) no longer seemed such a great idea.

So it became official Company policy from 1714 onward persons wishing to immigrate from Europe would have to do so at their own expense. The Cape's manpower needs, Company officials had calculated, could, as they arose, be filled by the importation of more slaves. As a result of that decision, the Cape's white population would remain small and, over time, become even smaller relative to its nonwhite population.

"In 1711, 1,781 slaves were owned by burghers, and 440 by the Company; by 1778 there were probably over 14,000, outnumbering the free population of 9,721" (Welsh 1999: 57–58). By contrast, in the United States after a generation or two of immigration from Europe, most settled areas had a preponderance of Whites over Natives, and that preponderance would increase over the years.

The Cape under Company rule ultimately became a slave society, its manpower needs in large part filled by slave labor. Even before the ending of Company-assisted immigration from Europe, it was mostly slaves who had built and maintained the settlement's military fortifications, administration buildings, and private homes. During the seventeenth and eighteenth centuries slaves did the work necessary to create roads and farmland out of wilderness. They then served the farmers as field laborers and domestic servants. Slaves also came to constitute the core of the urban labor force, serving as unskilled laborers, artisans and craftsmen, maids and butlers, wagon drivers, prostitutes, and the like. Some slave owners gave livestock and small land allotments to their slaves and allowed them to sell the products of their land and livestock. Some skilled slaves were allowed to live in Cape Town without constant supervision, selling their services as they could and paying part of what they earned to their owner.

What all slaves had in common was that they were not free to come and go, to do and be as they pleased. They were human beings who belonged to other human beings, and the owners had the right to be as nice or as inhumanely cruel to them as they wanted to be.

Not all persons who arrived in the Cape Colony as slaves remained slaves for life. Some were eventually **manumitted** or freed. A few former slaves were even able to acquire the means to buy land and themselves become slave-owning farmers (Welsh 1999: 59). Although,

> as time went on nearly all of them were squeezed out. The free Blacks were therefore concentrated in the relatively fluid [urban] society of Cape Town, where they made a living as artisans, cooks, innkeepers, and small-scale retail traders. They formed 16 percent

of the free burgher population of the Cape district population in 1750 and 13 percent in 1770 (Thompson 1995: 44–45).

During its early years, then, the population of the Cape settlement was more male than female, more slave than nonslave, and more Non-White than White. As a consequence, **miscegenation,** or interracial sex, was so widespread and common that it might quite accurately be called normative.

Free Blacks, black slaves, Asian slaves, urbanized Khoikhoi, European sailors from ships stopped off at the Cape enroute to other places, and permanent white male residents of the Cape sexually engaged each other with such frequency that there came into being a sizable mixed-race population that would come to be known as the Cape **Coloureds.** These people occupied an official status somewhere between that of Blacks and Whites. In fact, so common was miscegenation during the decades immediately following the arrival of the van Riebeeck contingent that "no less than 75 percent of the children born at the Cape of slave mothers were half-breeds" (MacCrone 1937: 11).

Nor were marriages across racial lines either unheard of or frowned upon during the years of Company sovereignty, as evidenced by the marriage of Eva, the Khoikhoi woman, to van Mierhoff, the Company surgeon. As a result, it has been estimated that "approximately 7 percent of the genes of the modern Afrikaner people originated outside of Europe and this occurred mostly during the Company period (Heese 1971: 17–24). It was also from this mix of slave, Khoikhoi, and Afrikaner that there would emerge the Dutch-variant language that would become known as **Afrikaans.**

During the early years of white settlement, then, interracial relations in and around what became Cape Town were not governed by widespread, firmly entrenched white supremacist ideologies that resulted in discriminatory laws mandating racial inequalities in all areas of life. Relations between Whites and Nonwhites of that period may be accurately described as loose, variable, unpredictable, unsettled, unstable, or otherwise ungeneralizable. Over time, however, they began to become less and less so.

Incidences of interracial marriage and cohabitation declined as the white male–female ratio became more even. And as the white population grew and free burghers thus came to occupy more and more territory over which the indigenous peoples had once roamed freely, there developed an increasing need for slaves and what were euphemistically referred to as "servants" and "apprentices" to support the free burgher way of life. In reality, the life situations of these Khoi-Bushman servants and apprentices were most often no different than the more formally enslaved nonindigenous Nonwhites.

As a consequence of the constant settler need for more slaves, servants, and apprentices, warfare between white settlers and indigenous

Khoi-Bushmen became increasingly more savage, the rate at which slaves were manumitted underwent a steady decline, and free Blacks became increasingly less free. For although "the free Blacks initially had the same rights as white settlers . . . the law began to discriminate against them in the 1760s, by the 1790s they were obliged to carry passes if they wished to leave town" (Thompson 1995: 37).

Life also worsened for the Khoikhoi and Bushmen. The steady settler encroachment onto lands that had traditionally been open to their use led to chronic warfare, resulting in the eventual disintegration of most indigenous communities.

In the absence of more attractive options, for instance, many Khoikhoi were enticed—by tobacco and brandy, mostly—to sell their cattle and go into the employ of white farmers as house servants and field laborers. Many of those who did so became Christianized, learned their masters' language, and acquired riding and shooting skills that would ultimately make them known as first-rate cavalrymen.

The destruction of the traditional Khoikhoi way of life was also hastened by smallpox epidemics that hit the Cape between 1710 and 1713 and then again in 1745, causing them to "die by the hundreds, so that they lay everywhere along the roads as if massacred" (Welsh 1999: 62).

But not all Khoikhoi died or adapted to life as servants to Whites. Some Khoikhoi, along with mixed-blood offspring of slaves and settlers and sailors enroute to lands beyond the African continent, trekked north and either formed more or less Europeanized communities of mixed bloods or lived by raiding both black and white lands and stealing their cattle.

Other displaced Khoikhoi with acquired riding and shooting skills took employment in the Company's militia or served in ad hoc Boer commando units, which often involved them in military campaigns against the Bushmen, whose traditional land was needed as grazing ground for the settlers' cattle. The Bushmen, in turn, often staged raids on white homesteads, stealing or maiming cattle. This resulted in ferocious retaliatory white commando attacks on Bushmen encampments, during which it was common for men and women to be killed and children taken into what the settlers euphemistically called "apprenticement."

By the end of the eighteenth century, large numbers of Afrikaners—particularly those in the farthest edges of settlement—had taken on starkly vicious predatory attitudes toward indigenous peoples, often using one group to help eradicate another. The extent to which this occurred can be discerned from a passage from Mike Nicol's *The Waiting Country* (Nicol cites Eve Palmer's *The Plains of Camdedoo* as his source for this passage):

> The colonists soon learned to regard the Bushmen as vermin, the most dangerous animals of all. In the 1790s a Graaff-Reinert [at the time located on the eastern frontier of white settlement] farmer,

when asked if he had found the Bushmen troublesome on the road, replied "with as much composure and indifference as if he had been speaking of partridges" that he had only shot four. [The explorer John] Barrow claimed that one colonist had boasted to him that he himself had killed nearly three hundred.

It was not only the Dutch colonists who regarded the Bushmen as game. Le Vaillant, the French ornithologist, for example, hunted Bushmen. . . . He had pitched his camp in excruciating heat in an open spot that the Bushman should not surprise him . . . and his Hottentots [Khoikhoi] kept constant watch, for, he said, "A Hottentot dreads a Boschman much more than a lion." From there he hunted them, and although he admired the way they flew over rocks with the nimbleness of monkeys, it did not stop him from shooting at them.

Farmers hunted the Bushmen in small groups, or in commandos. Barrow says one such party near Graaff-Reinert "prepared themselves for the enterprise by singing three or four hymns by William Sluiter and drinking each a glass of brandy." They probably needed both (1995: 18–19).

By the end of the eighteenth century white settlers had also begun to take control of lands beyond those traditionally inhabited by the Khoikhoi and Bushmen. These were lands occupied by Bantu-speaking and often internecine Xhosa tribes that had for centuries lived in stable mixed pastoral-farming communities or chiefdoms.

In the vanguard of the invading Whites were small groups of **trekboers**—seminomadic, white farmers-herdsmen-hunters who lived by supplying the Company and urban dwellers of various sorts with meat, ostrich feathers, ivory, hides, horns, whips, fat, and other pastoral products. Trekboers established themselves on Xhosa territory first as traders; increasingly they used force, sometimes engaging in armed clashes with the resistant Natives, sometimes fighting in alliance with one tribe against another, and at other times able to establish themselves alongside or in the midst of various native groups in an uneasy peace that was only occasionally interrupted by black raids on white livestock and white raids on black livestock.

One of the most notorious eighteenth century Boer commando leaders was Coenraad de Buys, who, like many other commando leaders, raided for "both cattle and women" (Welsh 1999: 81). When possible, though, trekboers sought to entice Natives to work on their farms without having to undergo the risks involved in trying to forcefully enslave or apprentice them. Liquor, tobacco, and promises of cattle were sometimes sufficient to induce natives to become trekboer farm workers. But the typical trekboer farm was hardly a farm at all in the modern sense.

The *trekboer*, the pioneering stock farmer, led a very different existence from his comfortable cousins at the Cape, managing their estates with the help of slaves, and living in elegant Cape Dutch

farmhouses. Once beyond the mountains life became hard and uncertain. Families lived around their ox-wagons, the only wheeled
transport possible in those roadless areas, or in the simplest wattle-
and-daub huts, their only valuables being their stock, horses and
guns; always moving in search of better grazing and game.

The further they moved from the Cape, the more primitive the
trekboers' existence became. Without schoolmasters, ministers, books
other than the Bible—and many in any case illiterate—life was centered around cattle and conflict. Towards the end of the eighteenth
century many of the frontier farmers represented the third generation of those who lived on the very edge of subsistence. During a
journey to the interior in 1776, Hendrik Swellengrebel, son of the former Governor, described a *trekboer* hut with clay walls three to four
feet high, a single room, no chimney, holes serving door and windows, "a floor of clay mixed with cow dung on which is placed
. . . butter, milk, freshly slaughtered meat, bread, etc., while hens,
ducks, piglets wander about." Swellengrebel worried that in time
such people "might become completely barbarous." (Welsh 1999: 78).

Apart from trekboers, by the end of the eighteenth century the
white population of the Dutch Cape Colony consisted of two other
groups. **Plaas boers** were settled wine, grain, fruit, and vegetable farmers who also kept livestock. Townsmen were either Company employees
("three of them to every eight burghers by 1740," [Patterson 1981: 6]) or
people who made their livings as artisans, traders, innkeepers, and such.

Boer expansion continued northward into Xhosa territory, but
Dutch control of the Cape Colony effectively ended in 1795 when French
revolutionary forces invaded the Netherlands, and Britain—then the
major European maritime power—sent troops to occupy the Colony, lest
it fall under French control.

The Dutch-speaking colonists, especially the rural Boers, disliked
being under British rule even more than they had disliked being under the
Company rule. Thus, the first contingent of British troops sent to take possession of the Cape met with armed resistance enroute from their landing
base at Simonstown to Cape Town. It wasn't heavy, all-out, bombarding
resistance; but it was sufficient to motivate the British to promise no new
taxes, a reevaluation of all existing taxes, and an end to Company monopolies and other Boer-perceived oppressions in hopes of making the Dutch
residents of the Cape more amenable to being under their authority.

This might have pacified the Dutch settlers had not the British also
outlawed all forms of judicial torturing of slaves, such as occurred on the
July 31, 1773, when a slave who had murdered his master was executed.

The delinquent [was] laid on the cross and tied fast to it, first his
arms and legs were burned in eight different parts with jagged
tongs, made red hot; afterwards his arms and legs were broken on

the wheel, and lastly, his head was cut off and fixed on a pole. The judge [who tried and condemned] the criminal [was] always present, and walk[ed] in procession to the place of execution, in order to give solemnity to the ceremony (Thompson 1995: 43).

The outlawing of judicial torture was greatly resented by a great many Boers, especially those in the outback who had migrated far northward and eastward from the Cape just so they wouldn't have to obey any laws, Dutch or English, except their own. They were especially opposed to laws that inhibited their treatment of their slaves.

General Craig, commander of the first British forces to arrive in Swellendam, found residents there on the verge of declaring themselves politically, administratively, judicially, and otherwise independent of Britain. They had gone so far as to elect a National Assembly, "with Hermanus Steyn, a respectable farmer, as president in an enormous cockaded hat. Among the fraternal demands of what had been claimed to be the first Afrikaner republic was one requiring that any captured Khoikhoi women should 'henceforth be the property of the farmer, employing them, and serve him for life.' " (Welsh 1999: 92). The Boers also deemed that "all Bushmen captured by commandos or by private individuals might be retained in perpetual slavery by the Boers—they and their children after them" (Marais 1939: 113).

Fortunately for the Bushmen and Khoikhoi, the demands of the Swellendam rebels were not met. Faced with the prospect of having to defend themselves against superior British forces, the rebels gave up the idea of an independent Swellendam republic without so much as even a most cursory exchange of gunfire with the British. A similar episode occurred when Graaf-Reinet attempted to become an independent republic. It never quite came into existence for the same reasons that prevented the Swellendam attempt. But future nationalistic Afrikaners would recall both cases as the first heroic attempts by their freedom-loving ancestors to rid themselves of the British yoke.

A violent revolt against British authority did, however, occur in the eastern region of the Cape in 1799. The cause of this revolt was the arrest of one Adriaan van Jaarsveld for forgery. Enroute to Cape Town, van Jaarsveld was forcibly liberated from his British military escorts by a group of Boers led by Martinus Prinsloo. This short-lived revolt was put down by British troops with assistance from Khoikhoi auxiliaries, which added insult to Boer injury.

As one of the provisions of the Treaty of Amiens—which brought a temporary end to British–French warfare in Europe—the Cape Colony came back under Dutch dominion in 1802. Then in 1806, only four years later, violations of the Treaty of Amiens led to a resumption of the war between Britain and France, and British forces returned to assume control of the Cape Colony—for the next hundred years or so.

CHAPTER 2

Early British Rule and the Great Trek

The British reassumed control of the Cape Colony, first establishing their rule in the rebellious eastern frontier region, then expanding into Xhosa lands north and west of the Colony's boundaries at the Fish River. Their ultimate objective was to replace native farmers with European farmers. Thus, in 1811, with help from Boer and Khoikhoi military units, British troops "ruthlessly expelled the Xhosa inhabitants from the land through to the Fish River, burning crops and villages and making off with thousands of heads of cattle" (Thompson 1995: 55).

But even with access to more land, the Boers still resented being under British rule. For one thing, many British at the highest levels of government held strong antislavery sentiments, believing that Nonwhites should have all of the same rights and privileges enjoyed by Whites. British officials sent to administer the affairs of the Cape Colony not only promulgated laws giving Nonwhites the same rights as Whites, they sometimes made strenuous efforts to enforce those laws—occasionally using soldiers to do so.

With the British administrators and soldiers had also come British missionaries of various Protestant stripes. The collective goal was to bring Nonwhites up to the spiritual, social, political, and economic levels of whites. Missionaries came in for particular detestation by the Boers. Among the complaints of the 1799 Graaf-Reinet rebels, for instance, had been that missionaries were not only allowing the Khoikhoi to attend the local churches, they were were also teaching them to read and write, "thereby put[ting them] on an equal footing with Christians" (Le May 1995: 38). Apparently in the minds of the complainants, "Christians" was a term that could and should only apply to Whites.

Graaf-Reinet was on the unruly, unsettled eastern frontier, but there was also friction between Boers and missionaries in the more settled western Cape (Patterson 1981: 11). Not only were the Boers there opposed to efforts to Christianize and educate the Khoikhoi, they were also outraged by the propensity among missionaries to champion the rights of the "noble Kaffir."

The **Black Circuit of 1812** stands as one of the most staunch attempts by missionaries to protect the rights of the Cape Khoikhoi. Black Circuit was the name given to proceedings of courts created, at the urgings of Drs. van der Kemp and Read of the London Missionary Society, to hear Khoikhoi allegations of mistreatment by their masters in the districts of George, Uitenhenge, and Graaf-Reinet. Although some of the Khoikhoi complaints were found to be justified, others turned out to be either entirely groundless or greatly exaggerated, perhaps due to the overenthusiastic coaching by the well-intentioned missionaries.

The truth or untruth of the Khoikhoi accusations was not the main issue, though. What so greatly outraged the Boers was having to answer any charges, groundless or otherwise, from their servants. In their view, they had the right to do as they pleased with their servants, and no court had the authority to impose a fine or other punishment on them for doing so.

Not only did the Black Circuit proceedings result in massive Boer protests, they were in later years recalled by Afrikaner nationalists as one of the earliest and most blatant of a long line of examples of the injustice of British rule. The **Slagters Nek Rebellion of 1815** was also precipated by an attempt to protect Khoikhoi rights; and in later years its leaders, like those of the Black Circuit protests, would rise to the status of early Afrikaner patriots in heroic rebellion against British oppression.

What precipitated the Slagters Nek Rebellion was an 1813 complaint filed with a magistrate in Cradock by a Khoikhoi charging his Boer employer, F. (in some accounts written "Feek," in others "Frederick") Bezuidenhout, with not paying him his agreed-upon wages and not letting him take away his cattle when his term of employment had expired. Bezuidenhout refused to answer the summons, so in 1815 he was sentenced in absentia to a month in jail for contempt of court, and a court official in command of 12 Khoikhoi troops was sent to arrest him. Refusing to be arrested, Bezuidenhout was ultimately killed in an exchange of gunfire with the Khoikhoi.

At Feek Bezuidenhout's wake, his brother Johannes (Hans) swore to avenge his brother's death by leading a rebellion that would end British rule in the Cape Colony. Besides looking to other Boers to assist him in expelling the British, Hans unsuccessfully attempted to enlist the aid of the Xhosa chief Gaika. This was rather ironic, considering that the black chief Gaika was Hans's former enemy and that Feek's death stemmed from his refusal to submit to both the indignity of responding to charges filed by a Nonwhite and being arrested by Nonwhites for that refusal.

Had Gaika assented to joining the 1815 revolt against the British, the Slagters Nek Rebellion would have probably gone down in sympathetic Afrikaner history as a most shameful episode of intraracial perfidy. It was the British, not the Boers, who enlisted the aid of Nonwhites in their battles against other whites. The Boers believed in keeping Nonwhites in their place. But Gaika and his warriors did not participate in the revolt. Neither, as a matter of fact, did most Boers in the region.

In the end, Hans Bezuidenhout was forced to go out and meet the British at Slagters Nek (i.e., Butcher's Pass) with less than 200 armed Boers behind him. Some of those men had black common-law wives; others were professional outlaws. Among the Slagters Nek rebels, for instance, were

> "Kasteel" Prinsloo, so-called because his father had been imprisoned in *Kasteel* or Castle in Cape Town for taking part in the Graaf-Reinet insurrection of 1799; Stephanus Botha, a convicted forger; and Cornelius Faber, Hans Bezuidenhout's brother-in-law, who had taken refuge with the Xhosa after the troubles of 1799 (Le May 1995: 39).

The confrontation between the Boer rebels and British regular troops aided by loyalist Boers took place on November 13, 1815, and like previous confrontations between armed Boers and armed British, it ended without a shot being fired. Before the Boers could disperse, a number of them were arrested. Among those who managed to flee was Bezuidenhout, along with his wife and 12-year-old son. Eventually cornered by a mixed force of Boers and members of the Cape regiment, Bezuidenhout and his wife and son were all wounded in exchanges of gunfire. The boy and Mrs. Bezuidenhout survived their wounds, but Hans's wounds were so severe that "he died in captivity that same day" (Le May 1995: 40)

Of the arrested rebels, 32 were found guilty by Dutch judges and banished from the frontier districts; six were found guilty and sentenced to be hanged, one of whom was pardoned. At the hangings, the "rope broke so that four of the five condemned men fell to the ground and had to be hanged all over again, despite their pleas for mercy" (Patterson 1981: 16). Thus were born more martyred Boer heroes in the struggle against British oppression.

> By the end of the [nineteenth] century the legend [of Slagters Nek] had become both anti-British and anti-Black and was used as a manifesto against both oppression and *gelykstelling* or racial equality. It was forgotten that Feek Bezuidenhout lived with a coloured woman and had a half-caste son, and forgotten too that his brother had tried to bring on a Xhosa invasion (Le May 1995: 41).

Three years later, in an attempt to regain lost lands, 10,000 assegais-(spear) bearing warriors swooped down on the area in the eastern Cape around Graham's Town. Their mission was not accomplished. British forces, once again with help from Afrikaner commando and Khoikhoi military units, succeeded not only in repelling the attackers but also driving other members of the Xhosa tribes from whence the attackers had come even farther back beyond the originally set Cape colonial boundaries.

BRITISH IMMIGRATION

With more lands in the Cape now cleared for white settlement, the British Parliament—in response to increased poverty, unemployment, and resulting social unrest in British cities—allocated funds for the transportation of a few thousand British subjects to the Colony. They were to be set up as independent farmers on lots of approximately 100 acres. Thus, in 1820 approximately 5,000 men, women, and children from England, Wales, Scotland, and Ireland—4,000 at government expense, 1,000 at private expense (Thompson 1995: 55)—arrived to take their own distinct place among the Dutch-speaking (i.e., Afrikaner) settlers and all the various indigenous African groups. These new farmers, members of the British Parliament hoped, would be more pliant and loyal subjects of British rule than were the Dutch Afrikaners.

Among the approximately 1,000 heads of the British immigrant families there were 72 former shopkeepers, 337 artisans, and four printers; most of them were carpenters and masons (Edwards 1934). Although brought to the Cape to become farmers, relatively few of this group of British immigrants remained farmers for very long. Being primarily from urban backgrounds, they could earn better livings doing things they were more skilled at doing.

There were other reasons the British settlers of 1820 might have had difficulty prospering as farmers. British settlers, unlike their French and Dutch predecessors, were prohibited from owning slaves, a result of the efforts of a strong antislavery lobby in Britain. In addition, "The soil of the area west of the Fish River where they were located was ill-suited to intensive agriculture" (Thompson 1995: 55).

Many of the 1820 British settlers quit their allotted lands to become artisans and tradesmen in and around military posts or the growing towns and villages in the areas of heavy Afrikaner settlement. Others journeyed back and forth across the frontier borders as traders in products from African tribes. Some, however, did remain on the land and eventually prospered by increasing the size of their holdings and producing wool for the market with merino sheep (Thompson 1995: 55). But most did not remain on the land. "By 1823, when the three years needed to validate the land grants had expired, only 438 of the original 1,004 families remained settled on their own farms" (Welsh 1999: 129).

The British settlers of 1820 also didn't have to become fluent in Dutch. An 1822 proclamation decreed "English would become the exclusive language of courts in five years time" (LeMay 1995: 43), and by the 1830s, English and only English was "authorized for use in government offices, law courts and public schools (Thompson 1999: 68).

As a result of their different occupational tendencies and other cultural differences, such as language, religion, cuisine, and historical nation-state identifications, the 1820 British settlers did not, in general, assimilate with the already-merged descendants of the earlier Dutch and French Huguenot immigrants, who by the nineteenth century had come to refer to themselves as Afrikaners.

Even today in the twenty-first century, English and Afrikaner (Boer) remain two distinct South African **ethnic groups.** Social mixing and intermarriage occur more frequently than they once did, but they are not the norm. The term *ethnic group* here is used to denote a group with a distinct self and social identity based on cultural charactertics. Among these characteristics are language, religious beliefs and practices, cuisine, allegiance to a specific geographic area, and a sense of shared history, all of which have, from the 1820 to the present day, distinguished Afrikaner or Boer from English.

Though maintaining cultural traditions quite different than Afrikaners and much less likely to harbor animosities toward the British government, the 1820 settlers and their descendants were nonetheless generally in solidarity with Afrikaners in matters concerning the Natives—how they should be treated, and what rights and privileges should not be granted to them.

Also during the 1820s, there came into ascendancy a powerful, militaristic Zulu nation headed by its dreaded king Shaka. This was in what is now South Africa's KwaZulu province, located above the Eastern Cape Province off the Indian Ocean. Under Shaka's leadership, the Zulu nation, as a result of its severely violent conquests and assimilation of previously independent tribal groups, grew from a few thousand to tens of thousands in less than a full generation.

The early nineteenth century years of Zulu conquest and resultant growth, known as the **mfecane,** resulted not only in the assimilation of other groups into the Zulu fold but also in the disintegration of old and the creation of new tribal groupings, such as the Sotho, the Swazi, and the Ndebele, and the expansion and reformation of others, such as the Pedi and the Tswana (Worden 1995: 13).

All in all, the mfecane was a period of great violence and severe social dislocation. Thousands of people, fearful of rapacious Zulu warriors, abandoned their fields and villages; and widespread famine, death from disease, exposure to the elements, and internecine tribal strife over scarce resources occurred.

During the 1820s, the Zulu kingdom became increasingly predatory. Shaka sent the army on annual campaigns, disrupting local
Chiefdoms to the north and south, destroying their food supplies,
seizing their cattle. . . . By the early 1830s organized community
life had virtually ended in some areas—notably in modern Natal,
south of the Zulu Kingdom (Thompson 1995: 85).

Of all the Zulu kings, Shaka stands as the most ruthless and widely
feared, and the mfecane stands as the most widely disruptive period of
southeastern South African tribal life.

Shaka's life came to an end on September 24, 1828. He was assassi-
nated by his personal servant and two of his half-brothers while his
army was away on a campaign, according to one account (Worden 1995:
85). One of the assassins, half-brother Dingaan (in some accounts written
Dingane), succeeded Shaka as Zulu king; he later became one of the
greatest of all villains in sympathetic accounts of Afrikaner history.
There is even an quasi-sacred Afrikaner national holiday named in dis-
honor of him: Dingaan's Day. To understand how this came about, it is
necessary to first understand who the Voortrekkers were.

THE VOORTREKKERS

The Cape Colony's Afrikaner population resented having been made
British subjects without having had a choice in the matter. They resented
being under British rule because official British policies were more
racially egalitarian than they wanted. This resulted in the events discussed earlier: the first British troops to land on the Cape having to fight
their way from Simonstown to Cape Town; the near-violent 1795 challenges to British authority in Swellandam and Graaf-Reinet; the Black
Circuit protests; and the Slagters Nek revolt of 1815, quelled by regular
British troops aided by Khoikhoi auxiliaries.

The Dutch-speaking Afrikaners also resented the imposition of
English as the one and only official language of the Colony.

Still another reason for Afrikaner hostility to British rule had to do
with the existence of slavery in the Cape Colony. Sentiment in Britain
was against the continuation of slavery. Even before the 1820 arrival of
British settlers, who were expressly prohibited from owning slaves, the
British Parliament had, in 1807, cut off the flow of slaves into the Colony
by banning all British participation in the slave trade.

Then in 1823, the British government ordered the governor of the
Cape Colony to set minimum standards of food and clothing and maximum hours of work for slaves. By the late 1820s, laws restricted the
rights of owners to punish slaves, and slave owners had to record punishments in special books subject to review by local officials. From the

slave-owning Afrikaner point of view, this was all a bit too much. It infringed on their right to do with their property as they saw fit. Slaves were property. Who ever heard of property having rights? Slaves with rights were not, properly speaking, slaves.

This cessation of the flow of slave labor into the Colony and the giving of rights to slaves was dangerous. In 1808, after the 1807 ban on importing more slaves into the Colony, there occurred an aborted but nonetheless ominous revolt involving more than 300 slaves and Khoikhoi servants (Thompson 1995: 58) in an agricultural region just north of Cape Town. It was led by a slave named Louis, who "having heard of the abolition of the slave trade, [and taken] this as a signal [of] emancipation, or at least a sympathetic hearing," prevailed on other slaves to take up arms with the intent of "establishing a government upon principles of their own" (Welsh 1999: 106).

There was also a smaller slave revolt in 1825, this one led by a slave named Galant. It too was quickly put down, but not before Galant and his followers—among whom were Khoikhoi servants—had taken over a farm and killed its white owners (Ross 1983: 109).

In 1828, further infuriating Britain's Afrikaner subjects and many of the Colony's English-speaking whites, the Cape governor, on order of the British House of Commons, issued **Ordinance 50,** which gave "Hottentots and other free people of colour" the same legal rights as Whites. Finally, in 1833, the British Parliament did what Afrikaner slave-owners had all along feared: It passed a law freeing all slaves residing within the British Empire.

Slaves were not, however, to become free all of a sudden. Freedom was to come gradually, in stages. For the first five years immediately following the emancipation, former slaves were to be "apprenticed" to their owners. It wouldn't be until 1838 that they would be totally free of all formal obligations of servitude.

Not only did the freeing of their slaves—no matter how gradual it was to be—cause outrage among the Colony's slave-owning population, so did the news that they would be compensated for their human property at only one-third of the assessed value. In addition, after the emancipation there were frequent Boer complaints of bands of ex-slaves and Khoikhoi roaming about the Colony robbing them of their livestock and other property.

A great many Afrikaners were also incensed by the British government's refusal to pass vagrancy laws restricting the free movement of Nonwhites. Such a law would have guaranteed the Afrikaners a more stable supply of workers. There was also resentment of the British government's unwillingness to grant representative government to the Cape's white residents.

As a result, during the 1830s there began the **Great Trek** of Afrikaners out of the Cape Colony, northward, beyond what they hoped would be the reach of the British government. By the end of the 1840s, at least 15,000 malcontented Afrikaners—along with upward to 5,000 of their Coloured (most of whom were Khoikhoi) and native "servants"—had departed the Cape Colony in ox wagons loaded with all their movable property, their cattle and sheep in tow.

In subsequent years, Afrikaner nationalists would depict these Cape Colony emigrants as heroic **Voortrekkers** (pioneers) whose flight from the Cape Colony was forced by the intolerable actions of unruly Coloureds and freed slaves set loose upon them by oppressive British governmental authorities. This is how the Voortrekkers wanted to be seen, as evidenced in a letter sent to the *Grahamstown Journal* by Piet Retief, the leader of a group that departed Grahamstown in 1837.

After bemoaning the loss of wealth resulting from the freeing of the slaves, Piet Retief (in whose honor two towns would be named) cites "the turbulent and dishonest conduct of vagrants . . . the plunder we have endured from the Caffres and other coloured classes," and

> The unjustifiable odium which has been cast upon us by interested and dishonest persons [i.e., missionaries], whose testimony [concerning the evils of slavery and Afrikaner mistreatment of non-whites] is believed in England, to the exclusion of all evidence in our favor, and we can forsee, as a result of this prejudice, nothing but the total ruin of our country (Eybers 1918: 143–145).

But Retief and his fellow Voortrekkers did not, he assured the British and all others who cared, intend to reinstitute slavery in the new settlements they hoped to establish. All they intended to do was "establish such regulations as may suppress crime and preserve proper relations between master and servant."

What of the native tribes already living on the lands that Retief and his fellow Voortrekkers intended to claim as their own? Not to worry. Retief intended to make them aware of "our intentions and our desire to live in peace and friendly intercourse with them." He concluded his letter by declaring: "We quit this country under the full assurance that the English Government has nothing more to require of us, and will allow us to govern ourselves without interference in [the] future" (Le May 1995: 45–46).

Apart from the reasons given above by Retief, some of his fellow Voortrekkers decided to quit the Cape Colony because of the dire economic circumstances they found themselves in, quite unrelated to the loss of their slaves. Others didn't even own slaves; and many "did not even own land in the Cape, but rather rented from the State and were heavily in arrears" (Worden 1995: 12) Retief himself, as noted in his letter, left the Colony "heavily in debt and being pursued by creditors." Land speculation may have also been a motive for the Voortrekkers, who were aiming at a "pre-emptive strike against the merchant houses of the Cape by claiming land in Natal for profitable resale" (Worden 1995: 12).

Despite the wishes of Retief and other Boers, their departure from the Cape Colony would not result in the British allowing them to establish themselves in new territories and conduct relations with the Natives and govern themselves as they saw fit. During the year preceding Retief's departure from the Cape (1836), the British had promulgated the Cape of Good Hope Punishment Act, claiming jurisdiction over all Europeans in all territories of southern Africa. This resulted from British fears that a too-rapid European intrusion into the lands of the Bantu-speaking Africans would precipitate all-out warfare between Natives and settlers, in which the combined forces of native tribes might prevail to the extent of imperiling the lives of Europeans throughout Africa. Thus, the British government, with the passage of the Cape of Good Hope Punishment Act, had reserved to itself the right to control European immigration and European–Native relations in areas of southern Africa even beyond the Cape.

The Voortrekkers trekked on anyway, engaging various tribes in battle after battle along the way, sometimes in alliance with other tribes with whom they had established cooperative relations. And despite an occasional setback, they ultimately emerged victorious.

Though in later years the Great Trek came to be seen as the birth of a nation, as an "Exodus with Retief as the Boers' Moses and Natal as the Promised Land" (Patterson 1981: 22)—the reality appears to have been much more complicated. The 15,000 or so Voortrekkers did not all depart en masse, under one leader, toward a common destination with the intent of forming one united Boer nation. The Great Trek actually occurred over a period of a few years, the Retief-led group being only one of many, not all even headed in the same direction. Like Retief, leaders of other groups of Voortrekkers—Hans van Rensburg, Louis Trichardt, Hendrik Potgieter, Gert Maritz, and Andries Pretorius, to name a few— would also have towns and settlements named in their honor.

Nor did any of the groups leave the Cape with the blessings of the Church. In fact, the Dutch Church was generally opposed to the Great Trek (Welsh 1999: 165). Tobias Herold, minister of Stellenbosch was so opposed that he "wrote a harsh denunciation" of it. But, "in vain did the Dutch Reform Church condemn the Trek as an Exodus without a Moses or the certainty of a Canaan, and refuse to send ministers to accompany the Boers in their flight from Pharaoh" (Pattersan 1981: 22). The Boers went anyway.

Piet Retief stands prominent among the Trek leaders in part due to his lack of success in reaching an accommodation with the Zulu king Dingaan, the same Dingaan who participated in the murder of his half-brother Shaka, who caused so much havoc and dislocation among African tribes in the areas surrounding present-day KwaZulu-Natal during the aforementioned mfecane of the 1820s–1830s.

The Retief-Dingaan episode began in October 1837 when the two met to discuss the possibility of Boers settling, as Zulu allies, on lands depopulated by the havoc caused by the brutality of Zulu armies. After the meeting, Retief returned to the Boer encampment at the foothills of the Drakensberg Mountains for approval of the agreement he thought he had reached with Dingaan. On February 16, 1838, he and 70 armed men went back to Dingaan's camp to formalize the agreement. According to an eyewitness, Francis Owen of the Anglican Church Missionary Society, Dingaan received Retief and members of his entourage hospitably, giving them food and drink; but afterward he had them seized and killed one by one (Welsh 1999: 170; LeMay 1995: 48–49).

After the Retief massacre, Zulu armies attacked the encampment of unsuspecting Voortrekkers awaiting Retief's return. During this attack, more than 500 people, including 186 children, were massacred in the district thereafter known as Weenen (weeping). Then, attempting a clean sweep of the whites, a Zulu **impi** (warrior unit) sacked Durban (a seaport settlement established by the British), slaughtering all those who had not been able to get away by sea (Welsh 1999: 171–72).

In April 1838, a Boer force led by Piet Uys and Gert Maritz went out to take vengeance on the Zulus for the massacre of Piet Retief and his men, women, and children followers. They were routed by the Zulu, and Uys and his son were killed.

The Boer revenge—or **Dingaan's Day,** as it would come to be called—came on December 16, 1838, when a new Boer force under the command of Andries Pretorius invaded the Zulu lands and engaged Dingaan's force in the **Battle of Blood River.** As a result of the Zulus' reckless charges into the Boer laager of circled ox wagons, the Battle of Blood River ended with 3,000 Zulu killed and only three Boers wounded.

Dingaan's demise came in 1839, when a combined force of Afrikaner commandos led by Pretorius and Zulu warriors led by Dingaan's half-brother Mpande met Dingaan's Zulu forces in a battle. Dingaan fled northward, where he was killed by Swazi warriors (Thompson 1995:91). The Boer price for helping Mpande bring about the death of his half-brother and their bitter enemy Dingaan was 40,000 cattle and nearly 1,000 children to be "apprenticed" to Boer families (Welsh 1999: 174).

But the Battle of Blood River, not the subsequent skirmish at which Dingaan was killed, is the one most remembered and commemorated. From 1864 (beginning in Natal) to 1938, December 16 was celebrated annually as Dingaan's Day, an officially recognized day of prayer and thanksgiving for the victory of the Voortrekkers over the armies of the treacherous Zulu king Dingaan. Then in 1938, Dingaan's Day became, officially, the Day of the Covenant. In 1980 it became the **Day of the Vow** (Akenson 1992: 66).

Why Vow or Covenant? It was believed that at least some of the participants in the original battle took the following vow, which came to be known as the Afrikaner Covenantal Oath:

> My brethren and fellow countrymen, at this moment we stand before the holy God of heaven and earth, to make a promise, if he will be with us and protect us and deliver the enemy into our hands, so that we may triumph over him, that we shall observe the day and the date, as an anniversary in each year and a day of thanksgiving like the Sabbath, in His Honor; and that they must take part with us in this, for a remembrance even for our posterity; and if anyone sees a difficulty in this let him return from this place. For the honor of His name shall be joyfully exalted, and to Him the fame and Honor of the victory must be given (Akenson 1992: 47).

Thus, involving what was purportedly a covenant with God—similar, it would be held, to the covenants made between God and Abraham and God and Moses—the Battle of Blood River stands as one of, if not the most, sacred events in Boer hagiography. Not only did it result in the demise of Dingaan and the opening up of Natal for Boer settlement, it would also come to stand, in the minds of Afrikaner nationalists, as historical evidence that the Afrikaner people were among God's chosen, possessed of a special mission and destiny to rule over the African land and all its indigenous peoples.

In 1839, the triumphant Boers proclaimed the newly conquered northeastern lands (extending westward from the Indian Ocean to Drakensberg Mountains) the independent Republic of Natalia. Citizenship in this new republic was limited to "Dutch-speaking people of European descent who had quit the Cape Colony to found an independent state" (Thompson 1992: 92). Activity by non–Dutch Reform Church missionaries was forbidden.

The independent Dutch-language Republic of Natalia didn't last very long, however. The British annexed it in 1843, turning it into the Natal Colony, another component of the worldwide British Empire. Prominent among the reasons for this annexation were reports to the British of Voortrekker use of slaves, despite the late Piet Retief's denial of such intentions on his leaving the Cape Colony. For the British, slavery was far more than just a cause for moral outrage; it could compel previously hostile tribal groups to unite into massive fighting that might make life precarious for all Whites on the African continent. Besides, annexation of the independent Republic of Natalia gave the British control of Durban, which was to become a major seaport.

The annexation of Natal also resulted in another great trek of Boers, this time north and westward of the formal boundaries of the Natal Colony, where they would engage native tribes in combat for the right to occupy these lands and ultimately emerge victorious. But these lands didn't remain beyond British control for much longer than had the lands that now constituted the Natal Colony. The first to be formally brought into the Empire were those between the Orange and Vaal Rivers. This occurred in 1848, following bloody British–Boer combat, from which the British emerged the winner. The British declared the contested area, which would later become the Orange Free State, now part of the British Empire, just as were the Cape and Natal Colonies.

The annexation of the lands between the Orange and Vaal Rivers resulted in still another large migration of Boers hoping to escape British oversight. Further northward they headed, into lands over which the British had not yet proclaimed sovereignty; however, Xhosa tribes had for millenia occupied these lands. As a consequence, there began another series of fierce battles between Boers and Natives, resulting in white possession of more fertile lands over which Xhosa tribes had once ruled and more African tribespeople being turned into house servants, farm laborers, or labor apprentices on white farms, or even, in some cases, renters of small parcels of land from white farmers.

Trekker migration out of Natal, following annexation by the British, not only resulted in Boer settlements in what would become the Orange Free State and the Transvaal Republic, it also led to a decline in the white population of the Natal Colony. To reverse the decline, the British offered inducements to immigration from Europe; as a result, between 1848 and 1852 approximately 5,000 immigrants—mostly from Britain, but some from Germany and Mauritius—arrived in the Natal Colony (Welsh 1999: 212; Thompson 1995: 96; Worden 1995: 15). The arrival of this wave of white immigrants not only assured Natal's survival as a colony of white settlement, it also increased the number and percentage of English-speakers within its borders.

Meanwhile, not everything was going smoothly back in the Cape Colony. Though there seemed to be no danger of slavery being reinstituted and the British-ancestored population was both sizable and long-established, scattered Xhosa tribes in the border areas beyond Cape Town and Port Elizabeth were still in sporadic revolt, sometimes escalating into full-scale warfare, against still-increasing settler occupation of their ancestral lands.

Going to war still cost the British government money, too—lots of money. In 1850, for instance, it cost the British 3,000,000 pounds to emerge victorious from all-out warfare against rancorous Xhosa tribes on the eastern frontier of the Cape Colony (Le May 1995: 50). Afterward, the British government reevaluated its activities in South Africa, concluding that it was no longer in its interests to maintain direct, day-to-day, detailed territorial sovereignty over all of South Africa or to become directly involved the adjudication of each and every dispute that occurred within its borders. All of that required financial expenditures greater than were necessary to protect the British government's interests in

South Africa. Instead, to protect its interests in the region Britain really needed only secure naval bases at the Cape of Good Hope and the Port of Durban.

Therefore, Britain's parliamentary leaders decided to adopt a policy of "limited commitment" to South Africa, making the Boers more financially responsible for their own defense. Not only, it was hoped, would such a policy lead to more cordial race relations in the Colony, but it would serve as a check on the seemingly insatiable settler greed for native lands and their readiness to engage in warfare, often involving British support, to satisfy that greed.

As William Edward Gladstone argued before the British House of Commons:

> [T]he community which is exposed to the war is likewise responsible for its expenses. For the [financial] burdens of war are the providential preventives of war, and operate as a check upon the passions of mankind and lust for territorial acquisitions, and the heats of international hatreds (Le May 1995: 50).

In implementation of its policy of limited commitment in South Africa, the British Parliament granted representative government to the Cape Colony in the form of a bicameral parliament with authority to enact legislation, subject to British veto, related to all domestic affairs. Moreover, in keeping with Britain's other race-blind policies, the Cape Colony *franchise* (i.e., vote) was to be open to any adult male inhabitant, regardless of race, who met certain property or income requirements.

A franchise open to persons of all races was indeed a step forward and did bring some Khoikhoi, Blacks, and persons of mixed race into the political system, but never in numbers anywhere close to reflecting their percentage in the general population, which from 1711 onward, as already noted, was much greater than the white population (Thompson 1999: 36). The primary reason for this great underrepresentation of nonwhite voters was that few Nonwhites owned enough land or received large enough salaries to make them eligible to exercise the franchise. In all, "people who were not White never amounted to more than 15 percent of the colonial electorate and never produced a member of the colonial parliament" (Thompson 1995:65). But if they did meet the property and salary requirements, Nonwhites in the Cape Colony could and often did vote, which was not to be the case in other areas of white settlement.

In 1852, in further implementation of its policy of limited commitment in South Africa, the British Parliament gave formal recognition as an independent republic to the Boer-occupied lands north of the Vaal River. Thus came into existence the independent South African Republic, more commonly referred to as the Transvaal Republic. Unlike in the Cape Colony, the franchise there was restricted to Whites only.

In 1854, Britain renounced its sovereignty over the territory south of the Transvaal Republic—between the Orange and Vaal Rivers—and there came into existence the Orange Free State, a second independent Boer republic where, as in the Transvaal, only Whites had the franchise.

In 1856, representative government was given to residents of the Natal Colony. As in the Cape Colony, the franchise there was to be open to both Whites and Nonwhites, despite the objectives of white settlers, provided the Nonwhites requesting admission to the electoral rolls met certain property qualifications, and most could not.

Then in 1865, another obstacle to black political participation was erected by the Boer-controlled Natal legislature: apart from having to meet the property qualification, a Black could vote only after securing the approval of three Whites (Welsh 1999: 245).

Still, not everything went as Natal's colonists wanted. Their initial problem was a labor shortage. This was due to the British government's initial allocation of 2,000,000 acres for native occupancy as "native reserves" (Welsh 1999: 214) to be governed by black tribal chiefs, followed by British government's allocation of Crown lands to individual black farmers. Black access to so much land made it necessary for some white landowners to enter into **sharecropping** agreements with blacks, whereby blacks cultivated lands owned by whites in return for sharing in the profits from their cultivations. Thus, large numbers of Blacks enjoyed economic opportunities beyond low-wage work on white farms and plantations.

INDIAN IMMIGRATION

Faced with a shortage of cheap black labor, in 1860 the Natal colonists began recruiting laborers from British India, primarily to work on Natal's newly established sugar plantations. Indian workers generally came under contracts to serve their employers for five years, after which they could remain in Natal and branch out on their own or receive free passage home if they so chose. Most chose to remain.

By 1866, the Indian population of Natal was 6,000 (Thompson 1995: 100), and another racial group had established itself in the South African colonies. Soon after the arrival of Indian contract workers,

> Traders, artisans and even professionals began to make their own way from India to Natal . . . where they integrated into the white community much more readily than did the blacks; but always as servants or subordinates to white masters. Indians [however] did not attract missionary attention in the same measure as Africans. As was the custom in India the many Hindu—but with a a fair measure of Muslim and some Christian—immigrants were left to their own devices, and began to contribute to the modest prosperity of Natal (Welsh 1999: 247).

CHAPTER 3

The Fight against Racial Equality

The British policy of limited commitment in southern Africa was in force only from the early 1850s to the late 1860s. It ended in 1867 with the discovery of large diamond fields on lands in the Witwatersrand region, claimed simultaneously by the Griqua (a mixed-race, Afrikaans/Dutch-speaking tribe), the Orange Free State, the South African Republic, and the Cape Colony.

The question of ownership of the diamond fields was put to arbitration, and ultimately decided in favor of the Griqua. The Griqua chief then offered to put the territory under British protection. The British were pleased to accept his offer, and thus began a period of deep British commitment to southern Africa. Because of the rich diamond fields, the region was to undergo rapid industrialization and population growth and become a source of substantial income for the British government as well for individual British subjects, one of whom was Cecil B. Rhodes.

Not only would Rhodes become extremely wealthy, he would also become prime minister of the Cape Colony and one of the most politically powerful men of his day. A portion of the wealth he amassed as head of the de Beers (diamond) and Consolidated (gold) mining companies would be used to establish the Rhodes scholarships, which for the past 100 or so years have funded numerous scholars, one of whom was former U.S. president William J. Clinton.

Cecil B. Rhodes would also bring two new vehemently racist southern African countries into being—Rhodesia and Southern Rhodesia—and play an instrumental role in bringing about the Boer War. And during Rhodes' tenure as Cape Colony prime minister, the diamond region would be formally annnexed to the Cape Colony and divided into two distinct parliamentary districts.

But back to the late 1860s. As a result of the economic boom brought about by the discovery of the Witwatersrand diamond fields and the consequent growth and development of the southern African diamond mining industry, the city of Kimberly came into being. Known as "the diamond city," its population just five years after the discovery of the first Witwatersrand diamond was already 20,000 Whites and 30,000 Blacks (Thompson 1995: 115).

The 30,000 blacks were indigenous to Africa. The 20,000 Whites were mostly English-speakers from Australia, the United States, England, Scotland, Ireland, and Wales; some were fortune seekers from the Scandinavian countries and the other regions of Europe.

Among the German-born fortune seekers were Alfred Beit and Julius Werhner, who would become as powerful and wealthy in the diamond and gold industries as Cecil Rhodes himself. Their firm, Wernher, Beit & Co., would also give significant financial support to the British troops during the Boer War.

There were Afrikaners who had migrated to the diamond region in hopes of striking it rich, but they generally remained apart from the foreign-born people, whom they referred to as **Uitlanders** (outsiders). Most Uitlanders were English-speakers. Apart from language, lineage, and a feeling among Afrikaners that their land was in danger of being taken over by the Uitlanders, the two groups tended to be separated by occupational, social class, and lifestyle differences. Uitlanders were more likely than Afrikaners to be skilled laborers and craftsmen, professionals, small businesspeople, and mine owners and supervisors, whereas residents of outlying rural, food-producing areas surrounding the diamond fields were almost all Afrikaners.

All in all, then, while Afrikaners dominated in the rural areas, Uitlanders dominated in the urban areas, typically living in greater material comfort than the typical Afrikaner. The recreational pursuits and daily cuisine of the two groups generally differed also.

What English and Afrikaners did hold in common, though, was a fiercely militant desire to keep Nonwhites from having the same opportunities as they themselves had to acquire wealth, political power, social status, or anything else of value.

At first Blacks and Whites staked acknowledged claims to diamond fields and worked them as independent claimholders. In fact,

the diamond diggings were a focal point for the ambitions and aspirations of hundreds of Africans and Coloureds from different parts of the Cape and beyond who shared common interests, values and experiences as a result of education at the hands of the Christian missionaries. On one mine, Bultfontein, blacks owned 80 percent of the licensed claims (Thomas 1996: 83).

But that was only at first, and only for a very few years. By the early 1870s, competition between black and white claimholders had led to increasingly more violent militant white actions to restrict black ownership rights. The rationale for these restrictions was that "It would be almost impossible for white men to compete with natives as diggers; there were differences between their general wants and necessities; their character and position of the two races utterly forbid it" (Wheatcroft 1985: 38).

Unfortunately for Blacks, it was not only the small, independent white diggers who felt the need to prevent Nonwhites from acquiring wealth from the diamond fields; the owners and directors of the large mining companies were no less desirous of reducing competition. Being in constant need of cheap black labor, the large companies had an interest in rescinding black ownership rights; they also had something to gain from undercutting the bargaining power of native workers by restricting their right to change employers whenever they saw fit.

Thus by the late 1870s, Blacks could no longer hold claims in the diamond fields. They could not barter or trade in diamonds. Black, but not white, mineworkers had to sign contracts binding them to their employers for specific periods of time. In order to travel about from one area of the city or region to another without fear of imprisonment or corporal punishment, Blacks had to carry passes authorizing them to do so. They were required to live in racially segregated areas—or if employed in the mines, in closed all-male compounds or "hostels" linked to the mines by tunnels. Black, but not white mineworkers, were subject to daily strip-searches as they left the mines. Sir Charles A. Payton, a visitor to Kimberly in about 1870, wrote of a "curfew [being] enforced and any [black] labourer found outside his quarters after the 10-o'clock bugle receiv[ing] 15 lashes." In addition, "Savage punishments were also meted out to Blacks found 'guilty' of IDB [i.e., illegal diamond buying] often on the flimsiest evidence." And after 1885, "African mineworkers, unlike white mineworkers, were not allowed outside the compounds for the duration of their contracts" (Thomas 1996: 84).

African workers were also prohibited from engaging in collective bargaining or other organized labor union activities. Nor were they permitted to compete with white workers for the high-paying, skilled jobs within the diamond industry. They were restricted to either the most menial aboveground work or the most grueling, dangerous, unhealthful underground work. As a result, during the 1870s their annual mortality rate was 8 percent, with pneumonia being "the principal killer" (Thompson 1995: 119).

Though during the 1870s the situation of Blacks in the diamond region deteriorated from promising to pitiful, it did not do so uninterruptedly. There was a valiant attempt by a valiant man to turn back the tide of racism in the diamond mining area. Though unsuccessful, this attempt is worth mentioning here to provide relief from enumerations of viciously racist actions by South African Whites, as well as to show that though the British government was officially committed to racial egalitarianism in southern Africa, British immigrants and other nineteenth century Uitlanders were typically no less racist than were their fellow white Afrikaners.

Sir Richard Southey was a British official who took to heart his government's officially proclaimed intention of extending full citizenship rights to its black subjects. Southey arrived in Kimberly in 1873 as the new lieutenant governor of the Cape Colony. Over the objections of white diggers, he "restored the rights of black claim-owners. Kangaroo courts and the 10-o'clock curfew were abolished, as were the residential restrictions white diggers had imposed on blacks" (Thomas 1996: 85).

The restoration of black rights was short lived. The white diggers, the majority of whom were English-speakers rather than Afrikaners, wouldn't stand for it. By early 1874, the day of the small-time digger was coming to an end. "Mechanization and large-scale organization were now essential if mining was to remain profitable at deep levels" (Thomas 1996: 95). As a consequence, the exodus from the diamond mines, which had in actuality begun a few years earlier and continued during the years in which black ownership rights were rescinded, continued throughout 1874.

Who was blamed for bringing the day of the small digger to an end? Not large mining companies such as the Cecil B. Rhode–controlled de Beers. It was Blacks who were blamed. Blacks engaged in illicit diamond buying. Lieutenant Governor Southey, too, was blamed, for having made it possible for them to have resumed doing so.

According to a newspaper editorial written by a Mr. Alfred Aylward—"alias Rivers, alias O'Brien, alias Nelson, a convicted killer and Fenian who [apart from being a small claims digger] had the unlikely sideline of acting as Kimberly correspondent for the London *Daily Telegraph*" (Thomas 1996: 95)—there was also the pure, simple, indisputable fact of black inferiority.

"Ruin," railed Aylward,

> financial ruin for the whites, moral ruin for the natives, these are the results of the attempt to elevate in one day the servant to an equality with his master . . . [C]lass legislation, restrictive laws and the holding in check of the native races, till by education they are fit to be our equals is the only policy that finds favour here (Thomas 1996: 95).

At a January 1875 meeting of miners, Aylward called for an armed rebellion as soon as a black piratical flag was hoisted on the Kimberly mine. At subsequent meetings, miners tried to reach a consensus as to what should be their ultimate objective: An independent digger republic? Or annexation to the Orange Free State, where Blacks weren't even allowed to walk on the same pavements as Whites?

Though still not having reached a consensus as to what should be their ultimate objective, by March 1875 white miners had nonetheless organized themselves into armed military units. Then in April 1875, a Mr. William Cowie was arrested for supplying guns to Aylward without a permit. For this breach of the law, the court fined Crowie 50 pounds and sentenced him to three months hard labor. In response to the fine and sentence imposed on Crowie, the gaunt, bushy-bearded Aylward, black flag in hand, rode out toward the Kimberly mine to lead the white miners in revolt (Thomas 1996: 96–98).

Once at the mine, however, Aylward himself did not hoist the flag and thereby commit treason. He had one of his followers, a Mr. Albany Paddon, do it. After which, approximately 300 armed men proceeded down the rutted streets to magistrate court to free Cowie before he was taken to jail to serve his three-month sentence for having supplied guns to Aylward and his followers without a permit.

After a tense face-off between the rebels and the greatly outnumbered colonial police, Cowie was released on bail, Colonial Secretary John Blades Currey having agreed to review Cowie's sentence. With Cowie, a canteen owner by profession, set free, the crowd dispersed. Aylward, however, didn't know of the temporary truce between the rebels and Crown officials until long after its occurrence; for immediately after the black flag was hoisted, he and Albany Paddon left the territory headed for the Transvaal, where they took secret refuge in a farmhouse, from whence the bold Alyward sent notice of his death to the area newspapers.

Though they dispersed after the freeing of Cowie, the rebels in Kimberly did not disarm. Sir Richard Southey, then, organized a new volunteer constable force, in case the temporarily quieted but still armed rebels made another attempt at establishing an independent republic. The rebels were most outraged by the human composition of this new volunteer constable force. One of its members was the diamond magnate Cecil Rhodes; others were Black, and armed. After stern threats of violence by the rebels unless the black constables were disarmed, Southey requested and was granted troops from the Cape government to help deal with the threat.

A day after the arrival of the troops from the Cape, five of the most vociferous rebel leaders were arrested without resistance. That was the end of the **Black Flag Rebellion.**

But there is also

an interesting footnote to the black flag rebellion in the form of a police report prepared for Southey which showed that no fewer than 13 of the rebel ringleaders had criminal records and seven of them were suspected of, or had actually been imprisoned for, illicit diamond buying. If ever proof was needed that the campaign to stamp out IDB [illegal diamond buying] was an excuse for oppressing blacks, one need look no further (Thomas 1996: 98).

Having successfully squelched the putative Black Flag Rebellion, racial egalitarianist Southey was then dismissed as lieutenant governor for what his superior, Sir Humphrey Barkly, considered his mishandling of the situation. Military intervention had cost the Crown 20,000 pounds, and "in a long dispatch to Lord Carnavon, the colonial secretary in London, Barkly made it clear that he did not consider morality and justice to be worth such a high price." Southey returned to England, replaced by a Colonel Grossman, who was most assuredly not a racial egalitarianist. "[Africans] must be treated as children," said Grossman in an official report, "incapable of governing themselves" (Thomas 1996: 99). Thus ended the brief attempt to restore black rights in the diamond mining regions.

The arrested black flag rebels were all acquitted in state trials.

Of much greater concern to British officials than the denial of basic human and economic rights to Blacks in the diamond mining area was the physical security of the diamond fields themselves.

THE FREEDOM WARS

Located 350 miles from the nearest coast, the diamond area lay contiguous to the two independent Boer republics, which were themselves bordered to the north by foreign powers (Germany and Portugal) desirous of extending their own influence in southern Africa. This meant that Germany, Portugal, a spiteful Boer republic, or a hostile native tribe could, if it so desired, block trade and transportation routes to the diamond fields and disrupt the supply of African labor to the mines.

With the aim of preventing that from happening, in 1877 the British government proclaimed the annexation of the South African Republic, bringing it back into the British Empire as the Transvaal, so named because it was located across or on the northern side of the Vaal River.

British forces then set out to subdue the Zulu kingdom, which at the time constituted far and away the most powerful African state in South Africa. After a series of Zulu victories, British forces finally defeated a massive Zulu army at Uluni. In the aftermath of the British defeat of the Zulu at Ulani, the Zulu chief Cetshwayo was exiled to the Cape Colony and his kingdom divided into several smaller chiefdoms. As a consequence, the Zulu would never again pose a formidible military threat to the British or any other European-dominant political entity.

Not so the Transvaal Boers. Their annexation turned out to be only temporary. Resentful of having once again been placed under British domination, in 1880 they staged an armed rebellion, consisting of a series of battles in which British regiments suffered relatively heavy losses. After calculating the various financial, political, and human costs that it would entail, the British chose not to avenge their losses. Thus in 1881, Britain withdrew its troops and accorded the Transvaal "complete self-government subject to the suzerainty of Her Majesty" (Le May 1995: 91), and in 1883 the former Transvaal colony was once again the South African Republic. In later years Afrikaners, with some justification, would take pride in calling the 1880 rebellion the **First Freedom War.**

"Complete self-government subject to the suzerainty of Her Majesty" did not, however, bring tranquility to the South African Republic (formerly Transvaal Colony). In 1886, rich gold deposits were discovered in and around the vicinity of Lyndenburg, a town located 30 miles south of Pretoria, the capital city of the South African Republic; and thus began the South African gold rush and rapid growth of the city of Johannesburg, the "city of gold," located approximately 30 miles south of Lyndenburg.

As in the diamond mining region, Africans in the gold mining region were prohibited from holding claims. Africans were obliged to sign contracts binding them to employers for fixed periods of time. The best and highest-paying jobs in the industry were reserved for Whites only. Pass laws limiting the movement of Africans in and around the region were instituted. African mineworkers were bound by contract to live in closed company-owned and managed worker compounds for the duration of their contracts. White workers, on the other hand earned about eight times as much as Africans (Thompson 1995: 121) and were free to come and go as they pleased, live where they pleased, and change jobs whenever they pleased.

All in all, then, the period of rapid industrialization immediately following the establishment of the diamond and gold mining industries in the late nineteenth century did not lead to great improvements in the life conditions of South African Blacks relative to South African Whites. In fact, in many ways the life conditions of Blacks actually worsened.

Labor contracts mandating that black mineworkers live in closed company-owned compounds away from their families for months at a time, for instance, served to disrupt black nucleur family life and weaken affective bonds between father and children and husband and wife.

In addition, racial inequalities worsened. Rather than reducing them, nineteenth century industrialization resulted in preexisting patterns of racial inequality becoming more pronounced and much less flexible than they had previously been.

The discovery of gold within its borders was, however, a great boon to the South African Republic. It made it one of the wealthiest and potentially most powerful political entities in all of southern Africa. The discovery also, as we have seen, resulted in the immigration of large numbers of English-speaking people—or Uitlanders, as the Boers called them and all other non-Afrikaners—to the South African Republic. So rapidly did the Uitlander population increase that by 1890 they outnumbered Afrikaners by more than three to one (Thomas 1996: 277), thereby posing a dire threat to continued Afrikaner political and cultural dominance of what had become a quite financially solvent republic.

One way of preventing Uitlanders from becoming the politically dominant group in the South African Republic, at least in the short run, was to erect barriers to their exercise of the franchise. This was done in 1890, when "a drastic new regulation was issued . . . allowing the franchise only after a residence period of 14 years" (Welsh 1999: 307), which meant that Uitlanders applying for South African Republic citizenship would, for 14 years, be stateless—men without a country.

The raising of the voter residency requirement from 5 to 14 years was very much resented by the Uitlanders. But it was not their only cause for feeling unfairly treated by the Boer-dominated government of the South African Republic. Among the other grievances were, in the words of American-born Johannesburg gold mining magnate John Hays Hammond,

> exorbitant taxation, government grants to private monopolies, corrupt administration and legislation, the denial of personal rights [to] interests [i.e., Uitlanders] representing more than two-thirds of the population, more than one-half of the land, more than nine-tenths of the assessed property, and more than nine-tenths of the taxes paid in the Transvaal (Hammond 1900: 13).

In 1892, the Uitlanders formed an Uitlander political party, the National Union, whose primary objective was equal rights for all white citizens of the Republic through constitutional reform. Because of the franchise restrictions, however, there were not enough Uitlander votes to push through the reforms.

Enter Cecil B. Rhodes, prime minister of the Cape Colony legislature and, by virtue of being chairman of the de Beers (diamond) and Gold Fields (gold) mining companies and director of the chartered British South Africa Company, one of the wealthiest and most powerful men of his time—all by age 36.

Rhodes's position as director of the chartered British South Africa Company gave him sovereign rights over a "territory stretching almost the whole way across Africa from the Indian Ocean to within 200 miles of the Atlantic Coast and from the Limpopo northwards to Africa Lake" (Thomas 1996: 221). This territory would come to constitute the sovereign English-speaking countries of Northern Rhodesia and Southern Rhodesia (in the 1970s renamed, respectively, Zambia and Zimbabwe). But even without the charter, in 1890 Rhodes would have still "controlled all South African and thereby 90 percent of the world's diamond production" (Thomas 1996: 181).

If not for South African Republic president Paul Kruger and other Afrikaner nationalist members of the legislature over which Kruger presided, Rhodes would have been an even wealthier and more powerful man than he was at the beginning of the 1890s. But there *were* the elderly, stern-faced, white-bearded "Uncle Paul" Kruger and his parliamentary cronies. And their imposition of higher rates of taxation in Johannesburg (where there lived a preponderance of English-speakers) than in other regions, their imposition of heavy duties on all Cape Colony products entering the Transvaal, and their awarding of brick, soap, dynamite, and other manufacturing monopolies to select individuals and corporations all greatly increased the cost of running one of the largest gold mining operations in the world.

Rhodes was not, however, a man interested only in reducing costs. He was a man with a dream, a vision—a grand vision. He not only believed in the supremacy of the white race over nonwhite races, but he also believed in the supremacy of the English race over other white races. At its grandest, Rhodes's vision was of a single African nation, or confederation of nations, ruled and populated by English colonists loyal and committed to the British government and the propagation of the British race and British culture all across the continent.

Before that could happen, though, Rhodes had to do something about the Afrikaner nationalist South African Republic headed by Paul Kruger, rumored to be so ignorant and backward that he had read only one book, the *Old Testament,* and believed that the earth was flat. Rhodes had to do something soon, too. All the wealth being extracted from the gold mines of the South African Republic presented a formidable obstacle to the realization of his vision.

What Rhodes eventually decided to do was finance a plan to bring the South African Republic back under British rule. Stated simply, the plan was for there to be an armed uprising of British miners in protest of intolerable mistreatment by the unjustly governing Boer political authorities. The miners would, in the process, appeal to Rhodes's close friend Dr. Leander Jameson—who would just happen to be just across the border in Bechuanaland with 600 mounted troops at his disposal—to come to their aid, lest they be slaughtered by the Boers. Jameson and his troops, recruited from the Rhodes-financed Rhodesian mounted force, would arrive as requested. Soon after would come the arrival of regular, uniformed Crown troops, and thus would end the relatively short life of the Boer-controlled South African Republic, it was hoped.

But what was supposed to happen didn't happen. There was no armed uprising of English-speaking miners, after all. Unfazed, Jameson and troops set out from Bechuanaland into South African Republic territory to rescue them anyway, making it to within 15 miles of Johannesburg before meeting, on January 21, 1896, vastly superior Boer forces and being forced into craven surrender. Jameson, according to Cronje, the Boer commandant, was "trembling like a reed" and surrendered unconditionally. Seventeen of his men were been killed and 55 wounded; the Boers lost only four men (Garrett and Edwards 1897: 113; Thomas 1996: 301).

Despite being almost hilariously unsuccessful, the **Jameson raid** nonetheless served to increase Boer fears of an imminent British invasion. And they began preparing for it, purchasing seige and field guns and cannon and Mauser rifles from French and German manufacturers and making haste to build fortifications for the defense of both Pretoria and Johannesburg.

Leaders of the South African Republic also conducted a treaty of alliance with the Orange Free State in the event of British invasion, thereby increasing British government and Uitlander concerns that the Boers were planning on taking offensive military action against them, perhaps with the intent of establishing Boer hegemony over all of southern Africa. Not wanting that to happen, the British Parliament authorized the dispatch of more British troops to both the Cape and the Natal Colony, it having been put forth in Parliament that annexation of the South African Republic was essential for the protection of British citizens, as well as for the maintenance of British hegemony in southern Africa.

The **Anglo-Boer War**—or **Boer War** to the British and **Second Freedom War** to Afrikaners—began on October 11, 1899. The most immediate cause of it was Britain's refusal to accede to demands presented in an ultimatum delivered by the government of the South African Republic, with backing from the Orange Free State, that it withdraw all British troops presently stationed along the South African Republic borders, remove from its southern African colonies all troops arrived within the past three months, and reroute all British troops currently at sea enroute to Britain's southern African colonies.

The war began with the Boer troops on the offensive, not only winning battles in the Transvaal but also invading Natal and the Cape Colony, where they lay seige to Ladysmith (Natal), Mafeking, and Kimberly (Cape), as well as Dundee (Natal) and smaller towns.

The first Boer-caused deaths in Kimberly occurred during the first day of Boer shelling of the town, when "an African woman['s] . . . head was blown off as she walked past the Kimberly Club, and an Afrikaans woman . . . died of shock when a shell burst near her home" (Thomas 1996: 340).

More African deaths occurred at the dawning of the second day of the shelling, when Lieutenant Colonel Robert Kekewich, commander of the British Army garrison in Kimberly,

> astonished to see a "living mass" of men approaching the town . . . gave orders for the field guns to open up at point-blank range. As the light improved, Kekewich suddenly realized that he had been shelling unarmed African mineworkers. [Cecil B.] Rhodes [who had assumed overall control of the defense and administration of Kimberly during the seige] had been emptying his [native diamond mineworkers'] compounds without bothering to inform the military authorities. The Boer shelling had put a stop to mining operations and Cecil Rhodes saw no reason why he should continue to feed an unproductive "hoard of savages" (Thomas 1996: 55–56).

The label Boer-Anglo War does not wholly describe what occurred on South African soil from 1899 to 1902. For starters, Boers and Brits were not the only participants in the hostilities. Thousands of Africans were involved. Nor did all Boers fight against the British. While some Cape and Natal burghers fought on the side of the rebel and Orange Free State burghers, others fought on the British side, against the rebel Boers.

Second Freedom War? Whose freedom? The Boers of the South African Republic and Orange Free State Boers were not in any way unfree. It was the Uitlander inhabitants who, despite being more numerous than the Boers, were without political representation in the South African Republic legislature.

By whatever name it is called, though, the 1899–1902 war in South Africa lasted longer than either the British or the Boers expected. The initial Boer victories only served to harden British resolve to defeat the rebels so decisively that they would have no choice but to accept unconditional surrender, which Britain felt was necessary to maintain its international prestige and aura of invincibility in the eyes of other colonials under its dominion.

British resolve notwithstanding, and in spite of being greatly outnumbered, the Boers were neither quickly nor easily defeated. Organized into civilian commando units of democratically elected officers and sub-officers, many of whom brought along native servants to provide noncombat support, the Boers were well armed, knew the terrain, had the active support of much of the surrounding noncombatant white population, and were driven by a vision of bringing all Afrikaners together in one unified South African Republic after driving out the British.

So the rebel Boers fought on, long after the tides of battle had turned against them and the British—after having gained control of Bloemfontein in the Orange Free State and Pretoria and Johannesburg in the South African Republic—proclaimed the reannexation of both republics. The war continued long after British victory was certain because proclamations of annexation did not by themselves result in effective control over either the South African Republic, which once again became the Transvaal Colony, or the Orange Free State, which was renamed the Orange River Colony.

British troops in the rural areas of these reannexed lands were still subject to guerrilla attacks from roving commando units whose members, because of their purported pledges to never surrender, under any circumstances, became known as **bitter-enders.**

Hoping that it would bring a quick end to the war, the British resorted to scorched earth tactics in areas of high Boer resistance, burning and looting farms, destroying and liberating Boer livestock. Men, women, and children made homeless by these tactics were rounded up and placed in what the British called "camps of refuge" and Afrikaners, with justification, now refer to as "concentration camps."

Also placed in the camps were the **hands-uppers,** that is, Boers who had laid down their arms in surrender to British troops. Africans, too, who had served as noncombatant auxiliaries to the Boer commando units and as workers on Boer farms and the like were placed in the camps.

Life in the camps was, to say the least, mean, nasty, brutish, un-healthy, humiliating, and shortened for thousands. According to some estimates, the Boers lost approximately 7,000 men in combat (Pakenham 1992: 607); but "official estimates" of the number of men, women, and children who died in camps, mostly from "pneumonia, measles, dysen-tary and enteric fever vary between 18,000 and 26,000" (Le May 1995: 118). In all, then, more Boers died in the camps than in combat.

Because no one kept close count, the number of Africans who died in the camps is open to broad speculation. One estimate is that the total number of Africans, or "black Boers," who died in the camps exceeded 12,000 (Pakenham 1992: 608). Another gives the total African deaths to be between 7,000 and 12,000 (LeMay 1995: 118). Yet another source gives a figure of 14,000 (Worden 1995: 29; citing Warwick 1980: 60–61).

Both the British and the Boers used natives as noncombatant auxil-iaries to their fighting troops; but the British also gave some of their na-tive troops rifles and used them as spies, scouts, and guardians of mili-tary fortifications and supply depots. How many of the 10,000 armed Africans who fought on the British side died in or as a result of having participated in combat? No one knows, because no one seems to have thought it worthwhile to keep count. What we do know is that "the Boers openly admitted killing the armed Africans when they captured them" (Pakenham 1992: 608). Captured Boers found guilty of having shot captured Natives could, however, in turn be charged with murder and themselves executed by the British—and some were.

In addition, sometimes Boer commandos killed unarmed, noncom-batant Africans. "For instance," reads a 1901 letter written by Canon Farmer, "one of the leading British missionaries in the Transvaal,"

> at Modderfontein, one of my strongest centres of Church work in the Transvaal, there was placed a garrison of 200 [white] men. The natives—all of whom I knew—were there in the village: the Boers under [General Jan] Smuts [who would one day become the Union of South Africa's prime minister], captured this post last month and when afterwards a column visited the place they found the bodies of all the Kaffirs murdered and unburied.
>
> I should be sorry to say anything that is unfair about the Boers. They look upon the Kaffirs as dogs and the killing of them as hardly a crime (Pakenham 1992: 608).

As their situation became more and more hopeless, some Boers were themselves executed by other Boers. The most common reason was for collaborating with the British, as they served—sometimes in return for release from prisoner-of-war camps—as **national scouts** in military units sent to do battle against their fellow Afrikaners pledged to fight the British to the bitter end of their lives. In fact, at the war's end there were 5,464 national scouts in British service (Le May 1995: 120), as opposed to the approximately 22,000 Afrikaners who had fought to the bitter end (Thompson 1995: 143). And amid all the postwar clamor for Afrikaner unity, "The fact that a fifth of the fighting Afrikaners at the end of the war fought on the side of the British was a secret that has remained hidden until today" (Pakenham 1992: 605–6).

Begun on October 11, 1899, the war officially ended May 31, 1902, with the signing of the **Treaty of Vereeniging,** in the Transvaal town of Vereeniging. Despite scores of thousands of British, Boer, and native lives having been lost in battle; scores of thousands of Boer and native men, women, and children having died in concentration camps; millions of horses, sheep, cattle, and swine having been destroyed; and hundreds, if not thousands, of farms having been burned to the ground, neither the Boers or the British, much less the participating Natives, came out of the war with all that they had initially hoped they would.

The Boers had surrendered, but their surrender had not been unconditional. There were no more independent Boer republics, but residents of the former Boer republics were granted the right to have the Dutch language taught in schools whenever requested by parents; the Treaty also proclaimed that the Dutch language "would be allowed in courts wherever necessary for the better administration of justice" (Thompson 1995: 144). Boers in the former republics were also to be granted representative government "as soon as circumstances permit."

The question of whether Natives in the former republics should be granted the franchise, the two parties also agreed, would not even be discussed, much less decided, until after the establishment of self-government in the former republics. In the meantime, the Cape Colony would be the only British South African colony in which anything close to significant numbers of Nonwhites were allowed to vote.

CHAPTER 4

Afrikaner Ascendance
1903–1946

Though there were concessions made to them in the Treaty of Vereeniging, Afrikaners emerged from the war a deeply embittered people. They were not about to forgive the British for the 6,000 men killed in battle; the upward of 26,000 women and children who died in the camps; the burned-out farmhouses and scorched fields; the loss of hundreds of thousands of head of livestock; and sending out of nonwhite troops to do battle against them.

There were also deep animosities among Afrikaners: between bitter-enders who had fought right up to the signing of the Treaty; the hands-uppers who had surrendered to the British long before the signing of the Treaty; and former national scouts, the Afrikaner members of volunteer regiments who had come out of the war actually having engaged in battle against fellow Afrikaners.

So deep were these Afrikaner–Afrikaner animosities that after the signing of the Treaty of Vereeniging, acting-president Burger of the Transvaal felt compelled to implore his fellow Afrikaners to "pray God to guide us and to direct us to keep our people together," to "be inclined to forgive when we meet our brothers" and to "not cast off that portion of our people who were unfaithful" (Le May 1995: 127).

Forgiveness did not come easily for many former battlefield veterans and camp survivors. Not all were immediately amenable to welcoming the unfaithful back into the fold. For example, many national scouts were shunned, sometimes even excluded from church services; and former Boer War general Christiaan de Wet, a bitter-ender, assaulted his brother, a hands-upper, on the platform of Bloemfontein station (Le May 1995: 126, 129).

Maintaining Afrikaner solidarity became the primary task of South Africa's early twentieth century Afrikaner leaders. If Afrikaners did not now become more united than ever before, they would cease to exist as a people. They would be politically, economically, and culturally eradicated from the face of the earth, forever—swallowed up by the British. So successful were these early twentieth century Afrikaner leaders in maintaining solidarity that they ended up creating a more unified Afrikaner **volk** (people) than had existed before the Second Freedom War.

The First Freedom War had been almost exclusively between Transvaal Afrikaners and the British. But the Second Freedom War had been a war of Afrikaners from all of Afrikanerdom against the British, and this was one of the sources of the increased Afrikaner solidarity, despite the large number of brethren who had fought on the side of the British.

Afrikaners emerged from the war not only bonded by a common language and a common allegiance to the Dutch Reformed Church; they also had common experiences of camp internment and common problems related to having to return to burned-out farms and reconstruct life as it had been before the war, some without livestock, seed, or farm implements.

Low levels of Afrikaner literacy, resulting in low levels of exposure to written English, coupled with geographic clustering, helped ensure the survival of the increasingly distinct (from Dutch) Afrikaner language. But more than preservation of their language was the need to ensure Afrikaner cultural and political dominance over South Africa's other racial and cultural groups. Especially in the face of British high commissioner Sir Alfred Milner's attempt to increase English immigration to the Transvaal and Orange Free State by convincing the British government to, in 1904, set aside "a million and a half acres . . . for English settler families, 10,000 of whom were expected." Fortunately for the country's Afrikaner residents, not as many English settlers as the high commissioner hoped would arrive actually arrived. Only 1,500 or so did, and then only "after a great deal of effort and expense" (Welsh 1999: 344).

But what if more British settlers had come?

Afrikaner unity did not, by itself, ensure that Afrikaners would remain South Africa's dominant cultural or political group. Nor did it ensure that Afrikaners would retain all the economic privileges that were denied to Nonwhites. What was required was a reconciliation with at least some sections of the resident South African English population, which was sad for many Afrikaners to contemplate but nonetheless necessary. Increasingly more Afrikaners came to believe it was in their interests to enter into some sort of coalition with certain segments of the English population. The English also benefited from, and were overwhelmingly in favor of, denying Nonwhites the same political and economic rights and personal freedoms they and other Whites enjoyed.

In that light, the goal of increased Afrikaner–English solidarity became more easily attainable in 1903, when, confronted with a shortage of unskilled black labor in Witwatersand mines, mine owners received permission from the British government to import indentured Chinese laborers into the country. This brought forth vehement protests from Afrikaners as well as from English-speaking miners who saw nothing positive to be gained from the presence of more Nonwhites in a land where Whites were a numerical minority already under constant seige from nonwhite economic competitors.

Though it provided impetus for greater soldarity among Afrikaners and British mineworkers, the importation of Chinese laborers actually weakened solidarity among the Transvaal's English-speaking population, dividing it more or less along social class and occupational lines. Mine owners and other employers of cheap labor were generally in favor of the importation of Chinese workers. English workers, like most Afrikaners, were generally opposed.

The arrival of the Chinese laborers occurred on the eve of upcoming elections of the self-governing political bodies promised in the Treaty of Vereeniging. In a series of meetings throughout South Africa, Afrikaners discussed their future as a people and the "Chinese issue." Out of these meetings came **Het Volk** (the People), a political organization explicitly committed to bringing bitter-enders, hands-uppers, and national scouts finally all back together as a united political force in hopes of dominating government policy-making and policy-implementing institutions at all levels in all areas of South African life.

In contrast, the English—whom Afrikaner nationalists would nonetheless forever view as rivals for political, economic, and cultural dominance—would remain more diverse in their political orientations. Not all were fervently in favor of representative government "as soon as circumstances permit." The **Progressives,** for instance, were content to wait indefinitely for representative government to come to the colonies. They were British. They wished to remain British. They didn't trust the Boers because of the Boers' distrust and resentment of the British government.

In contrast to the Progressives were the **Responsibles.** Primarily of the working and less affluent British classes, they were confident that Afrikaners could be trusted to accord them equal rights and, like most Afrikaners, were for immediate self-government.

There also came into existence a predominantly **English Labour Party,** preaching an all-white socialism and sufficiently trusting of Afrikaners to govern in their interests. They too were for self-government now.

Formal Afrikaner reconciliation with a large segment of the English population came in 1905, when the Responsibles made a formal announcement of their solidarity with Het Volk. The two organizations were in agreement that Nonwhites should not be allowed to vote. They both favored imposing severe restrictions on Asian entry into the country.

They both favored increasing political and economic restrictions on Asians already in the country.

On February 8, 1906, the cabinet of British prime minister Sir Henry Campbell-Bannerman voted in favor of self-government for the Transvaal Colony and Orange River Colony. The first election in these provinces, held in 1907, produced clear Afrikaner legislative majorities. Het Volk's affiliate party won 30 of the 38 Orange Free State and 37 of the 69 Transvaal seats, while 6 of the other Transvaal seats went to the Responsibles (renamed the National Association) and the remaining 3 went to the English Labour Party.

The importation of Chinese labor ceased in 1907, due to unabated white mineworker and Afrikaner nationalist objections to their continuing arrival, buttressed by reports back to London of Chinese workers being held in slavery by the mine owners and "horrifying accounts of buggery, prostitution, opium addiction and sadism [among Chinese mineworkers]" (Welsh 1999: 358).

Self-government became official for all white South Africans in 1909 when the British Parliament passed the **South Africa Act of Union,** making the Transvaal, the Orange Free State, Natal, and Cape Colony the four provinces of the Union of South Africa, a self-governing British dominion.

Louis Botha, commanding general of military forces of the Afrikaner republics during the Anglo-Boer War and an advocate of Afrikaner–English reconciliation, was the first prime minister of the Union of South Africa. He assumed office on May 31, 1910, as head of the **South African Party,** with overwhelming Afrikaner and substantial English support.

Not counting the more than 60,000 indentured Chinese laborers who had been brought into the gold mining region in response to black labor shortages, the population of the Union of South Africa in 1910 was approximately four million Africans, 500,000 Coloureds, 150,000 Indians, and 1,275,000 Whites (Thompson 1995: 153).

The South Africa Party's main opposition was the **Unionist Party,** headed by none other than Leander Jameson, M.D. leader of the aborted Cecil B. Rhodes–backed Jameson raid. A predominantly English party, it received approximately 25 percent of the vote in the first national election (Thompson 1995: 144; Welsh 1999: 373–74).

According to the constitution by which the union would be ruled, both Dutch and English would be the official languages. Except in the Cape Colony, the right to vote would be restricted to white men only. Only Whites could hold seats in the national and state legislatures.

Though the Act of Union gave white South Africans self-government and a constitutionally sanctioned right to practice racial discrimination, it was still not enough to satisfy the nationalist strivings of all Afrikaners. Some wanted to sever all affiliations with Britain. Moreover, they still harbored deep reservations about the Botha-led South African Party's alliance with country's resident English-speakers, who, though outnumbered by Afrikaners, still controlled more of the country's wealth and were generally more educated, more dominant in the professions, and more likely to be skilled artisans and urban white-collar workers than were Afrikaners.

A united Afrikaner-English front in opposition to Nonwhite strivings for social, political, and economic equality was desirable, but total reconciliation with English-speakers held the risk of Afrikaner **assimilation** of British cultural characteristics to the point that the descendants of present-day Afrikaners would for all practical purposes be English, that is, no longer speakers of the Afrikaans language or possessers of any other traditional Afrikaner cultural propensities. Assimilation is defined as "a one-way process in which an individual or group takes on the culture and identity of another group and becomes part of that group" (Theodorson and Theodorson 1969: 17).

Fearing that Afrikaners were losing the distinct cultural characteristics that set them apart from the British, in January 1914 a group of staunchly nationalistic Afrikaners under the leadership of J. B. M. Hertzog quit the Botha-led South Africa Party to form the **South African National Party.** The aims of the new party were to maintain white supremacy and preserve the Afrikaner language, culture, and national identity under conditions of total independence from the British Empire.

The South African Party was every bit as committed as the South African National Party to maintaining white supremacy in all areas of South African life and ensuring that Afrikaner culture was not swallowed up by English culture. The most fundamental difference between the two parties was that the South African Party's publicly expressed attitudes toward British rule tended to be acquiescent, whereas the National Party held firm to the goal of total independence from Britain. This was, however, a very important difference, leading to further divisions within Afrikanerdom with the outbreak of World War I.

As a member of the British Commonwealth, South Africa was pulled into the hostilities when, in 1914, Britain declared war on Germany. To no one's surprise, the small, predominantly English Unionist Party supported South African intervention on the side of Britain. Members of the newly formed (Afrikaner nationalist) South African National Party, however, tended to be either pro-Germany or, more publicly, for "minimal participation" in the war, although exactly what "minimal participation" meant was never made clear. Members of the more British-forgiving South African Party held the majority of the seats in the national legislature. It was they, headed by former Boer War hero Louis Botha, who cast the votes that resulted in South African troops being ordered into neighboring South West Africa, a German colony, to fight in support of the British.

The problem was that not all Afrikaner generals were amenable to going to war against Germany in support of Britain. General Maritiz, for instance, surrendered South African troops to the Germans as prisoners of war, proclaiming the South African provinces free from British affiliation and exhorting all South African Whites to take up arms in opposition to British forces. Generals de Wet and Beyers attempted to take troops into German territory to give direct aid and assistance to German forces, but they were met by other South African troops loyal to the government sent by Prime Minister Botha. The result: 124 rebels killed in action; 229 wounded; 5,400 captured (Le May 1995: 157).

There were many other Afrikaner tragedies. For example, General Koos de la Rey, a "veteran of many wars since the 1865 fight against the Basuto" but by 1914 "quivering on the brink of senility . . . [was] accidently shot in police block before he could take the field [against the British]"; and a young officer named Jopie Fourie was formally executed by an Afrikaner firing squad on orders of Boer War hero General Jan Smuts (Welsh 1999: 379–380).

All of this caused the South African Party to lose support among the country's most anti-British segments of the Afrikaner population, even though its leaders, former generals Botha and Smuts, had both distinguished themselves in combat against the British during the Second Freedom War. In the eyes of many Afrikaners, sending Afrikaner to do battle against Afrikaner in support of the British was among the most unforgivable of all sins. As a result, in the next general election, October 1915, the South African Party received 36 percent of the vote and lost seats in the national legislature; the South African National Party received 30 percent of the vote and gained seats.

When it came to matters related to race, though, the Afrikaner parties stood staunchly united, working cooperatively during the 1910s, 1920s, and 1930s to enact laws and implement policies designed to ensure that Nonwhites would never become their political, economic, social, or otherwise equals.

In 1911, one year after the Act of Union and three years before Hertzog and his followers split off from the South African Party to form the National Party, the Union government passed the Mines and Workers Act, which prohibited strikes by African workers. Also in 1911, the Union Government issued regulations prohibiting Africans from competing with Whites for the high-paid skilled jobs in the mining industry.

The Defense Act of 1912 created an all-white Active Citizen Force, restricting military training and the possession of firearms to Whites only. The only exceptions to this occurred during WW I, when Africans served as unarmed laborers (5,635 of whom lost their lives) in military campaigns in Europe, South West Africa, and East Africa and armed combat units of Coloureds (led by white officers) actually fought in the East African campaign. Most "white South Africans, however, remained quite intractably opposed to the arming of the Coloured batallions, and at war's end the government disbanded all the black units and failed to recognized their service" (Thompson 1995: 170–71).

Also during 1912 the **South African Native National Congress (SANNC)**—renamed the **African Nation Congress (ANC)** in 1923— came into existence. Its stated purpose was "to encourage mutual understanding and bring together into common action as one political people all tribes and clans of various tribes or races by means of combined effort and united political organization to defend their freedom and rights" (Worden 1995: 81–82; Thompson 1995: 48, 156).

Ultimately, the ANC did become the all-inclusive, interracial, mass-based organization that it set out to be. But for several decades, its membership consisted mostly of Africans, and African elites at that. Educated in Christian missionary schools, these were tribal chiefs and headmen, ministers, teachers, clerks, and other nonmanual workers who, though sincere in their determination to "defend their rights and freedoms," were disinclined toward participating in labor strikes or other openly militant protests against losses or denials of their political and other rights. Their hope was to effect change by writing English-language articles in native newspapers (that most natives could not read) and by politely submitting petitions to and requesting audiences with government officials who had absolutely nothing to gain by acceding to their requests.

The same was generally true of the early twentieth century Coloured and Indian civil rights group. They too tended to be organizations of elites living lives different than the lives of the average South African of their race. But Indians and Coloureds eschewed contact with each other, as well as with Blacks, because they suffered different types and degrees of discrimination and tended to hold the same negative stereotypes of each other as held by Whites.

The major Coloured civil rights organization was the African Political Organization (APO), founded in 1902 in response to the institution of pass laws restricting the movements of natives, which Coloureds feared might also come to be applied to them. They had good reason to fear, too. Already during the preceding years they had lost previously held rights and privileges and would continue to do so for decades to come. In 1895, for instance, "Coloureds were banned from the YMCA, in 1903 from the Tivoli Theatre, in 1904 from hotels, [and] in 1905 schools were segregated" (Welsh 1999: 541).

During the early years of the twentieth century the APO also protested the state policy of providing compulsory, government-subsidized education for Whites only and the denial of voting rights to Coloureds living outside the Cape Province. But like the ANC, APO protests were mild, confined primarily to speeches, petitions, letters, and audiences with responsible officials reputed to be sympathetic to their plight.

Coloured leaders did not seek to establish ties with African groups such as the ANC, because despite a few setbacks they held on to the hope that their life conditions could improve even as the life conditions of Blacks deteriorated. They were, after all, not Black. They were part-white and, therefore, "regarded [by whites] as superior to the 'aboriginal Natives' and often so regard[ed] themselves" (Welsh 1999: 356). Besides, at least Coloureds in the Cape Colony could still vote. Coloureds also, unlike Africans, were not subject to pass laws. Furthermore, Coloureds, like members of the country's dominant white group, spoke Afrikaans and went to the Dutch Reformed Church, even if not to the same Dutch Reformed churches as attended by Whites.

> The Indians' situation was hardly better than that of Coloureds. Natal had imposed an annual tax on . . . Indian [laborers] . . . and denied their tenuous right to vote on the excuse that India did not have representative government. . . . Further immigration was reduced by insisting on a test in a European language (which could be chosen by the authorities: few Indians were fluent in Norwegian). The Transvaal had discriminatory pass, trading and property laws, and the Orange Free State had since the 1880s enforced strict limitations on Indian immigration and enterprise. After Union little improvement had taken place [as] an iniquitous judgment in 1913 had banned the entry of all non-Christian wives—and formed only a modest proportion of Indian wives (Welsh 1999: 377–78).

Similar to SANNC and APO protests against discriminatory laws and regulations, most Indian protests tended to be studiously well mannered and carefully confined to speeches, petitions, and letters requesting the establishment of commissions of inquiry audiences with reputedly sympathetic officials. The exceptions to this were the civil disobedience (through nonviolent passive resistance) campaigns and the Indian miners' strike, both organized by Mohandas Karamchand "Mahatma" Gandhi, whose stay in South Africa spanned 21 years (1893–1914).

Like many Coloureds, large numbers of Indians were also holders of the prevailing white prejudices and perceptions of other nonwhite groups. Those of the Hindu faith, in fact, had a religious basis for holding Blacks to be inferior.

> In India, race prejudice manifested itself perhaps as long as 5,000 years ago. In the Rig-Veda there is a description of an invasion by the Aryas, or Aryans, of the valley of the Indus where there lived a dark-hued people. The god of the Aryas, Indra, is described as "blowing way with supernatural might from earth and from the heavens the black skin which she hates.". . . Having conquered

the land for the Aryas, Indra decreed that the foe was to be "flayed of his black skin" (Gosset 1997: 3).

Thus, as Welsh (1999: 379) writes: "Quite as much as any white, Gandhi and his followers resented the 'mixing of the Kaffirs with the Indians.' " This is the very same Mahatma Gandhi who left South Africa for India in 1914 and is widely lauded for having been instrumental in bringing an end to British colonial rule in that country by adopting a strategy of passive resistance that was later adopted by Reverend Martin Luther King as a weapon against discriminatory laws and practices in the United States.

During the early decades of the twentieth century, then, black, Coloured, and Indian civil rights organizations held their meetings and carried on their various activities for the most part quite independently of each other. But it was all to no avail. Rather than gaining more rights and freedoms, they continued losing them.

In 1913, the year after the formation of the SANNC and just a few months before the formation of the Afrikaner South African National Party, the Union government passed the Natives' Land Act, prohibiting Africans from purchasing or leasing land outside of designated areas known as native "reserves." In 1913 these reserves, generally located in the least fertile agricultural areas of the country, covered only 7 percent of the area of the Union. But with the addition of more acreage in 1936, they came to constitute 14 percent. This still, as Nelson Mandela notes in his autobiography, left Africans "deprived of 87 percent of the territory of the land of their birth" (1995: 99).

The 1913 Natives' Land Act required Africans to obtain official passes if they wished to move from town to country, country to town, or town to town. By doing so, it took away their ability to induce white employers to raise their wage level by threats of moving from low-paying jobs and regions to higher-paying ones. Also, since the amount of land set aside as native reserves or homelands was much too small and infertile to support South Africa's entire black population, the Natives' Land Act ensured white farmers, mine owners, and other employers of black workers of a steady, veritably inexhaustible, supply of Africans with no choice but to leave their homes and families for extended periods of time to work, wherever they were allowed, at low-paying jobs considered beneath the dignity of white men and women. As a result, black children in the homelands were, as previously noted, generally without fathers for long periods of time. In addition, the Status Quo Act of 1918 affirmed the right, granted by the 1911 Mines and Workers Act, of Whites to monopolize skilled and semiskilled positions in the mining industries.

Also in 1918, a group of Afrikaner clergymen, intellectuals, businesspeople, teachers, and university academics brought into existence the Afrikaner **Broederbond** (brotherhood). Its chief stated goals were to bring together Afrikaners into mutual assistance networks within all industries, professions, occupations, and governmental agencies; to propagate the Afrikaans language and culture; and to bring present and future Afrikaner leaders together for serious discussion of issues relevant to the preservation and prosperity of the Afrikaner people.

Prime Minister Botha of the ruling South African Party died in office in 1919. He was replaced by Jan Smuts of the South African Party.

In 1920, the South African legislature enacted the Native Affairs Act, which established separate tribal councils for the administration of each tribal reserve and separate tribal councils to help administer the various affairs of all the variously tribe-affiliated Natives in urban areas off the reserves. The purpose of these separate tribal councils was to halt the advance of native "detribalization," reflected in the tendency of increasing numbers of urban Africans to form friendships and come together in labor unions and political organizations that transcended traditional tribal divisions.

It was also in 1920 that, for the first time, the anti-British National Party emerged from the general election with more votes and more seats in the national legislature than did the South African Party. The South African Party remained the majority party only by effecting a merger with the predominantly English Unionist Party.

In 1922, the Afrikaner Broederbond began to go partially underground, the names of its members and their activities becoming loosely kept secrets. But its goals remained the same: the perpetuation of the Afrikaans language and Afrikaner culture; the creation of Afrikaner-preferential hiring policies in all the country's major social, political, and economic institutions; and, whenever the opportunity existed, Afrikaner patronage of Afrikaner business. In other, more contemporary, words: Primary among the goals of the Afrikaner Broederbond was the surreptitious establishment and perpetuation of Afrikaner mutual assistance networks and the covert implementation of Afrikaner-preferential affirmative action hiring and promotion policies.

In 1923, the National Government passed the Natives (Urban Areas) Act, permitting municipal governments, if they so desired, to impose residential segregation by race, if necessary, by the forceful removal of Blacks from designated white areas. This act also prohibited Africans from owning property in urban areas on the grounds that they were not, by virtue of having been placed on tribal reserve rolls, permanent urban residents and "Should only be permitted within municipal areas in so far and so long as their presence is demanded by the wants of the white population" (Koch 1983: 153). The costs of removing urban Africans from designated white locations were to be paid out of revenues from African rents and taxes on beer produced for native consumption in licensed beerhalls located in native areas.

The 1924 Industrial Conciliation Act gave trade unions the right to engage in collective bargaining but withheld from "migrant workers" (i.e., Africans) the right to do so. Also in 1924, the Broederbond-linked National Party entered into an electoral alliance with the white supremacist, primarily English, Labour Party. This resulted in the National Party, in conjunction with the Labour Party, winning a majority of House of Assembly seats in the 1924 general election. In addition, the country saw its first National Party prime minister, J. B. M. Hertzog.

The implementation of racially discriminatory policies and the passage of racially discriminatory legislation continued unabated. Shortly after coming to power, the Hertzog-led National Party–Labour Party coalition government brought into being what was called the **civilized labor policy.** This was made necessary by the existence of increasing numbers of poor Afrikaners during the first two decades or so of the twentieth century.

There had always been poor Afrikaners, but their numbers began to increase after the Anglo-Boer War. As a result of farmhouse, barn, and field burnings and livestock losses in the war, "not less than 10,000 individuals had been torn loose from the land which was their way of life and pillar of their self-respect" (Patterson 1981: 138). Some of these at least 10,000 individuals became sharecroppers, that is, persons who worked and lived on land owned by someone else in return for a share of the crop or cattle they raised on said land. But as the landless, rural Afrikaner population increased, sharecropping arrangements became more common, resulting in increasingly more landless Boers forced to leave the countryside in search of employment in and around the mining towns and other industrial centers.

Keeping these people poor and landless after their departure from the rural areas was their inability to compete with British and other European-ancestored Whites for the skilled "white" positions in the urban areas. And since both racial hubris and custom prevented them from competing for the low-wage, unskilled positions held by Blacks in the urban areas, they were unable to improve their life situations.

By the second decade of the twentieth century, Afrikaner leaders had begun to see white poverty as a potentially major problem, verified by a 1917 estimate by the minister of agriculture that "over 105,000 people or 8 percent of the total white population were living in poverty" (Patterson 1981: 139). Some of these people were living in close proximity to Blacks and no longer above offering themselves for low-wage, traditional Nonwhite employment.

With increasing numbers of Whites reduced to living under economic conditions increasingly similar to blacks, there arose a fear among Afrikaner cultural and political leaders that economic equality between the races, albeit at the lowest levels, would ultimately lead to social equality of the races and increasing numbers of poor Afrikaners "going Kaffir" or otherwise being lost to the volk as a result of losing their sense of solidarity with their more economically prosperous, more skilled, and better educated Afrikaner brethren.

Therefore, in 1924 there came into being the above mentioned civilized labor policy, the practice of paying white workers more than black workers even when they were engaged in the same work. Instituted in the interests of maintaining Afrikaner solidarity across social class lines, the civilized labor policy

> ensured the unskilled white workers a protected field of labor, mainly in such public services as the railways, and rates of pay which were related not to his productivity but his needs as a "civilized" person. Under these conditions "kaffir" work became acceptable as long as it was not done for kaffir wages or side by side with Kaffirs (Patterson 1981: 142).

One way of ensuring that black and white workers did not work side by side at the same tasks was to replace black workers with more highly paid white workers. South African Railways and Harbours, the country's largest employer of unskilled and semiskilled workers during the 1920s, stands as a good example of this. White laborers began being employed by South African Railways and Harbours in 1907, and their numbers came to increase rapidly thereafter. Between 1921 and 1928 the number of white laborers in its employ rose from 4,705 persons to 15,878 persons, "employed in separate gangs at 'civilized' wages . . . with free housing or a housing allowance [not given to Nonwhites]. [By] 1948, the railways were employing more Whites than Nonwhites" (Patterson 1981: 142).

Costly and inefficient though it was, the civilized labor policy nonetheless served its purpose of maintaining, despite broad Afrikaner social class divisions, Afrikaner group solidarity by providing avenues of mobility for large numbers of persons who might have otherwise fallen into poverty. By the 1950s, South African police and military forces had also become examples of affirmative action at work for Afrikaners, as they too became more and more Afrikaner-dominated.

In extension of the South African government's civilized labor policy, the 1926 Mines and Works Amendment Act not only gave the government the power to enforce the color bar in private industry, it also established differential wage rates solely on the basis of race or, in its own words, between "persons whose standard of living conforms to the standard of living generally recognized as tolerable from the usual European standpoint [and those] whose aim is restricted to the barer requirements of life as understood among barbarous and underdeveloped peoples" (Worden 1995: 74).

A follow-up to the 1920 Native Affairs Act, the 1927 Native Administration Act was meant to strengthen and perpetuate tribal divisions by giving tribal chiefs a stake in the survival and smooth administration of the tribal reserves by making them agents of the government. Apart from mandating that every African, even those living off the tribal reserves, would have a tribal identity over and above all other identities, it made African chiefs responsible for paying the taxes of all persons on tribal rolls.

Chiefs who failed to collect the required taxes were disciplined, and if the government so chose, their tribes could be relocated. On the other hand, chiefs who cooperated with Native Affairs Department were shown great respect by the agency and had the authority to determine how the tax burden was to be distributed among their individual tribal constituents, which gave them direct power over tribal members in the cities and on the tribal reserves.

The taxes levied on tribal members also ensured the cities a steady supply of cheap labor from the native reserves. Given the inability of the native reserves to provide substantive employment for most of its members, where else but outside the reserves would average members be able to earn the money to pay the taxes levied on themselves and their dependents?

In 1929, more National Party and South African Party members were elected to the national legislature, with a corresponding decrease in the number of British Labour Party members. In 1932, during the height of the Depression, the national legislature passed the Native Service Contract Act, requiring all native tenants on white-owned farms either to spend between three and six months of each year working directly for the owner or to pay the owner a flat tax of 5 pounds. This act also forbade native tenants and workers from leaving a farm without written permission from its owner, thereby guaranteeing white farmers a stable source of cheap, more or less captive, African farm labor.

In 1933, seeking even greater solidarity among Afrikaners, the leaders of the South African Party and the National Party (Jan Smuts and J. B. M. Hertzog, respectively) entered into a governing coalition, a diarchy, as it were, with Hertzog remaining prime minister and Smuts becoming deputy prime minister. Each had the right to nominate half of the lesser ministers in the cabinet. Though its combined members controlled 138 of the 150 House seats, the coalition didn't last out the year.

Not all National Party legislators were comfortable within the coalition. Their concern was that Hertzog had become too trusting of the British government and was, perhaps, now even willing to reconsider the goal of eventual secession from the British Empire. Thus in December 1933, under the leadership of D. F. Malan, an openly acknowledged member of the Afrikaner Broederbond, 19 National Party MPs left the South African Party–National Party coalition to form their own **Purified National Party.** In 1934, in response to the formation of the Purified National Party, the South African Party and the National Party merged to form the **United South African National Party.**

Three years after the formation of the Purified National Party, the House of Assembly passed the 1936 Representation of Natives Act, thereby taking the franchise away from Africans in the Cape Province. Now no Africans in any of the four South African provinces had the right to vote.

In 1937, hoping that it would stem the flow of Africans from the overpopulated, poverty-engulfed tribal reserves to impoverished, over-populated urban locations, the House of Assembly passed the Native Laws Amendment Act. It contained more stringent regulations concern-ing the issuance of passes governing the movement of native workers from one area to another and more detailed restrictions on when and where pass holders could and could not live or travel.

In the 1938 general election, the Purified National Party—though remaining the minority Afrikaner party—gained 10 more seats at the ex-pense of the less vehemently nationalist, Afrikaner-dominated United South African Party. This reflected an increasingly virulent Afrikaner racist nationalism.

Though indicative of things to come, the general election was not, however, the biggest event of 1938. The big event was the centennial cel-ebration of the December 16, 1838, Battle of Blood River, during which a contingent of greatly outnumbered Voortrekkers defeated a massive Zulu force under the command of the Zulu king Dingaan. (See Chapter 2 for details.) What had given the Boer victory at Blood River a sacred place in Afrikaner mythology and made December 16 a semireligious Afrikaner holiday was the purportedly holy vow, or covenantal oath, taken by the Boer warriors on the eve of the battle. The vow, many Afrikaner nationalists maintained, not only resulted in the Boer victory but also affirmed Afrikaners as a special people, entered into a covenant with God Himself and thus possessed of a divine right to the lands they had wrested from the Nonwhite peoples and were now in the process of ridding of British political influence.

The 1938 Broederbond-organized centenary celebrations began on August 8 in Cape Town with the departure of a couple of dozen or so ox-drawn wagons in a reenactment of the 1930s treks—following the abol-ishment of slavery in all British territories—from the Cape to what would become Natal, the Orange Free State, and the Transvaal. The wag-ons' drivers and passengers were dressed in replicated 1838 Voortrekker garb. Shortly thereafter, eight other ox-drawn wagons with similarly at-tired passengers set out for other cities.

During their treks toward the December 16, 1938, final celebrations in Pretoria (where the cornerstone of a Voortrekker Monument had been laid) or toward Natal (the actual place of the Battle of Blood River), the wagons and their passengers were met with even greater than expected enthusiasm and shows of Afrikaner pride. In the end, the centennial cele-bration of the Battle of Blood River turned out to be the greatest nonvio-lent Afrikaner happening ever.

Across the country, Afrikaner men took to affirming their ethnic identity by growing beards. Women made Voortrekker costumes and, as the procession approached, turned out their families in period dress. In hamlet and town, as the ox-wagons passed, there were proud ceremonies. . . . Long speeches were made, and frequently the covenantal oath was repeated. . . .

Approximately 100,000 people attended the Pretoria ceremony, slightly less than one-tenth of all Afrikaner men, women and children in the Union of South Africa (Akenson 1992: 46–47).

The celebrations also led to the formation of the **Ossewa-Brandwag** (ox-wagon sentinel), an Afrikaner nationalist group that in a few years would come out in militant opposition to the South African government's decision to go to war against Nazi Germany (Patterson 1981: 31).

Afrikaner poverty still being a concern to Afrikaner leaders, the 1938 celebrations also brought into being, in October 1939, "an Afrikaner Economic 'Volkskongres'. . . . [organized] as a means for the redemption of the poor White, its aims being to employ the mobilized capital of the Afrikaner, in the furtherance of his national interests in the sphere of commerce and industry, and to capture key positions "(Welsh 1999: 417)."

WORSENING CONDITIONS FOR NONWHITES

Steady improvements in the general conditions of Afrikaner life during the 1910s, 1920s, and 1930s, paralleled the increasingly worsening social, political, and economic conditions for Nonwhites.

How did the Nonwhites bear up under such a barrage of repressive laws and governmental policies? One reason was that not all laws and policies were always or everywhere enforced. Sometimes, they simply weren't enforceable.

The government didn't have the resources to keep track of everyone's doings. A few Blacks in some urban **townships** still held ownership to houses and small plots of land. A few continued operating small businesses and living as independent farmers in areas outside their officially designated tribal reserves. Many Blacks continued to leave the tribal reserves to find work in the city and create new lives of some sort for themselves without having official, government authorization to do so. All they needed was a White willing to break the law and hire them—and such Whites were apparently not so rare. Blacks unable to find a place to live in designated Black areas often set themselves up as squatters in wobbly shantytowns on land not officially open to native residency.

The degree and intensity of law enforcement was determined, in part, by economic conditions. If demand for native labor was high, enforcement was generally more lax than it was when the demand was low. In fact, a high demand for industrial labor during the Second World War (1939–45) led to a total suspension of the pass laws during the 1942 and 1943. Anyone could move about the country freely. And even before WW II, the number of natives living in urban areas had doubled between 1921 and 1936. Then between 1936 and 1948, it increased by two-thirds again. Thus by the 1940s, "the majority of the black urban population were no longer migrants but—despite the wishes of government officials—permanent residents who had broken economic ties with rural areas (Worden 1995: 61).

The biggest problem confronting native newcomers to urban areas was lack of housing of any sort, decent or indecent. Thus, the squatters' shantytowns developed—without electricity, running water, or other modern amenities, located on unoccupied land around Johannesburg, Cape Town, Bloemfontein, Durban, and other cities.

Many male workers separated from their families back on the reserve for months at a time had no choice but to live in all-male urban compounds or hostels owned and maintained by their employers. There intertribal hostilities, fighting, drinking, gambling, and both female and young male prostitution were part of normal, everyday life.

Other migrants were fortunate enough to rent rooms, or backyard spaces on which to construct makeshift shelters, in crowded, unpaved, officially designated native locations, where living conditions were no different than those in the squatter settlements. No electricity, no running water, no flush toilets or other modern amenities were facts of life in almost all areas of black residence; chronically high rates of unemployment, underemployment, and crime and violence of all sorts were common. Within the native locations and squatter settlements there also existed desultory, but nonetheless sometimes violent, intertribal conflicts, high rates of out-of-wedlock births and infant deaths, and all the other classic ills found in impoverished urban ghettos.

WORLD WAR II

Just as they had with the outbreak of World War I, inter-Afrikaner conflicts arose with the outbreak of World War II and Britain's declaration of war with Germany. Deputy Prime Minister Jan Smuts (of the coalitionist United Party) was for South Africa also declaring war on Germany, Prime Minister Hertzog was against it.

When put before United Party members of the the House of Assembly, the vote was 80 for going to war against Nazi Germany and 67 for semineutrality, that is, letting Britain continue using South Africa as a naval base but committing no South African military forces to battle.

The will of the majority carried: South Africa formally entered the war on the side of Britain. Hertzog resigned, and Smuts succeeded him as prime minister. But, as happened when South Africa entered WW I on the side of Britain against Germany, large numbers of Afrikaners remained firm in their unwillingness to go to war on behalf of "imperialist" Britain.

Hertzog reunited with D. F. Malan of the Purified National Party to form the Reunited National Party, henceforth referred to as simply the **National Party.** Most stridently nationalistic in orientation, the overriding goals of the new National Party were the severance of all ties with Great Britain; Afrikaner cultural and political dominance of South Africa; and the maintenance of white supremacy for all time.

In an even more militantly anti-British vein, leaders of the paramilitary Ossewa-Brandwag threatened violent rebellion against the Smuts-led government if the policy of neutrality was not followed. Those leaders were arrested and disarmed by government forces before they could carry out their threat. Some were imprisoned under the 1940 War Powers Act granting the government the right to do so.

The National Party went into the 1943 election with 27 House of Assembly seats (Welsh 1999: 418) but emerged much stronger, with 43 seats; the ruling United Party held 103 seats (Worden 1995: 92). The United Party's majority apparently resulted from overwhelming support from English-speakers; the National Party's gains apparently came from having received a majority of the Afrikaner vote.

Also during World War II, nonwhites mobilized even more in resistance to the low-wage levels and worsening urban living conditions even in the face of increased demands for their labor. In 1943, with leadership from the increasingly more militant and mass-oriented African National Congress, Africans staged a successful boycott of buses serving Alexandra, a native township near Johannesburg, resulting in the bus company's decision to rescind its fare increase from four pence to five.

Foreshadowing things to come, there were also African rent boycotts and work stayaways in towns all across South Africa (Worden 1995: 63). There was also the emergence of the Non-European Unity Front, organized by the Communist Party. In addition, the South African Indian Congress and the African Political Organization (the country's main Coloured civil rights group) joined the ANC in calling on all people of all races opposed to segregation and racial discrimination to come together in militant support of extending the full range of both human and civic rights to all of South Africa's peoples.

WW II ended in September 1945, by which time there were perhaps as many blacks as whites living in South Africa's urban areas.

CHAPTER 5

Apartheid

When the Second World War ended in 1945, the Jan Smuts–led United Party held the majority of seats in the national House of Assembly, but the more clamorously white supremacist National Party was gaining strength on its right. During the following year, the United Party was presented with an opportunity to show that, contrary to what its political rivals might want others to believe, it too was committed to the maintenance of racial inequality in all areas of South African life.

This opportunity arose when 70,000 African miners went on strike for higher wages. In response to the miners' demands, the government authorized actions resulting in the arrests of the leaders of the African Mineworkers Union, the destruction of the union's offices and files, the deaths of 12 miners, and none of the miners' demands being met (Mandela 1995: 101).

The Smuts-led national government also found itself faced with another labor problem in 1946: a shortage of skilled workers. But rather than try to solve the problem by breaking the color bar and allowing nonwhites to be trained and employed as skilled workers, it implemented an "immigration assistance" program, which, within a couple of years, resulted in approximately 60,000 more Europeans coming to South Africa, the majority of whom were English-speakers.

Also in 1946, the South African House of Assembly passed the Asian Land Tenure Act, which restricted the rights of Indians, who were already prohibited from residing in the Orange Free State, to own property and engage in trade in other provinces. The Asian Land Tenure Act also brought South Africa under condemnation at the first meeting of the UN General Assembly for denying "fundamental rights to its citizens." That was ironic, too, since it was South African prime minister Smuts "who had drafted the preamble to [the UN] Charter . . . committing the organization 'To reestablish faith in fundamental human rights, in the sanctity and ultimate value of human personality, in the equal rights of men and women of nations large and small'" (Welsh 1999: 422). Then again, maybe it wasn't so ironic. This was, after all, the same Jan Smuts who during the Anglo-Boer had rode at the head of a commando group reported to have gratuitously slaughtered approximately 100 unarmed Africans (Pakenham 1979: 608)

Though the government intended the opposite, more repressive laws and harsher treatment of those who protested such laws led to more rather than fewer militant protests by heretofore relatively timid nonwhite civil rights groups. In protest of the Asian Land Tenure Act, the Indian community initiated a two-year campaign of passive resistance that included mass rallies and occupation of lands that had become officially reserved for Whites only.

A result of one peaceful Indian demonstration was an anti-Indian riot in Durban, during which white civilians attacked the passively resisting Indians. Another result of the campaign was the arrest of the white Anglican reverend Michael Scott, for protesting in sympathy with the Indian community. It was the first but not the last arrest for Scott, who is today remembered as one of the earliest and most committed anti-apartheid white activists.

Though ultimately unsuccessful, Indian protests against the 1946 Land Tenure Act did, however, according to future South African president Nelson Mandela, "come to serve as a model for the type of protest actions members of the Youth League [of the African National Congress] had long been calling on the Congress's older, more conservative leaders to endorse" (1994: 104).

The unsuccessful 1946 African mineworkers strike had also deepened divisions within the African National Congress. Youthful members of the ANC tended to favor militant strikes, boycotts, and other acts of open resistance to the government's racist policies, whereas many older members still thought it possible to effect change by going through proper channels, writing articles, and submitting petitions requesting meetings with what they hoped were responsible, sympathetic government officials.

These same types of divisions between militants and nonmilitants were also beginning to surface within the leadership of the coloured African Political Organization (APO) and within the South African Indian Congress (SAIC). In the end, the militants would carry the day, primarily because of the insurmountable problem confronting the nonmilitants: there were no sympathetic, responsible government leaders.

The Native question was the big issue in the (Whites-only) 1948 elections. The United Party and the National Party were the major contestants. Though both parties were for continued racial discrimination, racial segregation, and white supremacy in all areas of South African life, the National Party advocated taking it one step further, by enacting laws and implementing policies that would lead to total, absolute **Apartheid,** which, in rough translation, means "separateness." *Die kaffer op sy plek* (the nigger in his place) and *die koelies uit die land* (the coolies [i.e., Indi-- ans] out of the country) were among the slogans on which National Party candidates ran.

Full apartheid, as described three years after the 1948 election by W. W. Eiselen, secretary of Native Affairs under cabinet minister and fu- ture prime minister H. F. Verwoerd, would consist of the separation of South Africa's racial groups "into separate socioeconomic units inhabi- tating different parts of the country, each enjoying in its own area [and only its own area] full citizenship rights" (Le May 1995: 208). In other words, regardless of whether they resided in their designated tribal re- serves or homelands, or ever had, Africans would no longer be citizens of the Union of South Africa and, thus, no longer in any sense entitled to the same citizenship rights of white South Africans while living, work- ing, or journeying through the 87 percent of the country's landmass not designated "tribal homelands."

If they received official permission, natives could, of course, live and work outside of their homelands, but without any of the basic rights of cit- izenship. Citizenship rights would be available only to natives living within the boundaries of their designated homelands. Those living outside of their homelands would be migrants, guests, pests, necessary evils, or something worse—but not citizens of the Union of South Africa, denied even basic rights. All of this was pretty much already the case for blacks long before 1948 and the use of the word *apartheid* arose to describe it.

The natives were to be encouraged to "develop along their own lines," which meant that if economic development of any consequence was to occur on the reserves, the natives themselves would have to bear most, and then ultimately all, of the financial and other costs involved. And though there were to be no designated Coloured or Indian home- lands in the full-fledged apartheid state, in the interest of preserving "the character and future of every race" (Le May 1995: 202), Indian and Coloured interactions with Whites, Blacks, and each other would also be kept to a minimum. Coloureds and Indians would also lose rights and privileges previously denied only to blacks.

On the eve of the May 1948 election, Afrikaners made up approxi- mately 12 percent of South Africa's population; English-speaking whites, approximately 8 percent; Coloured, 8 percent; Indians, 2 percent; and Blacks or Natives, 70 percent. After all the votes had been cast and tal- lied, it was—contrary to general expectations—the National Party [of apartheid], in alliance with the small right-wing Afrikaner Party, that emerged as the majority, having won 79 House of Assembly seats as op- posed to 65 for the United Party, 6 for the Labour Party, and 3 Native representatives (Welsh 1999: 428).

Although it came out of the election holding the majority of House of Assembly seats, the National Party had not won a majority of the popular vote. The United Party had, with 60 percent. But due to a provision in the 1910 constitution, rural votes were given a heavier weight than urban votes. And it was in the rural—that is, heavily Afrikaner—areas that the National Party's strength was greatest. Thus, the National Party won the 1948 election, despite not having received a majority of the popular vote, its leaders committed to making apartheid a total, complete, irreversible reality.

In 1949, pursuing its objective of reducing interracial interactions to the barest possible minimum, the National Party–dominated House of Assembly passed the Prohibition or Mixed Marriages Act, which, as its name suggests, prohibited marriages between persons of different races.

Also in 1949, violent Indian–black conflicts erupted in the coastal city of Durban in Natal Province. The cause was black resentment over the Indian monopoly over commerce, transport, and property ownership in black townships. One hundred and forty-two people were killed, "over a thousand injured and many trading stores and houses looted" (Worden 1995: 104–5; Welsh 1999: 431). White racists used this as evidence that since the different races would "obviously" never be able to live together in peace and harmony, apartheid was very much in accord with human nature. A growing sentiment among members of the African National Congress was that it might be in everyone's best interests if the ANC established tighter links with Indian and Coloured organizations, if for no other reason than to show the world that South Africa's diverse racial groups could indeed live in peace and harmony.

In 1950, the House passed the Immorality Act, making sexual contact between whites and nonwhites a felonious crime, punishable by imprisonment. That same year, the House also passed the Population Registration Act, requiring that all residents of South Africa be officially labeled by race; the Group Areas Act, mandating not only residential segregation of whites and nonwhites but also separate areas of residence for each of the different categories of nonwhites; and, finally, the Suppression of Communism Act, outlawing the Communist Party and any other group or organization guilty of "statutory communism." Seeking to effect political, industrial, social, or economic change by creating disturbances of *any* sort is what made a group or individual guilty of statutory communism.

In pursuit of its long-held goal of increasing Afrikaner control of all the country's major institutions, the National Party legislated Afrikaner-favoring affirmative action, making bilingualism (Afrikaans-English) a consideration in granting state employment. This gave the advantage to Afrikaners because they were more likely to speak English than were English-speakers to speak Afrikaans. Whenever possible, the National Party–led government also awarded state contracts to Afrikaner firms.

In the interest of protecting Afrikaners from an emerging threat to their numerical superiority, and thus their political dominance, the National Party–led government suspended the United Party–instituted immigration assistance program, which had brought mostly English-speaking immigrants to the country. Government leaders also reinstated "nationally minded" Afrikaner military officers who, in 1939, had resigned their commissions rather than fight World War II on the side of the British (Le May 1995: 204).

But by the 1950s, Britain and English-speakers were no longer the main concern of the National Party. Their overriding concern was, and would continue to be, Nonwhites: keeping them down, more separate and subordinate than even before; making Apartheid an irreversible reality.

Well aware of the National Party's intentions, Nonwhites began to organize mass mobilization campaigns in united opposition to Apartheid laws and institutions.

On May 1, 1950, **Freedom Day,** thousands of nonwhite workers did not report for work as part of a strike jointly organized by black, Indian, Coloured, and communist-affiliated groups. That night, in Johannesburg, groups of militants and their supporters gathered together in defiance of a government ban on such gatherings. They were fired on by police on foot; and as they fled in panic, they were beaten about the head and body by police on horseback. The final bloody tally: 18 Africans dead; many wounded (Mandela 1995: 117).

On June 26, 1950, in response to the Freedom Day killings, the ANC (black), the APO (Coloured), and the SAIC (Indian) staged a National Day of Protest, which, in the words of Mandela, then a member of the National Executive Committee of the ANC, was "a moderate success. In the cities, the majority of workers stayed home and black businesses did not open" (Mandela 1995: 118).

Mandela also writes (119) that Freedom Day was the beginning of the end of his long-standing opposition to allowing Communist Party members to become members of the ANC. One of the few nonracially exclusive organizations in South Africa, the Communist Party was offering its unequivocal support of anti-Apartheid activities, and Mandela and others were beginning to see no reason for rejecting its support, as long as its members refrained from efforts to play a dominant role in the ANC.

Apartheid was instituted to maintain and, when possible, deepen and widen the divisions between Whites and Nonwhites, Blacks, Coloureds, Indians, and different African tribal groups. So in 1951, the House of Assembly passed the Bantu Authorities Act, the purpose of which was to maintain indirect rule of tribal homelands through traditional chiefs appointed and subsidized by the South African government, whose white officials would oversee and have veto power over all decisions made by the appointed chiefs. In return for their cooperation, governmental authorities took care to accord cooperative tribal chiefs all due respect and to provide sufficient financial rewards to allow them to lead lives at levels of material comfort beyond that enjoyed by their subjects.

In 1951, the ANC made an official announcement of its new policy of cooperation with Coloureds and Indians. It did so despite the fact that Mandela and other ANC leaders "still feared the influence of Indians . . . [and] many of [their] grassroots African supporters saw Indians as exploiters of black labor in their role as shopkeepers and merchants" (Mandela 1994: 123).

Passed in 1952, the Abolition of Passes and Coordination of Documents Act did not abolish passes. Instead, it mandated that African women and men carry **reference books,** as passes were euphemistically called, giving their name, tribal affiliation, and other life and work history data.

Another 1952 legislative act, the Native Laws Amendment Act of 1952, limited the right of natives to live permanently in urban areas to persons born there; persons who lived there for 15 continuous years; or persons who had worked for the same employer for at least 10 years (Le May 1995: 213).

April 6, 1952, was the 300th anniversary of the arrival of the first group of white settlers at Table Bay in the Cape Province. Knowing this, the ANC, in coalition with Indian, Coloured, and other black groups, chose that as the day on which to launch the **United Defiance Campaign** that began nationwide demonstrations against Apartheid. Though intended to be peaceful, the demonstrations soon became violent. The violence began in the city of East London, located on the eastern coast of Cape Province, with the deaths of 26 Nonwhites. Then, as the demonstrations turned increasingly violent, six Whites, including a nun, were killed (Mandela 1995: 127–43, 210).

The East London deaths did not, however, put an end to the United Defiance Campaign. It continued for five months, during which, as a result of worker strikes and other acts of defiance, thousands were arrested and ANC membership increased from 20,000 to 100,000 (Mandela 1995: 132).

Though the Defiance Campaign led to more rather than less cooperation between black and Indian anti-Apartheid groups, there were, at least at first, still Indians who didn't think it in their best interests to enter into coalitions with black groups. Mary Benson, a white South African journalist, novelist, and anti-Apartheid activist for many years, recalls being present at a meeting of leaders of the Indian congress: "To judge from the vehemence of some Indian delegates, there was considerable doubt about whether Africans were capable of sustaining nonviolence. One of them [Mahatma Gandhi's son Manilal] opined that it would be a disaster for untutored people to attempt such disciplined resistance" (1996: 84). But Manilal Gandhi was wrong. After the 1952 Defiance Campaign, Black and Indian anti-Apartheid activists continued working in concert with each other.

Also in 1952, the UN General Assembly passed the first of decades of annual resolutions condemning South Africa's Apartheid policies. The leaders of South Africa's ruling party didn't care; they continued doing what they had set out to do.

In 1953 it became a crime for African workers to go on strike, and the legislature passed the Public Safety Act, empowering the government to declare martial law and detain people without trial whenever it deemed it in the national interest to do so. There was also, during 1953, the passage of the Criminal Laws Amendment Act, authorizing the infliction of corporal punishment on those who defied the country's Apartheid laws.

Also in 1953, the legislature passed the Bantu Education Act, which placed native schools under the direction and supervision of the newly created Department of Bantu Education, one of whose main purposes was to ensure that Africans "develop along their own lines." This meant that henceforth there would be no pretense of providing the same type of education to Natives as provided to Whites. According to a 1954 statement by Dr. H. F. Verwoerd, one of the architects of Bantu Education and a man who would soon be party prime minister,

> The Native child must be taught subjects which will enable him to work with and among his own people; therefore there is no use misleading him by showing him the green pastures of European society, in which he is not allowed to graze. Bantu education should not be used to create imitation whites (Mathabane 1986: 193).

The Bantu Education Act also prohibited teachers at native schools from criticizing the government or any school official (Mandela 1994: 167).

The 1953 Extension of University Education Act established separate colleges for nonwhite groups and prohibited their attendance at the Universities of Cape Town and Witwatersrand, previously open to all races. In addition, the 1953 Reservation of Separate Amenities Act decreed that separate facilities for South Africa's different racial groups did not have to be in any way equal. In that same year it became unlawful for African workers to go on strike.

In 1954, D. F. Malan, age 80, resigned as head of the National Party and Johannes Strijdom became the country's new prime minister. Chief Albert Luthuli was the elected president of the black African National Congress. Nelson Mandela became one of the ANC's four deputy presidents.

During the following year, 1955, there emerged two white anti-Apartheid groups: the **Torch Commando** and the **Black Sash.** The Torch Commando was formed by a group of World War II veterans who during the coming years would hold and participate in small-scale parades and demonstrations in opposition to Apartheid. The Black Sash was an all-female, mostly English-speaking group committed to passive resistance to Apartheid. Apart from writing protest letters and putting other kinds of nonviolent pressures on cabinet ministers and other influential government officials, Black Sash members provided advice and legal assistance to persons seeking help after arrest or help to violate the country's pass laws. Unfortunately, neither the Torch Commando nor the Black Sash was large or influential enough to make a substantive difference.

In June 1955, a meeting of the Congress of the People was held in Kliptown, located just outside of Johannesburg. In attendance were 3,000 or so delegates from the ANC, the South African Indian Congress, the National Union of the Organization of Coloured People, and the Congress of Democrats (a white organization with communist affiliations). One of the products of this meeting was the **Freedom Charter,** a document calling for the abolition of all forms of Apartheid, universal suffrage, land redistribution, and the nationalization of South African banks and other private sector industries. The government's response to the Freedom Charter was a series of police raids on the homes and organizational offices of those who attended the meeting. In all, 156 people of all races were arrested and charged with having committed treason.

By the middle 1950s, South Africa's Apartheid laws and methods of enforcing them were making the country's policies the object of increasingly widespread international condemnation and disgust. But confident of the support of the overwhelming majority of South African whites, the National Party continued enacting and enforcing Apartheid laws that were making it, in the words of E. H. Louw, its minister of external affairs (1954–66), "the polecat [skunk] of the world" (Le May 1995: 212).

In 1956, the right to vote was finally taken away from the Cape Coloureds. Now no Nonwhites anywhere in South Africa had the right to vote in any municipal, provincial, or national election. It was also during the mid-1950s that Nelson Mandela and other ANC leaders began to reconsider their organization's disavowal of violence as a means of shattering the strictures and structures of Apartheid.

In 1957, the ANC Women's League organized nationwide demonstrations in protest of female residents of urban areas having to carry passes, or reference books, as they were officially designated. Almost 2,000 protesters were arrested in Johannesburg alone. A few days before the 1958 election, the state decreed gatherings of more than 10 Africans in any urban area to henceforth be illegal (Mandela 1995: 217).

The National Party emerged from the 1958 election stronger than ever, among English-speakers as well as Afrikaners. The number of House of Assembly seats held by its members increased to 103 out of a total of 159 (Le May 1995: 213). Increasing English support for the National Party, plus a higher Afrikaner than English birthrate, was beginning to give rise to talk of the future Afrikanerization of the English.

But the National Party still had problems. Prominent among them was that Apartheid wasn't accomplishing what it was supposed to accomplish. There was no way it could. The African tribal homelands simply could not support the entire African population, not even half of it. The African population was still growing faster than the white population. Despite "influx control" measures, periodic "population removals," pass laws, and the Group Areas Act, the African townships or "locations" situated on the fringes of all of the country's areas were every day becoming larger and more densely populated. And, in truth, there was a great need for Africans in the urban areas. How could the country's industries survive without cheap African labor? How could white workers be paid wages that allowed them to enjoy one of the highest standards of living in the world, if not at the expense of lowly paid African workers?

Apart from their high rates of population growth and the lack of paved roads, electricity, running water, and such, the urban African townships were becoming more problematic in other ways. Most alarmingly, they were becoming increasingly militantly politicized, despite the presence of government-paid informants in the ANC and other anti-Apartheid groups. There were also a lot of idle, unemployed young people, defiantly swaggering about, running amok, disinclined to show proper respect for the police and other agents of the white South African government.

The townships were also home to illegal stills and **shebeens** (bars and beer joints) and criminal gangs and others involved in all manner of illegal activities. But as long as black criminal activities remained nonpolitical and had no negative impacts on the lives of Whites, they were not of primary concern to the police. Political criminals were their primary concern.

On August 24, a few months after the 1958 election, Prime Minister Strijdom died in office and was replaced by former minister of Bantu education Hendrik Verwoerd. Under Verwoerd's leadership, the National Party held firm to its commitment to attaining total and complete racial Apartheid, no matter how unattainable clearer heads might have seen it to be.

In 1959, the legislature passed the Promotion of Bantu Self-Government bill, authorizing the creation of eight "nation units," or "ethnic bantustans," to be located in the discontiguous 13 percent of the country's landmass set aside for the native population, who constituted approximately 70 percent of the country's total population. These new African nation units were to eventually become, according to government plans, independent states, part of an interrelated cluster of southern African states, of which white South Africa would be the dominant member.

WINDS OF CHANGE

During 1959, South Africa came under increasingly widespread condemnation during meetings of the UN General Assembly. British prime minister Harold Macmillan disassociated himself and the British government from Apartheid by declaring in a speech following a tour of the African continent that the "winds of change" were sweeping through the continent and that Verwoerd's Apartheid policies would find no support from Britain, which was now committed to rapid decolonization (Worden 1995: 107). "Individual merit alone," Macmillan asserted, "should be the only determinant of how far and in what direction a person can advance" (Le May 1995: 218).

April 6, 1959, was the 307th anniversary of Jan van Riebeeck's arrival at the Cape. Anti-Apartheid groups were becoming more militant, one of the most militant being the **Pan Africanist Congress (PAC),** a black political group. Formed by disillusioned members of the ANC, the PAC came into existence in 1959, rejecting multiracial cooperation in its labeling of both Whites and Indians as "foreign minority groups" with no "natural" or "earned" place in South Africa. They advocated a South Africa ruled by and for black Africans and black Africans only.

On March 21, 1960, South Africa came in for another torrent of worldwide condemnation as a result of nationwide demonstrations organized by the PAC in protest of the country's pass laws. Police fired into a mass of unarmed Africans marching through the township of Sharpeville, located near Vereeniging in the Transvaal. Sixty-nine people were killed; hundreds were wounded (Le May 1995: 221). Two Africans were also killed during a protest in Cape Town (Mandela 1995: 231).

The **Sharpeville masacre** set off a series of protest marches and general strikes that threatened to shut down the country. The government dealt with the threat by declaring a state of emergency, mobilizing its Active Citizen (Police) Force, arresting close to 18,000 people of all races, and declaring both the ANC and PAC banned, or illegal, organizations.

In October 1960, South African whites voted on whether their country should immediately declare itself an independent republic or remain a British dominion within the British Commonwealth. South Africa became an independent republic on May 31, 1961, but having become the "polecat of the world," the country was denied membership in the British Commonwealth.

Albert John Luthuli, Zulu chief and head of the banned African National Congress, was awarded the 1960 Nobel Peace Prize for his nonviolent efforts to end Apartheid. Though he was **banned,** Luthuli was given special dispensation to leave the country to receive his prize firsthand.

Luthuli was neither the first nor the last anti-Apartheid activist to be banned. Thousands of people were. To be banned was, among other things, to be prohibited from making speeches and from being in the simultaneous company of two or more people. In 1963, it would become illegal to publicly quote a banned person and illegal for a banned person's picture to appear in public.

In 1961, the African National Congress dropped its commitment to attaining its objectives through nonviolent means, authorizing Nelson

Mandela to form a military force separate from the formal ANC organizational structure. **Umkhonto we Sizwe** (Spear of the Nation) was the formal name of this new organization, but it was usually referred to simply as **MK.**

The membership of MK was racially diverse and included communists. Its mission was to engage in the sabotage of government buildings and facilities, making "selective forays against military installations, power plants, telephone lines, transportation links," all with the aim of frightening National Party supporters, scaring off foreign investors, and thereby weakening the economy (Mandela 1995: 274, 283).

During the 1960s, MK training bases were set up in sympathetic neighboring countries, and the ANC entered into intense competition with the Pan African Congress (PAC), whose leaders charged MK with being the brainchild of white communists and members of the white Liberal Party (Mandela 1995: 284).

The National Party emerged from the 1961 general election with its members still holding the overwhelming majority of House of Assembly seats. The white, racially liberal Progressive Party—consisting of former United Party members—whose slogan was "merit not color," won one seat; but it would not win another until 1974.

In 1962, National Party member B. J. Vorster became South Africa's minister of justice. The National Party, as he saw it, stood "for Christian Nationalism, which is an ally of National Socialism. You can call the anti-democratic system a dictatorship if you like. In Italy it is called Fascism, in Germany National Socialism, and in South Africa Christian Nationalism" (Malherbe 1977: 106).

Among other 1962 happenings were the arrest of Nelson Mandela, after his return from a trip abroad in solicitation of money and training facilities for MK, and a UN General Assembly vote in favor of imposing sanctions on South Africa. Then, to ensure a continued supply of arms to its police and military forces, the South African government established ARMSCOR, its very own arms manufacturing firm.

Even with Mandela and other of its founding leaders in prison, MK continued its hit-and-run guerrilla tactics against the South African government. The PAC and African Resistance Movement (ARM) also engaged in periodic acts of sabotage. In response, the House of Assembly passed the 1963 General Law Amendment Act, giving police the right to detain and place in solitary confinement anyone suspected of a political crime without formally charging them. It was also in 1963 that the House of Assembly made it illegal to publish photographs of and speeches by banned persons. Speaking of banned, because of its Apartheid policies, South Africa was banned from participation in the 1964 World Olympic Games. This ban would be in effect until 1992.

In 1964, Nelson Mandela was found guilty of numerous acts of sabotage and sentenced to life imprisonment at Robben Island, located just across the bay from Cape Town. Once there, he found that the same divisions existed within the prison community as on the outside: Whites with guns, Blacks at their mercy; the Africa-for-Africans-only PAC versus the multiracial ANC.

In the South Africa beyond the prison walls, acts of sabotage continued and the National Party continued to draw more support from English-speaking whites. The results of the 1966 general election were 126 House of Assembly seats for the National Party, 39 for the United Party, and only 1 for the Progressive Party (Mandela 1994: 432).

During the late 1960s the Africanist PAC, still in fierce competition with the multiracial ANC, opened its membership to both whites and Indians. Then in 1970, the House passed the Prohibition of Political Interference Act, making it a crime to be a member of a multiracial political party. In 1973, the UN General Assembly expressed its condemnation of South African Apartheid by declaring it to be a crime against humanity.

Then there appeared a crack in the walls of Apartheid. Recognizing that laws and policies preventing Blacks from competing with Whites for skilled jobs limited the development of a larger black consumer market for South African goods, thus keeping demand for these goods lower than it would otherwise be, Prime Minister Vorster, in 1973, acknowledged that "Blacks should be allowed to do skilled work in white occupations, as long as white workers didn't object to their doing so." Soon, Blacks were doing work previously reserved for Whites only, regardless of whether white union members concurred.

> Previously, one white businessman recalls, "you couldn't make Blacks heavy-metal crane drivers, because Blacks had no depth perception. But the moment the law was changed, Blacks acquired depth perception overnight" (Waldmeir 1998: 26).

Also during the 1970s there arose in the urban townships the Black Consciousness Movement (BCM), its members advocating a nonracial society, but one in which whites would not be allowed to play leading roles. Later, in 1974, black policemen in the urban townships became authorized to carry guns.

Soweto is the acronym for Southwestern Township, one of the sprawling, densely populated black ghettoes located on the southwestern periphery of Johannesburg. On June 16, 1976, African students all over the country went on strike in protest of the issuance of a government decree mandating that half of all instruction in native schools be conducted in the Afrikaans language. An illegal 15,000-student march took place in Soweto.

The marchers came to a stop at a police roadblock. The police ordered them to disperse. Some of the student marchers threw stones at the police. The police opened fire, killing over 20 students (Welsh 1999: 474) and wounding scores of others, some felled by bullets fired at their backs as they fled in fright. Video footage of South African police shooting at fleeing schoolchildren was shown on TV news programs around the world.

The most immediate response to the **Soweto massacre** in South Africa itself was a nationwide student boycott of classes and a seemingly endless wave of student demonstrations, riots, and violent confrontations with the police that continued into the following year, 1977. According to official government estimates of the time, between June 1976 and February 1977, 575 people were killed and 2,389 wounded in protest actions engendered by the Soweto massacre (Le May 1995: 237; Worden 1995: 119).

Also in 1977, Steve Biko, a Black Consciousness Movement leader, died of massive head and body wounds received while in police custody (Truth and Reconciliation Commission). African students again took to the streets, participating in another round of school boycotts and protest actions that led to violent reactions by the police and more worldwide condemnation of Apartheid as a crime against humanity. Thousands of black nonstudents began refusing to pay the rents and service fees the government charged for allowing them to live in rickety, corrugated iron-roofed shanties in unpaved, rutted-road townships like Soweto.

Still, despite all the nonwhite protests against Apartheid policies, most South Africans seemed quite content with the way the National Party was handling things. In the 1977 general election, the National Party won 134 seats in the House of Assembly (Le May 1995: 237), which was more than it had ever before won.

Then in 1978, the National Party was hit with a financial scandal involving the misuse of funds by party leaders within the Department of Information. Prime Minister Vorster was forced to resign. P. W. Botha, former minister of defense, became the country's new prime minister. Another crack in the walls occurred in 1979, when black trade unionism was legalized. Black workers could now organize.

By the beginning of the 1980, as a result of successful liberation movements in Mozambique, Angola, and Rhodesia, South Africa now bordered independent black-ruled states. Sympathetic to MK and other armed groups seeking to bring an end to Apartheid in South Africa, these states allowed them to operate military bases from which to launch operations calculated to strike terror in the hearts of white South Africans. Nelson Mandela has estimated that in 1980 MK was "orchestrating an explosion a week at some strategic site or another [in South Africa]" (1995: 506).

Even so, according to the then head of the South African Defense Force, General Constand Viljoen, MK was never a really very serious *military* foe. "[A] long drawn out war was completely possible from a military point of view," he is quoted as having said (Waldmeir 1998: 34–35). "But from the country's psychological point of view it was not possible and one had to find a solution."

General Viljoen meant that while MK was nothing like a formidible military foe, its very existence and the small physical damage that it did inflict on the country served to strike fear in the hearts of Whites. This gave a psychological uplift to Blacks, which was exactly what MK leaders intended. The once a week or so MK explosions helped the anti-Apartheid cause; but by the 1980s, Afrikaner leaders had other reasons for questioning whether they still should, or even could, continue to maintain racial Apartheid in its existing form.

Things had changed since the Anglo-Boer War. The social, political, and economic situations of Afrikaners had greatly improved in relation to all other groups within the general population, English-speakers included. The National Party's use of the state to raise the general economic status of the country's politically dominant Afrikaner constituents through affirmative action–type hiring programs and the awarding of, whenever feasible, state contracts to Afrikaners had been successful. Afrikaners were now dominant at all levels of government, and particularly in the country's police, military, and other state security agencies. And while the majority of the country's rural and small town whites were Afrikaners, Afrikaners were no longer primarily a rural people. They had become primarily urban-dwelling and were becoming duly represented in the country's white-collar and managerial classes. By 1977, 65 percent of all Afrikaners were engaged in white-collar work.

As a consequence of all of the above, by the 1980s a great many Afrikaner business, cultural, and political leaders, many of whom belonged to the Broederbond, had come to see Apartheid as standing as the gravest threat of all to South Africa's continued economic prosperity. South Africa had become a full-fledged industrial nation in which manufacturing industries were the largest contributors to the gross national product. Now, however, these industries were at an impasse: They were faced with chronic shortages of workers qualified to fill skilled-labor positions because Apartheid policies prevented large numbers of blacks from filling them and a too-low rate of white immigration because not a lot of Europeans were eager to immigrate to a country that seemed to be on the verge of a violent race war the likes of which the world had never seen. Plus, the low wages paid to black workers limited the size, as well as the potential size, of the domestic market for goods manufactured in South Africa. In addition, boycotts of South African products were greatly reducing the international market for its goods. Also, pressures from anti-Apartheid forces in their home countries were forcing more and more foreign firms to shut down their plants and suspend all business dealings within South Africa.

Being the skunk of the world was not only a great hindrance to further growth of South Africa's manufacturing sector, it also took its toll on the physical and mental health of South Africa's White population. Under Apartheid, South African Whites had come to have the highest rate of coronary heart disease in the world, as well as one of the highest suicide rates (Thompson 1999: 203–4).

The enforcement of Apartheid laws and policies also required great financial expenditures. It cost money to maintain a huge national defense force and the police and internal security forces necessary combat the seemingly intractable foes of Apartheid. It also cost money to incarcerate the foes of Apartheid. Moreover, government bodies at all levels would have more money to spend on other things if they didn't have to maintain separate administrative agencies, separate buses and public accommodation facilities, separate parks and beaches, and separate practically everything else for each of the country's four designated racial groups.

Thus, by the 1980s there had begun to a develop a widening split among persons within the higher circles of Afrikanerdom. Some were amenable to constitutional change resulting in some form of power sharing with the nonwhite population.

A new constitution, some pondered might, for instance, grant persons of all races the right to vote without thereby ushering in black majority rule. Majority rule could perhaps be avoided by (1) executive power sharing between Whites and Nonwhites; (2) an equal distribution of House seats and positions in other public institutions to members of the different racial groups, regardless of their respective numbers within the general population; (3) the granting of veto power to each minority party within the House of Assembly; or (4) some combination of the three.

With the right kind of restructuring of government, some thought, the National Party might be able to remain dominant by gaining the support of the country's Coloured and Indian voters. Coloureds, after all, were Afrikaans-speaking and Dutch Reform Church–affiliated, and though it pained some Afrikaners to acknowledge, Coloureds carried a bit of Afrikaner blood in their veins. Indians? It was only within recent decades that Indians had shown a willingness to accept Blacks as their equals. Maybe they still weren't truly ready.

There were also, however, other influential Afrikaners who most adamantly rejected the concept of power sharing, which they saw as going against all that the National Party had come into existence to preserve. Andries Treurnicht was one such member of the House of Assembly. After being expelled from the National Party for his virulent opposition to power sharing, Treurnicht and his followers went on to form a new **Conservative Party.**

There was also former policeman Eugene Terreblanche, who during the 1980s formed the paramilitary, vigilantist **Afrikaner Weerstandsbeweging** (Afrikaner Resistance Movement, or **AWB**), whose insignia contains three sevens arranged to resemble a swastika. To counter black guerrilla attacks on government facilities and White-owned farms and other private White-owned business enterprises was the publicly announced goal of the AWB.

In 1982, Nelson Mandela's eighteenth year of incarceration, he and four other ANC leaders were transferred from Robben Island to less crowded quarters at Pollsmoor Prison, a maximum security facility located a few miles southeast of Cape Town. Also in 1982, South African Defense Force troops conducted a raid on an ANC compound in Maputo, Mozambique, which resulted in the deaths of 13 African ANC affiliates, some of whom were women and children. Another raid in Maseru, Lesotho, resulted in the deaths of 42 Africans, some of whom were also women and children. In retaliation, MK (the military arm of the ANC) set off its first fatal car bomb, at an air force and military intelligence office in Pretoria, resulting in 19 deaths and 200 injuries. There were also MK bomb explosions at the Koeberg nuclear power plant near Cape Town and "other military targets" (Mandela 1995: 518).

In November 1983, two-thirds of the South African electorate voted for a referendum to create a tricameral legislature consisting of a House of Assembly for Whites, a House of Representatives for Coloureds, and a House of Delegates for Indians. There was a catch, though; the white House of Assembly had veto power over decisions made by members of the Coloured and Indian Houses. But this attempt to separate the Coloured and Indian populations from the black population did not work. "[O]nly 14 percent of the former and 16.6 percent of the latter voted in the first [1984] election" (Welsh 1999: 483). Apart from creating a tricameral legislature, the 1983 referendum also brought into existence a new constitution, which, among other things, changed the title of the country's chief of state from prime minister to president.

In 1984, for his courageously nonviolent challenges to apartheid—such as his call for international economic sanctions against South African, even while still in residence there—black South African archbishop of the Anglican Church Desmond Tutu was awarded the Nobel Peace Prize. Also in 1984, Nelson Mandela, still in prison, began to receive visits from high government officials wanting to know exactly what the ANC wanted. A unitary state led by persons elected in one person–one vote, nonracially exclusive elections, was Mandela's reply.

Other noteworthy 1984 occurrences were the emergence of the interracial **United Democratic Front (UDM),** representing 575 separate groups ranging from trade unions to sports clubs (Thompson 1995: 228) and the all-black **Congress of South African Trade Unions (COSATU).** Both groups were committed to the use of nonviolent means to end Apartheid.

On January 31, 1985, Prime Minister Botha offered Nelson Mandela his freedom on condition that henceforth the ANC reject the use of violence as a political instrument. Mandela rejected Botha's offer.

On March 21, 1985, the twenty-fifth anniversary of the Sharpeville massacre, there began a new, intensified wave of political violence that continued on into the 1990s. The most direct instigators of this new wave of violence were the Cape Province police, who opened fire on a group of blacks participating in a funeral procession that their superiors deemed a threat to law and order.

In response to the shootings, ANC leaders instructed their supporters to commence making the country "ungovernable." Thus, not only did there begin a new and more intensive wave of raids and acts of sabotage against government facilities, there also began an increase in acts of political violence within the townships. The township rent and service fee strikes continued, too. There were also, within the townships, increasing numbers of attacks on the persons and property of black township councillors, black policemen (who usually did not belong to the same tribal groups as the people they policed), and others either known or suspected to be government agents or informants.

Fighting between members of the ANC, the Pan African Congress, the Black Consciousness Movement, and other groups competing for leadership in the black communities became common.

Vigilante "people's courts" sprung up in the townships, self-empowered to summarily impose and implement death sentences. **Necklacing**—placing a gasoline-soaked rubber tire around a person's neck and setting fire to it—was one of the most brutal means of carrying out these death sentences

"Liberation before education" became the slogan of the tens of thousands of school-age children who gave up attending school to join the fight against the municipal police, black collaborators and informants, and all other perceived agents of the detested Apartheid state.

In November 1985, after his release from the Volks Hospital in Cape Province Town, where he had undergone surgery necessitated by an enlarged prostate gland, Nelson Mandela had an audience with Kobie Coetsee, South Africa's minister of justice, police, and prisons, and General Johan Willemse, commissioner of prisoners. Though no substantive political issues were discussed at this meeting, it ended with the Afrikaners having developed a favorable impression of Mandela, and he of them.

After his release from the Volks Hospital, Mandela was informed that he had been assigned new quarters at Pollsmoor Prison. It was a private cell in the prison hospital on the ground floor,

> eight yards by six, painted pale green, comfortably furnished, with a private bathroom next door and a second cell across a hallway equipped with a gymnasium with an exercise bike for the 65-year-old fitness fanatic. By South African prison standards, this was unheard-of luxury (Sparks 1995: 31).

During subsequent years, there would be a reported 46 more secret meetings in "hospitals, prisons, and a cabinet minister's home" between Mandela and top South African officials (Sparks 1995: 36). Most prominent among these officials were the above mentioned Kobie Coetsee and

Johan Willemse, as well as Niel Barnard, head of the National Intelligence Service, Barnard's deputy Mike Louw, and civil servant Fanus van der Merwe. They wanted to know what they, white South Africans, would have to give up in order for the ANC to cease hostilities against the South African government. And since they wanted detailed answers to this question, their talks with Mandela sometimes lasted for several hours. Sometimes the talks took place in state automobiles, during drives through the Western Cape countryside, arranged to gradually accustom Mandela to life back in the world from which he had been officially banished for life.

But even as the secret talks between Mandela and high National Party officials continued, so did the political violence beyond the narrowly circumscribed world of Nelson Mandela, who was still very much a Pollsmoor Prison inmate, despite receiving highly preferential treatment.

Political and economic conditions continued to deteriorate in 1986, another tumultuous year. Prime Minister Botha declared the country under a state of emergency and ordered a **total onslaught** against the enemies of Apartheid. The ANC stepped up its bombings and attacks on White-owned farms and government installations. The South African Defense Force made more retaliatory raids on suspected ANC bases in neighboring countries. Yielding to pressure from shareholders, foreign firms began to dispose of their South African assets. As more and more countries instituted trade sanctions and boycotts of South African products, the value of the South African rand declined in relation to foreign currencies. "Free Mandela!" became a demand heard from all corners of the world.

In all, "Nearly 1,000 people died in political violence in 1986, 20,000 were detained, and there were about 200 guerrilla attacks by Umkhonto we Sizwe [MK]" (Le May 1995: 247). There were also reports of secret white right-wing groups seemingly unworried about governmental interference as they went about taking violent clandestine action against enemies of apartheid both at home and abroad.

There still occurred more cracks in the wall, though. Amid all the township violence and the government's "total onslaught," 1986 was also the year in which South Africa's pass laws were abolished. Blacks of both sexes could now travel about and change jobs without being in possession of passes, or reference books, giving them official authorization to do so. The repeal of the pass laws was followed by the repeal of the Prohibition of Mixed Marriages and Immorality Acts and the repeal of the Reservation of Separate Amenities Act, which mandated "petty Apartheid," or racially segregated parks, theaters, buses, libraries, beaches, toilets, and other places of public recreation, conveyance, and accommodation.

But it was not enough. Antigovernment protests, violent and nonviolent, continued. The state of emergency remained in force.

The 1987 general election was the first one in which the Conservative Party ran candidates. It won 22 seats, attacking the National Party for not doing all that could be done to combat black terrorism. Having received 52 percent of the vote and a majority of House of Assembly seats (Le May 1995: 247), the National Party was still the majority party; but its majority was shrinking and divisions with Afrikanerdom was widening. MK guerilla attacks, township violence, township rent and service fee strikes, and the government-declared state of emergency continued.

In January 1989, President Botha suffered a mild stroke. As a result, members of his cabinet forced him to resign his position as leader of the National Party, but he remained president of the Republic of South Africa. F. W. de Klerk, the former minister of national education, became the new leader of the National Party.

Mandela and Botha finally met, secretly, on July 5, 1989, at Tuynhuys, the president's Cape Town residence. The meeting was cordial, mostly polite small talk; nothing substantive was decided or discussed, but at least it had occurred. It was a good sign that the two had shook hands upon being introduced, not a common thing for blacks and Afrikaners to do.

By the time of his meeting with Botha, Mandela was not the only ANC leader holding meetings with members of the Afrikaner governing elite. By the early 1980s, a majority faction within the Afrikaner Broederbond had come to see Apartheid as no longer serving Afrikaner interests. It wasn't worth the costs, they were beginning to think. Maybe it wasn't even necessary for continued white economic control of the country and the preservation of the Afrikaans language and Afrikaner culture. Maybe. But maybe not. They would have to see.

There were communists among the top ANC leaders. The Afrikaners needed to know how serious those leaders were about nationalizing the economy and carrying out a massive land redistribution scheme.

Peter de Lange, who while principal of the Rand Afrikaans University in Johannesburg became chairman of the Broederbond in 1983, made his initial contact with leading members of the ANC (in exile) at a Ford Foundation–sponsored conference in Long Island, New York, 1986 (Sparks 1995: 72–90). De Lange first sought out Thabo Mbeki, who would one day succeed Mandela as president of South Africa but was then the ANC's director of information to lunch with himself and his wife.

At a luncheon with Mbeki, de Lange is reported to have explained the evolution of the Broederbond position regarding the granting of citizenship rights to blacks, saying in the effect that while in the past Afrikaners had seen laws mandating separate living areas and laws prohibiting interracial marriages and other forms of race mixing as being essential to the survival of the Afrikaner people and Afrikaner culture, present-day realities were such that they could now rescind all Apartheid laws and very little would change as a result. According to reports, de Lange gave the Group Areas Act as an example of this: "We can remove [it] tommorrow," he told Thabo Mbeki,

> and it's not going to make any difference, because your people don't have the money to move into the expensive white suburbs. So from your point of view it will be a meaningless change, but for us Afrikaners it will mean we will wake up one day and realize nothing has changed, that we are still all right, we've not perished as a people because the Group Areas Act is not there. That will open the way to asking the question: Why do we need a white government anyway? (Sparks 1995: 73).

In other words, by the mid-1980s leading members of the Broederbond were amenable to working out a power-sharing agreement with black African leaders, one in which blacks had full citizenship rights, and Afrikaners and other Whites maintained their economic dominance and thereby their distinct cultural identity. But for this to happen, the Broederbond leaders had to be certain that the ANC leaders were not really the wild-eyed, fire-breathing, died-in-the-wool communist terrorist radicals that they and other leading Afrikaners had been making them out to be all these past years.

Thus between November 1987 and May 1990, members of the Broederbond and other nonofficial Afrikaner leaders (Church, intellectual, business, and so on) held a series of 12 meetings with Mbeki and other ANC leaders in exile in Europe and Africa (Sparks 1995: 82–87). These meetings assuaged Afrikaner fears that if blacks came to political power under ANC leaders, South Africa would go communist and Afrikaners and other Whites would lose everything, including their identity and very existence as culturally distinct people. It wouldn't be that way at all, de Lange and other influential Afrikaners became convinced. Mbeki—the holder of a master's degree in economics from the London School of Economics—and the other ANC leaders with whom de Lange and other unofficial Afrikaner leaders had met were well educated. They seemed to be reasonable and practical men with whom the Afrikaners could work something out. Also by 1989, communism, in decline all over the world, even in Russia, was hardly the threat it had once seemed.

The only remaining questions were: Exactly what kind of power-sharing deal could Afrikaner leaders make with black leaders? With which black leaders should the deal be made?

The ANC leaders didn't speak for all Blacks. There was the **Zulu Inkatha Freedom Party (IFP),** headed by Māngosuthu Buthelezi. Like some other tribal group leaders, Afrikaners included, Buthelezi was bent on securing guarantees that his group would receive sufficient territorial sovereignty and representation in the National House of Assembly to ensure survival of its distinct cultural identity in any new political dispensation.

Maybe it would be best for Afrikaners if the Buthelezi-led IFP was the black party that came to power in the new dispensation, a sizable number of influential, staunchly conservative Afrikaner elected office-holders and civil servants were beginning to think. Maybe both the Broederbond and the National Party had become too liberal for the good of Afrikanerdom, many non-Broederbond and more than few nonelite Afrikaners were beginning to think. Maybe it was time for a change, a switch over to the Conservative Party.

Then in October 1989, the National Party found itself in the eye of a scandal that began when, on the eve of his execution for the murder of a white farmer, black African Butana Almond Nofomela, gained a stay of execution by confessing to his involvement in eight political assassinations by order of active state security personnel. In an attempt to save himself after hearing of Nofomela's confession, Captain Dirk Coetzee, Nofomela's former commanding officer, gave reporters employed by the Afrikaans-language newspaper *Vrye Weekblad* detailed information "not only about his own involvement in 23 serious crimes, including six murders, but also about **Vlakplaas,** the special—officially nonexistent—counterinsurgency unit he had commanded for nine years" (Sparks 1996: 162). Vlakplaas was the name of the "isolated farm where he [Coetzee] converted former ANC members into police informers and assassins" (Waldmeir 1997: 43). Most people had long suspected that South African military, police, and national security agencies had been behind the murders of perhaps thousands of anti-Apartheid activists and alleged activists, but now they knew of specific instances, names of some of the individuals involved in the murders, and something about the agency for which these individuals had worked.

Disaffection with the National Party was evident in the outcome of the 1989 general election. It came out of it having lost 27 seats, 11 to more racially liberal parties and 16 to the white supremacist Conservative Party, which had increased its percentage of Afrikaner vote from 26 to 40.

February 2, 1990, was the day de Klerk, now both president of the House of Assembly and National Party leader, announced the unbanning of the ANC, the PAC, the South African Communist Party, and other previously banned anti-Apartheid organizations.

Seven days later, February 11, 1990, Nelson Mandela was unconditionally released from prison, having been incarcerated for 27 years, and given assurances that, in his view:

> Whites are fellow South Africans, and [in any new political dispensation] we want them to feel safe and to know that we appreciate the contributions they have made toward the development of this country. Any man or woman who abandons Apartheid will be embraced in our struggle for a democratic South Africa; we must do

everything we can to persuade our white compatriots that a new nonracial South Africa will be a better place for all (Mandela 1995: 568–69).

Shortly after his release from prison, Mandela stood in a Soweto stadium addressing a crowd of over 100,000, calling on black children to return to school, urging that rampant crime be brought under control, and deeply grieved to have heard of criminals going about in the guise of freedom fighters.

On February 27, 1990, Mandela was elected deputy president of the ANC.

The release of Mandela and other ANC leaders did not, however, lead to the suspension of the ANC's military operations inside South Africa. That would not happen, its leaders declared, until the state of emergency was lifted, *all* political prisoners were released, and *all* Apartheid laws were repealed.

CHAPTER 6

Postapartheid South Africa

POLITICAL STRIFE AND SOCIAL DIVISIONS

Mandela's release from prison was immediately followed by a period of increased Black-on-Black violence. The main participants in the violence were members of the ANC, the Zulu Inkatha Freedom Party, and the "Africa for [black] Africans" Pan African Congress, fighting to the death for dominance in both the urban townships and the tribal homelands. The group that emerged dominant would be the one with which National Party leaders would negotiate whatever power-sharing arrangement they could prevail on them to accept.

Zulu participation in the violence was particularly intense because Zulu chief Māngosuthu Buthelezi, head of the IFP and chief minister of the KwaZulu homeland in Natal Province, and his supporters were most adamantly against the establishment of a unitary, multitribal, multiracial state. Such a state, they feared, would result in the Zulu being at the mercy of a national legislature dominated by Xhosa tribal groups. The Zulu wanted for themselves what white right-wing groups wanted: If not a completely independent homeland then at least a federated South Africa, in which specific tribal (racial, in the case of the white right-wingers) group rights were guaranteed.

The Zulu had reason to fear a Xhosa-dominated legislature. Many government-armed and -abetted migrant Zulu hostel-dwellers in non-Zulu urban townships had come forth in violent opposition to the student strikes of the 1970s and 1980s, acting in effect as agents of the Apartheid state.

Zulu were also, more often than members of other tribes, employed as municipal policemen in non-Zulu urban townships. For that reason they were resented by many of the people they policed, some whom perceived the Zulu to have taken pleasure in helping their white masters impose Apartheid law and order on other blacks. Zulu also had reason to fear other Zulu. Most were IFP members, but not all. Some were ANC members. Some were PAC members.

Mandela, partisan though he was, aptly described the predominantly Zulu Natal Province of the early 1990s as a "killing ground." As a result of IFP supporters declaring war on ANC strongholds, "entire villages were set alight, dozens of people were killed, hundereds were wounded, and thousands became refugees. In March 1990 alone, 230 people lost their lives" (Mandela 1995: 576).

Behind much of this violence, it was suspected and later verified during the Truth and Reconciliation Commission (TRC) hearings, was the nefarious **Third Force.** There were members of police and government intelligence agencies, such as the aforementioned Vlakpaas, who surreptitiously flamed the violence by supplying the Zulu-dominant IFP with money and weapons and protecting its members from reprisals by its enemies; sometimes they themselves carried out assassinations of ANC and PAC activists. There was, of course, no Third Force or white right-wing support for PAC attempts to become a dominant force in the black communities. Its slogan, "one bullet, one settler," was too scary, as were its terrorist bombings in white areas.

Despite its complicity in Black-on-Black violence, and amid threats of insurrection by armed white right-wing groups, in June 1990 the government suspended the state of emergency it had declared in response to the upsurge in anti-Apartheid violence following the Sharpeville massacre and the subsequent ANC call to make the country ungovernable.

The government's suspension of the state of emergency notwithstanding, the political violence continued. By July 1990, the number of deaths from political violence since the beginning of the year stood at 1,500, and government security forces had arrested 40 members of the ANC on charges of being part of a communist plot to overthrow the government.

Encouraging news came in August 1990. The ANC announced that it was suspending its armed struggle against the government. In return, the government had promised to set dates for the release of more political prisoners and to consider granting amnesty for all persons guilty of political crimes.

An end to the ANC's armed struggle against the government did not mean an end to Black-on-Black violence. It continued even as the ANC and government leaders continued negotiations for some mutually acceptable system of power sharing between the country's Whites and Nonwhites. All of this occurred in the midst of more stories, later verified in petitions to the Postapartheid Truth and Reconciliation Commission—of gross police brutality, roving white right-wing death squads, and government aid to and protection of attacking Zulu IFP members.

In November 1990, the Zulu—and Zulu only—were given government permission to carry traditional Zulu weapons (**assegais,** or spears, and **knobkerries,** or wooden sticks with heavy wooden heads) to political rallies and meetings.

In July 1991, the ANC held its first conference inside South Africa in 30 years. Nelson Mandela was elected without opposition to the office of ANC president. During its first 17 months of resumed legal activity, the ANC increased its membership by 700,000 members, albeit disproportionately in the urban areas. Government support of the Zulu Inkatha Freedom Party notwithstanding, the ANC was clearly the choice of most Blacks.

The final blow to lawfully mandated Apartheid was delivered in 1991, with the repeal of the Group Areas Land and Population Acts. The repeal of these acts meant that Blacks, on and off the homelands, were once again officially acknowledged citizens of South Africa, possessed of the same legal rights as Whites. There was great rejoicing around the world. South African athletes were invited to participate in the 1992 Olympic Games. Countries began resuming commercial relations with South Africa. South African political exiles returned home from abroad. The National Party began participation in a series of meetings to work out the exact details of political reform with the ANC and 21 other anti-Apartheid organizations, which together constituted the Convention for a Democratic South Africa, or CODESA. Missing from the CODESA meetings were IFP and PAC representatives, their leaders having decided not to participate.

Then, in perhaps its most unequivocal show of commitment to political change, the National Party opened its membership to persons of all races. This was the same National Party that had come to power in 1948 under slogans such as *die kaffer op sy plek* (the nigger in his place) and *die koelies uit die land* (the coolies [Asians] out of the country).

If the National Party were to survive elections in which members of all races could vote, it had to open its membership to persons of all races. It was not out of the question that by admitting Nonwhites into its membership, the party that had given the world Apartheid could emerge from an all-race election still dominant in South Africa. There was a chance.

Blacks were divided, however. The ANC might have more supporters than the Zulu IFP and other black political parties, but it wasn't clear that most Blacks were ANC supporters, or would still be so by the time elections were held.

Could a new multiracial National Party pull a sizable percentage of the black vote, as well as a majority of the Coloured and Indian votes? Though there were Coloured and Indian occupants of leadership positions in the ANC, interpersonal relations among the Black, Coloured, and Indian masses had never been close and cordial. Indians and Coloureds had fared better than Blacks both before and during Apartheid. As a result there had always been a general tendency among them to look down on Blacks, and for Blacks to resent them for it. Remember the Black anti-Indian riots of 1949?

It did not seem at all out of the question that a majority of Indian and Coloured voters could be wooed to the National Party, especially if the party convinced them that, as minorities, they would fare better under a democratic coalition government controlled by a racially integrated Afrikaner-dominant party than under the governance of a black-dominant party. This was especially true for Coloureds, most of them spoke Afrikaans, were members of the Dutch Reformed Church, and were sometimes referred to by liberal white Afrikaners as "brown Afrikaners." Coloureds might easily be brought to see that they had more in common with white Afrikaners than they did with black Africans.

A coalition government dominated by the National Party was not out of the question. Within that coalition there could also be the Zulu IFP, as well as Coloureds, Indians, and other groups in opposition to the ANC. It could happen.

If that didn't happen, something else could. Perhaps the franchise could be extended to Blacks, but not all Blacks. Perhaps an arrangement could be worked out whereby, in the interests of protecting white rights, all votes were not equal: one white vote would carry more weight than one nonwhite vote. There were a great many possibilities. In its negotiations with the ANC and other CODESA members, National Party representatives would explore them all.

After a Conservative Party victory in a by-election at Potchefstroom, the National Party presented white South Africans with a referendum on whether or not it should continue working toward social and political accommodation of the nonwhite majority. A clear majority, 69 percent, voted to continue the negotiations (Mandela 1995: 601).

In May 1992, the National Party–headed national government was embarrassed by the release of information implicating leading members of its security forces in the 1985 murders of four United Democratic Front anti-Apartheid activists. Then came the release of information indicating that the Department of Military Intelligence was still conducting covert operations against the ANC (Mandela 1995: 601).

On June 17, 1992, a Black-on-Black confrontation involving Zulu IFP members resulted in the deaths of 46 non-Zulu, most of whom were women and children. No arrests were made, and the government undertook no investigation.

Shortly after, the CODESA talks broke down. The ANC then organized a mass action campaign in support of its demands put forth during the CODESA negotiations and in protest of "state-supported violence." On September 7, 1992, native troops opened fire on a large contingent of ANC supporters marching through Bisho, the capital of Ciskei, one of the eastern Cape homelands, whose leaders were known to be anti-ANC. The result was 29 dead and more than 200 wounded.

The CODESA talks resumed despite the ongoing violence, and on September 26, 1992, de Klerk and Mandela signed a record of understanding that, among other things, created an independent body to review police actions and banned the use of "traditional weapons" (of the kind Zulu had been given permission to carry) at rallies.

In the interest of making it easier than it otherwise would be for regional or minority parties (e.g., the National Party) to win legislative majorities and thus executive control at the provincial and local levels of government, ANC and National Party negotiators agreed to divide the country's then four existing provinces (Cape, Orange Free State, Natal, and Transvaal) into nine new provinces: the Western Cape, the Eastern Cape, the Northern Cape, the Free State, KwaZulul-Natal, Gauteng, North-West, Eastern Transvaal, and Northern Transvaal.

The National Party government also agreed to allow for the multiracial election of a constitutional assembly to create a new constitution and serve as a transitional legislature for the next elected government. During talks lasting into 1993, ANC and National Party negotiators agreed on the first multiracially elected South African government, the **Government of National Unity (GNU).** In acquiescence to National Party demands for some form of power sharing, all parties receiving 5 percent or more of the vote in the general election would be proportionally represented in the new government's presidential cabinet. But this would be only a short-term arrangement. There were to be no special rights, guarantees, or accommodations made for the white or any other minority group after the country's second national election, to be held five years after the first. From then on, the elected government would be either a simple majority government or, if no party received a majority of votes, a coalition government.

Māngosuthu Buthelezi, KwaZulu chief and leader of the IFP, and other rulers of tribal homelands, as well as the leaders and rank and file of the Afrikaner Weerstandsbeweging, the Conservative Party, and other white right-wing groups, were not at all pleased that in the long run there would be no special rights granted or accommodations made for racial and ethnic minority groups. They wanted self-determination in their own separate, sovereign homelands and, as a result, were adamantly opposed to subordination in a unified state in which their respective groups would each constitute a relatively powerless minority.

There was talk, and fear, of an alliance between the Zulu IFP, conservative black leaders of native homelands, and right-wing Afrikaner groups. But it didn't happen. It was just talk, part of a general fear of ominous things to come, as the political violence continued unabated.

In 1993, thousands of deaths resulted from political violence, most of which occurred between IFP and ANC supporters. There were also innumerable acts of violence by the PAC and AWB, as well as by more covert, nefarious persons, both black and white, in the employ of police and intelligence agencies.

Perhaps the closest South Africa came to an all-out race war occurred in April 1993, when Chris Hani, the young, popular, former MK chief of staff and current top-level ANC and South African Communist Party member, was gunned down in front of his house in Boksburg, a recently racially integrated upscale suburb of Johannesburg. But thanks to information provided by one of Hani's female Afrikaner neighbors, police soon arrested a Polish immigrant who belonged to the AWB. Also arrested for complicity in Hani's murder was Clive Derby-Davis, a nationally known member of the Conservative Party.

ANC–National Party negotiations continued until everything that could be negotiated had been negotiated.

For their efforts in helping to bring an end to Apartheid, in October 1993 Frederick de Klerk and Nelson Mandela were announced as joint recipients of the Nobel Peace Prize. On that same October day, however, South African Defense Force soldiers conducted a 27-minute assault on a suspected PAC stronghold in Umtata, resulting in multiple deaths. In response, Mandela condemned his fellow Nobel Peace Prize recipient. Also on that day, "the *Weekly Mail and Guardian* reported that between July and September 85 commuters had been murdered in Witwatersrand and 105 people had been injured" (Nicol 1995: 95).

At close to midnight on November 18, 1993, the CODESA negotiations came to an official end with the approval of the new constitution hammered out by Mandela, de Klerk, and other ANC and NP officeholders. After the passage of the new constitution, "The rest of the National Party team retired exhausted, but Roelf Meyer stayed on [at the World Trade Center]. In the bowels of that grim building, he and Cyril Ramaphosa [a high-ranking black trade union leader and ANC official] joined exhausted delegates and journalists to dance for hours, waltzing in the new South Africa" (Waldmeir 1997: 218).

The violence continued into 1994, with the ANC campaigning for the April elections on the slogan "A Better Life for All." One of the PAC campaign slogans was "One Settler, One Bullet." "We Made the Change, We'll Make the Difference," was the most stridently upbeat of the National Party slogans. Although, at one point during the election, the NP was accused of distributing a comic book in Coloured areas of the Cape declaring the ANC's slogan to be "Kill a Coloured, Kill a Farmer."

The Zulu IFP, on the other hand, seemed quite intractably firm in its resolve not to participate in the election without promise of an independent Zulu homeland. By the end of 1993, there had been over 20,000 deaths as a result of ANC-IFP fighting (Waldmeir 1997: 226).

The Afrikaner Weerstandsbeweging and other white right-wing groups continued about their business of making sure rural Afrikaners were armed and trained to defend themselves against attacks by black groups. When opportunity arose, it also launched nondefensive attacks on Blacks.

One of the AWB's most spectacularly failed attempts at intimidating Blacks was when, at the behest of a tribal headman about to be ousted by people for forbidding them to vote in the upcoming election, they set up a roadblock and instituted commando patrols on the tribal lands. A result of this failed intimidation was video footage and newspaper photographs of a carload of overweight AWB commandos pleading for their lives before being shot by unforgiving uniformed black tribal commandos.

In early April 1994, an IFP march through Johannesburg turned into a violent clash between IFP and ANC supporters, resulting in 53 dead and hundreds wounded.

A MULTIRACIAL, COALITION GOVERNMENT

In the end, a coalition of AWB members, Conservative Party members, and other right-wing Afrikaner groups calling themselves the Freedom Front (FF), along with members of the IFP, led by Zulu chief Buthelezi, participated in the election after all. Though it was not known by persons outside of higher circles of the National Party until after the election, three million hectares signed over to the trust of Zulu king Goodwill Zwelithini was the price of IFP participation. With the Zulu having made out like the proverbial bandits, South Africa's first multiracial elections took place as scheduled, and with very little attendant violence. All in all, things went more smoothly than many people had expected.

The ANC came out of the election clearly the victor: 62 percent of the popular vote; 252 of the 400 National Assembly seats; and the majority of legislative seats in all but two of the country's nine provinces.

Among other things, it had promised to create new jobs through public works projects; build one million new houses with electricity and flush toiliets by the year 2000; extend primary health care to all citizens; provide 10 years of free education to everyone; institute a land redistribution program through a state land claims court; and take "extensive affirmative action measures in both the private and public sectors" (Mandela 1995: 613–14).

The National Party came in second, having won 20 percent of the popular vote, 82 National Assembly seats, and control of the Western Cape legislature, a result of having captured a majority of the Western Cape Coloured vote.

The Zulu Inkatha Freedom Party came in third, having won 10 percent of the popular vote, 43 National Assembly seats, and a majority in the KwaZula-Natal provincial legislature.

Coming in fourth, fifth, and sixth were the right-wing Afrikaner Freedom Front, with 2 percent of the popular vote and nine National Assembly seats; the left-wing Democratic Party, with slightly less than 2 percent of the popular vote and seven National Assembly seats; the PAC, with 1 percent and five seats; and African Christian Democratic Party, with 0.45 percent and two seats (Thompson 1995: 252; Worden 1995: 114; Le May 1995: 259).

Nelson Mandela, as head of the party that had won a majority of the National Assembly seats, was elected president of the Government of National Unity. He then appointed Thabo Mbeki, fellow ANC member and son of one of his oldest comrades in arms, his first deputy president. Frederick de Klerk, leader of the party that had finished second in the popular vote and captured the second largest number of legislative seats, assumed the office of second deputy president.

South Africa's population, at the time of the first multiracial election (April 1994) was 12 percent white, 8 percent Coloured, 2 percent Asian, and 78 percent black (Economist Intelligence Unit 1995–96: 47). Though most ANC and IFP support came from Blacks and most National Party support from Whites, all three parties received at least some votes from members of all four of the country's designated racial groups. And the National Party did, in fact, win a majority of the Cape Coloured vote.

The secretary general of the United Nations and representatives from 45 of the world's nations were present at Mandela's swearing in as South Africa's first president to be democratically elected by a multiracial electorate. South African Defense Force fighter planes piloted by white officers flew overhead in celebration of his swearing in. Mandela's swearing in as president, however, did not end the violence.

CONTINUED POLITICAL VIOLENCE

Even though it did so with decreasing intensity, political violence continued all through Mandela's term of office, up to almost the eve of the 1999 elections. As before, it was most consistently between IFP and ANC affiliates. The latter were still intent on gaining greater KwaZulu-Natal autonomy from central government control. There were also white groups and individuals still clamoring for a white homeland.

According to a report by the Human Rights Commission, during November 1994—six months after the election of the Mandela-led government—106 South Africans were killed in political violence, with 56 of the deaths occurring in KwaZulu-Natal (Economist Intelligence Unit 1995: 12).

During the spring of 1995, two officials of the predominantly Zulu IFP were arrested by a police task force investigating hit squads in KwaZulu-Natal. IFP officials charged the government with not investigating the assassinations of several hundred of its own officials with the same vigor.

The deaths resulting from the IFP-ANC violence in KwaZulu-Natal during the June 1995 totaled 44, and 500 KwaZulu homes were gutted by politically motivated arsonists between April and August 1995 (Economist Intelligence Unit 1995: 5).

In November 1995, the IFP launched its election campaign for control of seats in the KwaZulu provincial legislature with a warning that their defeat could lead to increased violence. On Christmas Day, ANC supporters were killed at Shobashobane, a small ANC stronghold in a predominantly IFP area. Eighty-seven homes, of presumably ANC supporters, were also razed. A source cites police estimates of 20 violent deaths per day in KwaZulu-Natal during most of Mandela's term of office (Economist Intelligence Unit 1996: 10).

Nor were Zulu and white groups wanting a separate white homeland the only immediate problems confronting ANC leaders during their first years of political hegemony. Conflicts of interest and seemingly irreconcilable differences between President Mandela and Deputy President de Klerk and their respective constituents began to emerge almost immediately after they came together as coalitionists in the new Government of National Unity. One of the first and most publicized of sources of these disagreements concerned the establishment of a **Truth and Reconciliation Commission (TRC)**.

THE TRUTH AND RECONCILIATION COMMISSION

Shortly after the election of April 27, 1994, Minister of Justice Dullah Omar proposed the establishment of a "truth" commission to determine the content and extent of political murders of Nonwhites by police, military personnel, civil servants, and other Whites acting in defense of white hegemony during the Apartheid era. The stated purpose of the commission was not, however, to prosecute persons responsible for the murders and other blatant violations of human rights; it was to determine who, if anyone, should receive state compensation for these violations.

Persons determined to be guilty of having committed such violations, but who confessed to them, would not be prosecuted if they confessed to each and every crime they committed. Persons who did not confess to all of their crimes would, however, be prosecuted.

Reflecting the concerns of many of his constituents, de Klerk, in January 1995, threatened to pull the National Party out of the presidential cabinet of the Government of National Unity if it acted on Minister Omar's proposal to establish such a commission. In de Klerk's view, such a commission would only serve to subvert attempts to establish the sense of national solidarity that had begun to take root after the election, that is, it would rip "out the stitches from wounds which are only now beginning to heal" (Nicol 1995: 187).

In order to go forward, de Klerk said, the country must forgive and forget. Furthermore, he maintained, he and others had entered into the final deliberations, resulting in the acceptance of the interim constitution and the holding of an all-race democratic election, under the impression that they were doing so with unconditional amnesty for past actions by government officials assured.

Others further argued that if such a committee were established, it would, in all fairness, also have to call forth Blacks guilty of terrorist acts in opposition to Apartheid. But many Blacks shot back with the argument that terrorist acts committed in order to bring down a nondemocratic terrorist regime were not crimes.

As the debate over the establishment of the commission continued, Safety and Securities Minister and ANC member Sydney Mufamadi forced the resignation of white police commissioner Johan van der Merwe, an outspoken opponent of a truth commission who had recently come to the defense of a group of military and police officers charged with Apartheid era crimes.

Perhaps with van der Merwe's resignation in mind, in his opening address to the legislature in February 1995, President Mandela once again felt it necessary to give assurances that there would be no retribution for illegal Apartheid activities reported to the commission, only for those not reported (Economist Intelligence Unit 1995: 7).

Shortly after Mandela's reassurances, de Klerk restated the National Party's commitment to remaining in the GNU; at the same time, he made it clear that he would continue to insist that the constitutional assembly ultimately produce a new constitution carrying guarantees of minority party representation in the cabinets of all future governments and that the NP was still vehemently opposed to the establishment of the proposed truth commission.

National Party members of the National Assembly were not alone in opposition to the establishment of such a commission. Members of the white right-wing Freedom Front also voted against its establishment, wanting amnesty extended to Whites convicted of crimes occurring right up to the April 27, 1994, general election (Economist Intelligence Unit 1995: 9).

Nonetheless, on July 12, 1995, the Promotion of National Unity and Reconciliation Act was signed into law, authorizing the establishment of the Truth and Reconciliation Commission. Headed by Bishop Desmond Tutu, the TRC was to exist for two years, during which time it would deal with human rights violations occurring from 1961 to December 5, 1993.

On May 8, 1996, the National Assembly adopted a new 140-page constitution, despite members of the Zulu-dominant IFP having withdrawn from participation in the deliberative body that produced it.

Apart from giving official recognition to South Africa's four Apartheid-era racial groups and 11 of the country's spoken languages, the new constitution gave South Africa a federal system with a strong president and bicameral legislature. It also denounced past racism and gave guarantees of freedom of speech, movement, and political activity, as well as rights to housing, health care, water, food, and education, including basic adult education; it also contained a comprehensive bill of rights.

But because it gave no guarantees of minority party representation in future presidential cabinets and made no provision for the continued government support of single-language (Afrikaans) schools, the new constitution failed to satisfy the Zulu chief and his followers. Nor did it satisfy white right-wingers, such as those affiliated with the Freedom Front, or de Klerk and members of the National Party.

The new constitution was the last straw for de Klerk. So dissatisfied was de Klerk that the day after its adoption, May 9, 1996, he and other members of the National Party resigned from the presidential cabinet. With no guaranteed representation in the presidential cabinet, no guaranteed government commitment to the survival of the Afrikaans language, and the establishment of the Truth and Reconciliation Commission, de Klerk, National Party members, and their constituents no longer had anything to gain from National Party representation in the interim cabinet in the Government of National Unity. Rather than remaining in the cabinet and thereby giving the appearance of agreeing with decisions with which they strongly disagreed, they felt they could best serve the country as members of a loyal opposition.

Members of the National Party had also wanted the new constitution to carry, among other things, straightforward affirmation of the inviolability of private property, affirmation of the death penalty, and a ban on abortions. It did not. All the new constitution had given the National Party's constituents were more reasons for dissatisfaction with de Klerk's leadership. In their view, he had given away everything without having received any guarantees or anything of substance in return, and now he was withdrawing from the cabinet. Why hadn't he done so earlier? Why had he participated in the first place? Why had he agreed to relinquish power to the ANC?

At first, withdrawal from the government seems not to have hurt the National Party. In a special provincial election held on May 31, 1996, in the heavily Coloured Western Cape province, the party emerged the clear victor, having won almost all rural areas and four of six metropolitan areas.

Nobel Prize–winner Desmond Tutu resigned as archbishop of the Anglican Church in Southern Africa on Sunday, June 2, 1996. He was 64 years old and had held the position since 1986. Now he would be devoting most of his energies to the fulfillment of his duties as chairperson of South Africa's Truth and Reconciliation Commission.

Like most major speeches by South African leaders, then as well as now, Tutu's farewell speech contained the warning that crime and corruption were so widespread in South Africa that they constituted serious threats to its survival as a democracy. "There are those who mistake freedom for license," he lamented, "[who] believe that they can do whatever they like. This is not freedom; that is chaos and disorder; that is lawlessness. We must not permit this to happen" (*San Diego Union Tribune*, June 3, 1996).

A month later, July 4, 1996, Tutu himself was saved from being a murder victim when police apprehended a black gunman trying to crash a meeting of the Truth and Reconciliation Commission over which he was to preside (*San Diego Union Tribune*, July 4, 1996).

The TRC hearings proceeded with Tutu as the commission's chairperson. The revelations that these hearings brought forth evoked a wide mix of emotions from both Blacks and Whites. Some felt cleansed by the revelations. Some were horrified. Some were outraged. Some were relieved that things that others had believed to be gross exaggerations where finally coming out as verified truths. The police and other government agents *did* torture and murder people; they *did* enlist other people to torture and murder people; and they *were* behind a great deal of the Black-on-Black violence. There was also truth in the rumors of mad scientists contemplating germ warfare against Blacks.

Apparently, most people felt that it would be best to get it all out so that everything that happened could be known, repented, and forgiven and the country could go forward assured that such things would never happen again. But not everyone felt that way. There were still many Whites who viewed the hearings with contempt. They resented that many people were brought to ruin and public disgrace for doing nothing more than what their jobs required they do. Many asked, what of the era of racial peace and harmony that the new government was supposed to usher in? Wouldn't the commission revelations create more rather than less racial animosity? Many argued both during and after the hearings, haven't the revelations, in fact, created more rather than less interracial animosity?

There were also black dissatisfactions with the Mandela government and the TRC hearings. Significant numbers of ANC members and affiliates were disappointed with participation of Whites in the first ANC-led presidential cabinet; later on, they were disappointed with the granting of tenure to white civil servants and police officers who had served the apartheid governments. Then, after the establishment of the TRC, there were those who argued that Whites found guilty of Apartheid crimes should be punished whether they confessed to them or not.

As early as February 1995, before the commencement of the TRC hearings, Winnie Mandela—President Mandela's former wife and, at the time, deputy minister of arts, culture, science and technology—publicly accused the GNU of "overindulgence" in its attempts at reconciliation with Whites (Thompson 1995: 274). As a result of this and her later criticisms of the ANC-led government for not doing enough for its core urban black constituency, she was dismissed from her government position. No longer a deputy minister, she nonetheless remained a stridently vocal member of the National Assembly and popular among young Blacks in the townships around Johannesburg and Pretoria.

In 1996, relatives of anti-Apartheid activist Steven Biko—who in 1977 was beaten to death while in police custody—instituted a class action suit challenging the right of the Truth and Reconciliation Commission to grant pardons to people who admit to murder and other human rights violations during the Apartheid era. Much to the disappointment of the Biko family and many other Blacks, in July 1996 the Constitutional Court upheld the right of the TRC to grant amnesty to persons guilty of Apartheid era crimes.

There was also widespread black and white dissatisfaction within the military and police forces. This dissatisfaction resulted from the GNU having come to power with a constitutional mandate to integrate soldiers from former black guerrilla units, former independent homeland armies, and members of the old South African Force into a new multiracial South African Defense Force. Given the pre-1994 election guarantees of job tenure to Apartheid civil servants, this multiracial force was destined to have a disproportionate number of white commanding officers and senior enlisted men for years to come.

There were rumors of secret cabals of white senior officers and enlisted men deeply resentful of having to serve with or under former guerrilla leaders and doing what they could to slow the restructuring process (Thompson 1995: 260). There are still reports of white military personnel involvement with paramilitary white groups who have not yet accepted black majority rule.

Concrete cause for distrust of the intentions of white military officers still in uniform after years of service to Apartheid governments arose on April 7, 1998, following the resignation of General Georg Meiring, South Africa's chief army general. Meiring resigned after it had been revealed that he had presented Mandela with a bogus report of a plot to overthrow the government "by former anti-Apartheid guerrillas who now hold high-level posts in both the military and the government as well as president's former wife, Winnie Madikezela-Mandela" (*San Diego Union Tribune*, April 7, 1998). General Meiring was replaced as head of South Africa's military forces by General Siphiwe Nyanda, a former ANC anti-Apartheid guerrilla leader.

Apart from resenting having to serve among and sometimes under the command of former guerrillas, white military men were also known to be deeply opposed to affirmative action appointments within the military. "Once past imbalances are redressed . . . appointments will be made on merits," General Nyanda promised on assuming command. He also promised that racism in the military would not be tolerated.

On November 12, 1998, a South African military spokesperson announced that during the next three years the army would reduce its troop strength from 90,000 to 70,000. But the reduction in armed forces strength was "not about chasing white officers away," said Major General Themba Matanzima. "We are looking for the best candidates to take the army into the new scenario" (*San Diego Tribune Union*, Nov. 13, 1990).

One of the most deadly eruptions of racial tension in the recently integrated South African Defense Force occurred on September 16, 1999, at the Tempe military base in Bloemfontein. An angry black lieutenant, Sibusiso Madubela, went on a rampage, killing six white soldiers and one white civilian and wounding five white soldiers. The rampage ended when Madubela was finally shot dead by other soldiers.

In explanation of Madubela's actions, another black soldier told South African reporters that "Those people [current South African Defense Force soldiers who served the Apartheid governments] are in charge and it seems their aim is to frustrate us. They had charged him [Madubela] with being AWOL [Absent Without Leave] but had not found him guilty. He went to them to try and put his case and they humiliated him. He has a family to feed. More of these things are going to happen unless this is put right" (*Daily Mail and Guardian*, September 17, 1999).

In the aftermath of the above shootings, black soldiers at the base where they occurred refused to stand as honor guards at the slain white soldiers' funeral. They stated their intention of attending the burial of the shooter, Madubela, who despite a request from the Pan African Congress did not receive a full military burial with honors. In its September 22, 1999, electronic edition, the *Johannesburg Star* reported that the "Pan African Congress and its former military wing, the Azanian Liberation Army (Apla) would give the shooter, Lt. Sibusiso Madubela a 'military' burial" and that all Apla cadres who were not serving in the South African Defense Forces would "honor Madubela because he was previously in an Apla cadre." Another source reported: "British military advisers [had] warned two years ago that the Tempe base was riven by racial tensions." The report cited several incidents, including one in which a white officer locked four black soldiers in a room and sprayed it with tear gas (McGreal, September 22, 1999).

So even though white-piloted military planes had flown overhead in salutation of Mandela's swearing in as the country's first black president, and even after the appointment of a black minister of defense pledged to end racism in the country's military forces, South Africa's defense forces still remain tense with potentially murderous racial divisions.

From the beginning, the ANC also had to deal with charges and incidences of political corruption within its ranks. In September 1996, for instance, Bantu Holomisa, a high-ranking ANC official and former deputy minister of the environment in the Mandela cabinet, was booted out of the ANC for revealing that in 1994 Mandela had accepted a campaign contribution from American businessman Sol Kerzner, who was currently under investigation for bribery. Mandela acknowledged the contribution, but neither Holomisa nor anyone else had any proof of Mandela having in any way tried to influence the outcome of the investigation into Kerzner's activities. Holomisa also told journalists that Kerzner had sponsored Deputy President Thabo Mbeki's fiftieth birthday party and that "the country's sports minister had accepted free hotel accommodations from Kerzner" (*San Diego Union Tribune,* September 2, 1996).

Among Holomisa's other accusations was that the then-current minister of public enterprises, Stella Sigcau—when she was minister in the homeland government of Transkei—had received part of a two million rand (approximately $350,000) bribe supposedly given to Transkei prime minister George Matanzima for gambling rights in the homeland.

Though no one accused by Holomisa went to jail or lost their party position, one result of his accusations was that Kader Asmal, chairperson of the ANC Disciplinary Committee, insisted that henceforth all submissions to the TRC first be routed through his committee. This, in turn, caused the TRC to issue a statement expressing incredulity that the ANC leadership would try "to muzzle its rank-and-file members by demanding to check their statements." Mathews Phosa, ANC legal adviser and premier of Mpumalunga Province (formerly Eastern Transvaal Province) then declared that ANC members do not have to apply for amnesty because whatever they did was in the service of a just cause. TRC chairperson Tutu did not agree. He said he would resign "if the ANC grants itself amnesty," refusing "to be abused by a party that will not accept equal treatment before a Truth Commission" (Krog 1999: 151–52).

It all came to nothing. ANC members continued to submit their amnesty applications to the TRC. Tutu did not resign. But from then on, relations between members of the TRC and members of the ANC were strained.

The first list of approved amnesty applications was released at the end of 1996. Included were the names of seven black ANC members and four white right-wingers, one black and four white appeals having been turned down (Krog 1999: 154). Not everyone was happy, but the commission continued reviewing applications.

In early September 1997, the TRC hearings still in process, de Klerk announced his retirement as head of the National Party. Despite all he had done to save his country from cataclysmic racial violence, he was, as he put it, still "demonized as a symbol of the Apartheid past and is therefore more of a liability than an asset to today's multiracial National Party." He said he would like to be remembered "As a leader who prevented hundreds of thousands of deaths and who made a quantum leap that fundamentally changed our country for the better and brought justice to all South Africans" (Hawthorne 1997: 67).

De Klerk was replaced as head of the National Party by 37-year-old Marthinus van Schalkwyk, and soon afterward, in an effort to dissociate itself from its apartheid past, the National Party was renamed the New National Party (NNP). Thus began in earnest the end of the National Party's reign as the country's leading opposition party.

There were soon defections at the highest levels, beginning with Roelf Meyer, a young National Party *verligte* (enlightened one, or liberal) who before the dismantling of the Apartheid state had been involved in negotiations with the ANC leadership in exile. Meyer left the NP-NNP to form a new multiracial political party with a black group led by the aforementioned ex-ANC dissident Bantu Holomisa. The United Democratic Movement (UDM) would be the name of this new multiracial party.

The Nelson Mandela–Winnie Mandela divorce became final in 1996. The following year, in September 1997, the former Mrs. Mandela was subpoenaed to appear before the Truth and Reconciliation Commission to answer charges that she been involved in the kidnapping of 14-year-old Stompei Seipei, a suspected police informant, and had also wielded the knife that led to his death. There were also reports that she had ordered the death of a Soweto doctor who refused to go along with her plan to discredit a white priest by accusing him of being a homosexual.

Then, in 1997, in the wake of all these allegations, the former Mrs. Mandela was nominated for a deputy position within the ANC, which if she won would put her in position to become the country's next deputy president.

In December 1997, at the ANC's fiftieth national conference in Mafikeng, Nelson Mandela announced that though he would remain president of the Republic of South Africa, he was giving up his position as president of the African National Congress. The new ANC president would be Thabo Mbeki, the current deputy president of the Republic of South Africa and Mandela's obvious choice to succeed him as the country's president.

In his speech before the delegates at the fiftieth ANC conference, Mandela lashed out at ANC members and grassroots supporters who criticized the party's leaders for still not having delivered on all of their campaign promises after being in power for three and a half years. Mandela challenged his critics to name a party that could have done better than the ANC. No one ventured an answer.

It was also in this speech that Mandela made his thus far harshest public criticism of the country's Whites—Afrikaners in particular—accusing many of them of still harboring white supremacist attitudes and "various elements of the former ruling group" and of working "to establish a network which would launch or intensify a campaign of [political] destabilization." Pulling no punches, Mandela also criticized the media as being servants of the "white bosses" and accused "some ANC leaders of [using] the party to further personal goals, of becoming corrupt, a comment that drew loud cheers" (*San Diego Union Tribune,* December 17, 1997).

The Mafikeng conference ended with Mandela no doubt relieved that his ex-wife had not, alas, been elected to the position of ANC deputy president. She was still, however, a powerful force to be reckoned with, strong among the country's urban poor, the ones who had so far received very few tangible benefits from the miracle that had brought the ANC to power.

Six weeks later, in a more conciliatory vein, Mandela suggested that those who had benefited from Apartheid might now repay their fellow countrymen by performing voluntary public service. As an example, he mentioned a South African businessman, later identified as Meyer Kahn, who stepped down from the chairmanship of a multibillion-dollar corporation to become the chief executive, without pay, of the national police force. "This country," Mandela read in quote of Kahn, "warts and all, has been good to me; it has clothed me; it has educated me . . . I think the very least I could do is put something back, and this is my kind of national service and I am enjoying it" (*San Diego Union Tribune,* February 17, 1999).

Two days later, the 79-year-old Nelson Mandela confessed to being in love with Graca Machel, the 52-year-old widow of former Mozambique president Samora Machel. "I don't regret the reverses and setbacks I've had because late in my life, I am blooming like a flower because of the love and support she has given me" (*San Diego Union Tribune,* February 9, 1998). Before the end of the year they were married.

On April 16, 1998, Apartheid-era president P. W. Botha appeared before a black judge in George, South Africa, on charges of refusing to cooperate with the Truth and Reconciliation Commission by answering questions regarding his knowledge of and complicity in Apartheid crimes. One report decribed the 82-year-old ex-president as having "sat stone-faced as prosecutors presented . . . evidence that the State Security Council he headed in the the 1980s may have ordered the killing of anti-Apartheid activists." Still he refused to cooperate, just as he had refused to cooperate with the Truth and Reconciliation Commission. He did not care if they charged him with contempt; he was not going to testify. "Even if they destroy me, they cannot destroy my soul and my convictions," he said (*San Diego Union Tribune,* April 16, 1998).

On November 16, 1998, the Mandela government's Human Rights Commission announced that it was beginning an investigation into "racism in the press." The commission's chairman, Barney Pityana, maintained that "Racism is endemic in South Africa. There is no reason to believe the media are somehow insulated." The source of the report described "some editors" as viewing the inquiry as a "carefully timed attempt" to stifle news media criticisms of the Mandela government during the six months preceding the June 1999 elections (*San Diego Union Tribune*, November 17, 1998).

Fears of intensified political violence during the months leading up to the June 1999 election were heightened by the January 23, 1999, assassination of Sifiso Nkabinde, secretary general of the United Democratic Movement, the multiracial political party brought into existence by the former National Party member Roelf Meyer and the ANC apostate Bantu Holomisa. Before becoming secretary general of the UDM, Nkabinde was expelled from the ANC for allegedly having been a government informant during the Apartheid era, supplying the government with information about ANC members and their activities. The year before his assassination he had stood accused of inciting political violence in the town of Richmond in KwaZulu-Natal and being responsible for 16 deaths (*San Diego Union Tribune*, January 24, 1999).

Later during the day of Nkabinde's assassination, gunmen broke into a house in the same area where he was murdered and killed 11 alleged ANC supporters. In addition, seven others were seriously injured and at least three homes burned. Police called it "retaliatory political violence" (*San Diego Union Tribune*, January 25, 1999).

In the past, most of the political violence in KwaZulu-Natal had been between the ANC and the Zulu-based IFP. People wondered if Nkabinde had been rubbed out by members of one of those groups, as a warning to the UDM to stay out of KwaZulu-Natal. Or did his assassination, followed so quickly by the murder of ANC affiliates, mean that with the election only four months away KwaZulu-Natal was in for another round of political violence, only now involving three main antagonists? Mandela was so concerned Nkabinde's assassination might be followed by a new wave of violence that he canceled a trip to Uganda to remain home and appeal for calm on all sides until Nbakinde's killers were found and brought to justice.

Four days after the Nkabinde assassination, Johann Kriegler, South Africa's chief election officer, handed in his resignation, expressing fears that the $91 million allocated would not be sufficient to provide the supervision necessary to ensure a fair election (*San Diego Union Tribune*, January 27, 1999).

On February 6, 1999, two weeks after Nkabinde's assassination and slightly more than a week after Kriegler's resignation, Mandela stood before Parliament calling on all South Africans of all races to not give in to the "merchants of cynicism and despair, to remain committed to building a better country for all." His message was that although there remained much to be accomplished, much had already been accomplished.

He talked of crime, the number one campaign issue. Though the country's murder rate stood at 52 per 100,000 (eight times that of the United States), it had nonetheless dropped 10 percent since 1994. There were carjackings every day and scores of farmers killed every year, but things were getting better and would continue to get better, he tried to assure his audience. "He also boasted [that] . . . in five years, his government [had] brought clean water to 3 million people, electricity to 2 million people and telephones to 1.3 million people" (*Los Angeles Times*, February 6, 1999).

February 1999 was also the publication date of *The Last Trek: A New Beginning*, by F. W. de Klerk, former president of the Republic of South Africa and Nobel Prize–winner for helping bring an end to Apartheid. "Despite all of its shortcomings, the new South Africa," de Klerk asserts in this autobiographical account of his life in politics, "is infinitely better than it would have been if we had not embarked on the course of fundamental reform nine years ago." In speeches promoting the book, de Klerk also put forth the hope that it would end " 'the demonization of the majority of white South Africans, by making clear the important role that Whites, including himself, played in undoing racial segregation" (Murphy 1999: A2).

During an early February visit to Cape Town, U.S. defense secretary William Cohen announced U.S. intentions of establishing closer military ties with South Africa, but he didn't see such ties being established in the immediate future. "It's going to take some time," he was quoted as having said (Burns 1999). This was before the September 1999 shootings by the black lieutenant of Tempe military base in Bloemfontein.

On May 21, 1999, South African police in KwaZulu-Natal province announced the seizure of more than seven tons of arms, ammunition, and explosives in a place called Nquthu, not far from the former headquarters of Chief Māngosuthu Buthelezi, head of the Zulu-based Inkatha Freedom Party. Phillip Powell, a prominent white member of the IFP, led police to this massive cache of arms, having explained that the weapons were supplied to him by white police officials *before the 1994 elections* (*San Diego Union Tribune*, May 22, 1999).

May 31, 1999, was the day of noncandidate Mandela's final speeches on behalf of ANC candidates. "Please become part of the majority," he entreated Whites in the crowd gathered before him at a shopping mall in an affluent white Johannesburg neighborhood, "and this country will become even more of a miracle" (*San Diego Union Tribune*, June 1, 1999).

The day before the election, June 1, 1999, an appeals court dismissed the contempt of court conviction of Apartheid-era president P. W. Botha, handed down in sanction of his refusal to appear before the Truth and Reconciliation Commission. The dismissal came on a technicality: The TRC's legal mandate to exist had expired on December 14, 1997, but it had issued a subpoena for Botha to appear on December 19, 1997. "Our beautiful country cannot afford to be in a state of despair," was Botha's bemusing response to the appeals court's decision. "Minority rights as well as cultural rights should be maintained. South Africa should press on in the knowledge that God is in control" (McNeil, 1999).

South African voters went to the polls on June 2, 1999, with 100,000 soldiers and police officers spread out around polling stations across the nation to keep the peace. Offering support for the peacekeeping troops and police officers were "100 aircraft, including helicopters" (*Daily Mail and Guardian,* May 31, 1999). The election went off with no major problems. There were scattered incidences of violence and intimidation, but not so many or on such a scale as to affect anything.

As expected, the ANC emerged from the 1999 election still the nation's governing party. Final election tabulations showed it to have won a larger percentage of seats in the national legislature than it had won in the 1994 election, 65 percent versus 62 percent (*Daily Mail and Guardian,* September 27, 1999).

Coming in far behind the ANC was the rightist white-dominated Democratic Party, with 9.56 percent of the vote. Next was the Zulu-based Inkatha Freedom Party, with 8.58 percent of the popular vote; the white-dominated New National Party, with 6.87 percent of the vote; and the more racially diverse United Democratic Movement Party candidates, with 3.42 percent of the vote. Coming in sixth was the African Christian Democratic Party, with 1.43 percent of the vote. Of the remaining parties winning one or more National Assembly seats, none received more than 1 percent of the popular vote. Also, as expected, Mandela's handpicked successor, British-educated economist and ANC president Thabo Mbeki, became the new president of the Republic of South Africa.

The ANC is, thus, still South Africa's ruling political by an even wider margin than before, but now it is the Democratic Party rather the New National Party that is the leading white vote-getter and leading opposition party nationwide.

The 1999 election brought forth no great changes in the provinces, either. The ANC won a majority of seats in all but two of the provincial legislatures. These are the same two in which they were not the majority party before the election: KwaZulu-Natal, where the IFP is still strong; and the Western Cape, where Gerald Morkel of the New National Party became prime minister. Of all the provinces, the Western Cape was where the New National Party ran the strongest, winning approximately 39 percent of the vote, compared to the ANC's 41 percent and the DP's 12 percent.

The big news was that the 1999 election took place in an overall peaceful climate, providing evidence of what Sir David Steele—head of the Commonwealth observer group sent to observe that the election proceeded without gross irregularities—called "the emergence of a mature democracy" (*San Diego Union Tribune,* June 6, 1999).

Steele, who also headed the observer group sent to observe the 1994 election, was particularly struck by the big contrast in the two elections: the first being "a liberation election and this [1999] . . . more like a normal election held in any country, with healthy debate . . . and [the] absence of the kind of terrorism . . . that occurred last time around" (*Dispatch Online,* June 6, 1999).

The 1999 election also, however, gave evidence of present-day South Africa's still deep racial divisions, most votes having been cast mainly along racial lines: the great majority of Blacks (77 percent of the population) voting for ANC candidates; the majority of Whites (12.7 percent of the population), Coloureds (8 percent), and Indians (2 percent) voting for candidates put forth by white-led parties.

In his speech on March 26, 1999, at the final sitting of the first South African parliament put in office by a multiracial electorate, Mandela said,

> In brief, we have laid the foundation for a better life. Things that were unimaginable a few years ago have become everyday reality. And of this we must be proud. . . . As I was reminded yet again on the visit which I have just made to the Netherlands and four Nordic countries, the world admires us for our success as a nation in rising to the challeges of our era. Those challenges were: to avoid the nightmare of debilitating racial war and bloodshed and to reconcile our people on the basis that our overriding objective must be together to overcome the legacy of poverty, division and inequity. To the extent that we have still to reconcile our nation; to the extent that the consequences of Apartheid still permeate our society and define the lives of millions of South Africans as lives of deprivation, those challenges are unchanged (Office of the President, 1999).

Mandela was right: Though the ANC has successfully met many of the challenges facing it when it took office, a great many formidable challenges still remain. Chief among these are the challenges of raising the generally low occupational skills and educational attainments of South Africa's black citizens, who collectively constitute somewhere between three-fourths and four-fifths of its current population.

CHAPTER 7

Religion and Schooling

From the Beginning to the Anglo-Boer War

South Africa's first formally organized school came into existence in 1658. It was established for the first contingent of slaves to arrive at the Cape so that they might more easily understand the wishes of their new Dutch East India Company masters and thereby more quickly become obedient servants. Under the tutelage of the Dutch East India Company chaplain (Welsh 1999: 35), slaves were given lessons in the "Dutch language [as well as] the rudiments of the Christian religion and were encouraged to be diligent [in their assimilation of the imparted knowledge] with rewards of brandy and tobacco" (Troup 1976: 8).

A second Company school was opened in 1663. Racially integrated, it was attended by 12 white children, four slaves, and one Khoikhoi. These students, like the ones in the first school, learned "mainly about religion and some basic reading, writing and arithmetic" (Christie 1989: 33) nonwhite children attended this school for free; white children paid to attend, if their parents could afford it.

It was not until 1676 that the "the [Dutch Reformed] Church Council was asking for a separate school for slaves" (Troup 1976: 8). They didn't get separate schools right away, however, because hardly anyone else saw a need for them.

Most colonists were opposed to schools of any kind for slaves, Khoikhoi, or any other Nonwhites. Schooling took them away from work. There was already a shortage of workers, which was why slaves were brought there in the first place. As a consequence, few slave or other nonwhite children attended either racially integrated or racially segregated schools. And those who did, didn't attend for long.

Nor, for that matter, did many white children attend school for very long. A little bit of education was all they needed, seems to have been the general sentiment. Moreover, what education they did receive wasn't of high quality. Though it occurred under Church auspices, the education of the Cape's first school attendees was

> entrusted to an official called the *sieckentrooster* or "sick comforter." The holders of this office do not seem to have been of intellectual distinction; it was not, after all, a calling which offered much hope of advancement. The first school was closed because all the pupils had run away [despite the brandy and tobacco]; the second was nearly ruined by the habitual drunkenness of the reigning *siecken-trooster*, Ernestus Beck . . . [who was] deported to Batavia in 1665 (Le May 1995: 22).

The prevailing attitudes toward education didn't change much during the next half century or so. It was not until 1714 that the Cape Colony's first high school was founded, for example. But it was soon abandoned because "it received little support" (Thompson 1995: 41).

That was formal education in early eighteenth century Cape Colony towns and villages.

Out in the frontier trekboer areas, there were no formally organized schools for anyone of any color or condition of servitude. Trekboer children who learned to read and write did so from family members, neighbors, or former Company employees turned itinerant teachers, most of whom were "so incompetent that the word *meester* (teacher) acquired a derogatory meaning" (Thompson 1995: 48).

Almost all of the formal schooling during the seventeenth and eighteenth centuries took place under the auspices of the **Dutch Reformed Church (DRC)** The Dutch Reformed Church was a Calvinist Protestant church, meaning its adherents, at least in theory, were believers in the religious doctrines and teachings of John Calvin. Calvin brought into prominence the notion of **predestination,** that human beings, individuals, as well as nations, are put on this earth for specific God-ordained purposes. In this view, all that is done by human beings is done in fulfillment of their God-given destiny, because God wills that it be done.

If the teachings of the Dutch Reformed Church were based on Calvinist doctrines and world views, and DRC was the Church of seventeenth and eighteenth century Boers, does this then mean that they saw themselves as having been sent to southern Africa by God to claim and rule over it and all its inhabitants in His name? Were their ruthless land seizures and brutal treatment of the indigenous people driven, guided, motivated, and justified by a belief they were God's chosen people, sent to the African continent to take control over its blessed lands and its cursed dark-skinned peoples by whatever means possible?

No. Most Boers of this period appear to have been Calvinist only in the sense that they came from regions where Calvinist religious denominations were dominant. Their low levels of educational attainment and correspondingly low rates of literacy make it highly unlikely that they had systematic knowledge of the basic tenets of Calvinism, much less of the Old Testament derivatives of these tenets. Moreover, there was no one coherent, comprehensive Calvinist worldview that would allow them to see themselves and their situation as analogous to God's chosen people in the Old Testament.

Slavery, for instance, was banned in Calvinist Scotland long before it was banned in either Calvinist South Africa or non-Calvinist England (Gerzina 1995: 39). Scottish Calvinist missionaries arrived in South Africa imbued with racial egalitarian ideals that they lived out to the point of taking nonwhite wives. Whereas back in 1714, members of the Cape's DRC council had asked for separate schools for slaves.

So not all so-called Calvinists shared the same beliefs. In fact, it is even likely that most Boers of the seventeenth and eighteenth centuries had never heard of John Calvin. True, Boer families are reported to have always had a Bible close at hand, and when they attended church, they attended Dutch Reformed Church services. But just as a great many present-day Americans attend Presbyterian Church services without knowing who John Calvin was, or the basic Calvinist tenets or world-view, or even that theirs is a Calvinist church, so apparently did most seventeenth and eighteenth century Boers attend Dutch Reformed Church services. The Afrikaner free burghers of this period were primarily concerned with acquiring as much land as possible, and ultimately becoming totally free of Company control, so that they could live and do as they pleased—not as the Church mandated that they live and do.

It was not that the Church was irrelevant, however, that it gave no depth, meaning, guidance, justification, or anything else of substance to their lives. The Church and religious gatherings played important roles in their lives. Church schools were attached to town and village churches. Church sermons offered concrete guidance and explanations of the meaning and purpose of human life. Gatherings presided over by itinerant ministers provided opportunities for frontier Boers to marry, have their children christened, and come together with other Boers to whom they might ultimately become related by marriage or alongside whom they might serve in commando units. Such gatherings also, alas, provided opportunities for members of commando units to learn hymns that could be sung before going out to kill Bushmen (see Chapter 1).

Otherwise, with so much to do and so many other concerns, the typical Boer head of household had no more time for ministers and abstract religious contemplations than his children had for formal schooling Besides, the ministers were salaried Company officials sent out to the frontier areas to encourage the Boers to abide by Company rules and restrictions pertaining to their dealings with the natives and their occupancy of lands beyond the boundaries of settlement set by the Company. Trekboers didn't want to listen to that kind of talk. Freedom from Company rules and restrictions was the reason they had migrated to the frontier in the first place.

From 1652 to the British takeover of the Cape at the turn of the nineteenth century, the DRC was effectively the only church in South Africa. Had it made greater efforts to convert black slaves to the faith and engaged in more serious missionary activities among the indigenous Xhosa peoples in the outlying areas of the Cape, South Africa would be in many ways different than it is today. For one thing, there would be more Afrikaans-speakers than there are now, and the long-term survival of that language would be more certain, as there would, for example, exist a larger, richer, more varied and widely read Afrikaner literature and more people able to carry on and develop its traditions.

MISSION AND GOVERNMENT SCHOOLS

Serious, intensive missionary activity in South Africa didn't begin until after the takeover of the Cape by the British and the subsequent arrival of Anglican Church–affiliated London Missionary Society representatives, who were soon followed by representatives from other missionary organizations, most of which were British.

Unlike the Cape's DRC religious leaders, these early British missionaries were racial egalitarians. They were strongly opposed to slavery and deeply committed to teaching Nonwhites to read and write and to accept the Christian faith so that one day they might be the social, political, economic, and spiritual equals of Whites.

In the missionaries' scheme of things, education and Christianity went together like the proverbial horse and carriage: education being the horse; Christianity, the carriage. It was in mission schools and through mission-schooled Nonwhites that they were most successful in spreading the faith in Africa.

Their belief that the Holy Bible was divinely inspired and that one can come to know God, Christ, and the Holy Spirit through the teachings of the Bible explains why missionaries placed such emphasis on spreading literacy among peoples they sought to convert. If one is literate, they felt, one has direct access to the Word of God and can pass it on to others, thereby becoming a Christian missionary oneself. The more people passing the Word on to others, the more people receiving the Word. The more people receiving the Word, the more people accepting the Word. That's what being a Christian missionary was all about: spreading the Word, serving as a disciple of Christ.

As a result of the first generations of Africans receiving their schooling at English-language mission schools, English became the common, unifying language of educated South African Blacks of all tribes. Before the establishment of English-language mission schools there was no language comprehensible to either elite or non-elite members of all African tribes.

Most literate Blacks of the early nineteenth century became literate as a result of attendance at mission schools. Others acquired their literacy at English-language government schools. Unlike their Dutch predecessors, the early nineteenth century British political administrators were very much concerned with the schooling of their Cape Colony subjects, both white and nonwhite.

The British government began setting up racially integrated schools on the Cape shortly after its final takeover of the Colony in 1806.

> [T]eachers were brought in from England. English became the medium of instruction . . . and the English system of education was introduced. New and improved schools were established for white and coloured children, free schools were for the needy and children were to be admitted to government schools without distinction of race. It was made compulsory for slave owners to send slave children between three and ten years of age for at least three days a week, but the colonists resented the loss of child labour and . . . the[se] regulations were not enforced (Horrell 1970: 10–11).

Ordinance 50 was issued in 1828, giving Khoikhoi the same rights and freedoms possessed by whites. Slavery was officially abolished in 1833. As a consequence, Khoikhoi and former slaves, having left the homesteads of their former masters, became more dispersed throughout the Colony. In the minds of British officials and missionary organizations, this created a need for more schools.

The Moravian Church, which offered classes in Dutch, responded to this need by estabishing a training program for Coloured teachers at its mission in Grenadendal. This was before the existence in South Africa of a state-sponsored or subsidized institute for the training of white teachers.

Administrators of the Lovedale School, established in 1824 by the Glasgow Missionary Society, responded by establishing an institute for the training of "catechists and teachers," its first students being 11 Africans and nine Whites, "mostly the sons of missionaries" (Wilson and Thompson 1971: 77).

Responding to the need to educate the newly emancipated Khoikhoi and Blacks, the Cape government brought more teachers over from Britain. It also set up, in 1839, a colonial Department of Education and, in 1841, authorized the dispension of state funds to sudsidize the salaries of teachers at needy secular schools. In addition, it provided state funds for support of pedagogical activities of mission schools. By the middle of the nineteenth century,

> a state inspectorate had been established . . . to give the natives the same education as Europeans were getting. . . . [A] very large large number of Europeans as well as natives had to work together

and they would work much better if they had a common basis and foundation of knowledge. If they were educated in different directions they would not understand each other (Interdepartmental Committee on Native Education 1936; (cited in Wilson and Thompson 1971: 224).

In the eyes of the Cape's early governors, money spent on native education was money well spent. It would help bring greater stability to the British Empire. Mission schools would bring the natives into the orbit of Western culture by instilling in them Western modes of thought and behavior and Western work habits and farming and artisan skills. Money well spent, indeed, felt early Cape administrators; in fact, Whites generally had to pay a fee for their children's schooling, whereas Nonwhites generally did not. As Cape governor Sir George Grey explained in an 1855 address to the Cape parliament:

> If we leave the natives beyond our borders ignorant barbarians, they will remain a race of troublesome marauders. We should try to make them a part of ourselves, with common faith and common interests, useful servants, consumers of our goods, contributors to our revenue. Therefore, I propose that we make unremitting efforts to raise the natives in Christianity and civilization by establishing among them missions connected with industrial schools.
>
> The native races beyond our boundary, influenced by our missionaries, instructed in our schools, benefitting by our trade, would not make wars on our frontiers (Rose and Tunmer 1975: 205).

Like government schools, mission schools were also racially integrated. Just as Nonwhites attended state schools at which mostly Whites were enrolled, it was not uncommon for Whites to be educated alongside Blacks and Coloureds at mission schools. "Toward the end of the century at the Anglican Zonnenbloem Training School, for instance, "half the students were African and half were White and Coloured" (Wilson and Thompson 1971: 221).

The Lovedale School also provided teacher training and other types of higher education for both Whites and Nonwhites. Racial integration at the mission schools was not, however, always total and complete. "At Lovedale, African and white students lived in the same building, but slept in different dormitories and ate different food at separate tables" (Horrell 1970: 10).

Still, despite the separate dormitories and dining tables, both white and African students attended the same classes and received the same relatively high quality educations: "Lovedale produced [during the nineteenth century] not only African men and women of distinction but also (before a more, modern systematic racial segregation took over) some eminent Whites" (Troup 1976: 11). The high quality of education received by Lovedale students is also evidenced by the fact that "Of some 3,448 Africans who passed through Lovedale [during the nineteenth century], 700 entered the professions" (Rose 1971: 74).

Apart from state-subsidized public schools and mission schools, there were also native schools, that is, schools attended by natives on native reserves. By the Cape Education Act of 1865, they were also recipients of financial aid from the state.

Thus was the state of education in the Cape Colony up into the 1880s under racially liberal British administrators: committed to educating both Whites and Nonwhites and to teaching Nonwhite pupils the same things taught to Whites.

Things were different in the lands north of the Cape to which thousands of Boers (Voortrekkers) had fled in anger at Ordinance 50, the freeing of the slaves, and other British attempts to put Nonwhites on an equal footing with Whites. The establishment of schools and their children's acquisition of the kinds of knowledge that could best be acquired in formal classrooms was not foremost among either the Voortrekkers' short- or medium-term concerns.

First of all, it took a while for the white populations in the lands that became Natal, the Orange Free State, and the Transvaal to become greatly concerned with establishing schools for their children. Their most immediate concerns centered on removing themselves as far away from British oversight as possible and establishing themselves as the dominant military and economic powers on lands over which native tribes had traditionally claimed as theirs. The fight for dominance over the lands required the full-time efforts of every Boer man, woman, and child. Even if there had been towns and villages large enough to make formally organized schools viable, children would not have had time to attend them with any degree of regularity. The Boers, of course, were adamantly against native education. It was the British missionaries who were for educating the Natives to the level of Whites.

The desire to prevent Nonwhites from acquiring the same social, political, economic, and basic human rights as they possessed was initially one of the few things the various groups of Voortrekkers held in common. Otherwise, they disagreed on many matters. Though in later years they would continue to all be spoken of in the same reverential breath, the Voortrekkers, it is worth restating, did not leave the Cape all together, at the same time, for the same destination, under the same leadership. Nor did they do so with the blessing of the Church. Tobias Herold, minister of Stellenbosch, wrote a stinging denunciation of the departure from the Cape of large numbers of persons under his spiritual purview. In removing themselves from British oversight, they were also removing themselves from his and the Church's oversight.

Nor did the various groups of Voortrekkers leave the British-controlled Cape intending to unite with other groups to form one united

Boer republic. Leaders of the various Voortrekker groups left with the intention of establishing their own republics, independent of those established by other groups.

Political divisions and personal rivalries between leaders of the various Voortrekker groups, as well as divisions within groups, were so pronounced that from approximately 1840 to 1880 there existed, for various short lengths of time, smaller republics within the territories that ultimately became Natal, the Orange Free State, and the South African (i.e., Transvaal) Republic. Among these smaller, short-lived, occasionally warring republics within the larger republics were Winburg/Potchefstroom, Lyndenburg, Stellaland, Utrecht, Goshen, and the New Republic, each with its own constitution and elected officeholders (Welsh 1999: 224).

Despite their differences, though, the different groups of Voortrekkers remained united with each other, as well as with Afrikaners still in the Cape Colony, by a common desire to be free of British rule, a common language, a common culture, and a common allegiance to the Afrikaner Dutch Reformed Church, which in 1824 became independent from the Dutch Reformed Church in the Netherlands.

THE AFRIKANER DUTCH REFORMED CHURCH

Independence from the Dutch Reformed Church in the Netherlands meant that the DRC in South Africa was now quite specifically and exclusively the Afrikaner church. As such, it would become the great, transcendent Afrikaner unifier: the Dutch-language repository of the beliefs, values, aspirations, and historical experiences shared by all Afrikaners, rural, urban, wealthy, poor, educated, and uneducated. As the Afrikaner population increased and dispersed out into areas beyond the Cape, so did the influence of the Afrikaner DRC.

Though the 1830s Voortrekkers left the Cape without the blessings of the DRC high clergy, once established in the territories that would become Natal, the Transvaal, and the Orange Free State they were soon joined by DRC-ordained ministers. The ministers came to give the Voortrekkers assurances of eternal life, if they followed the main behavioral prescriptions of the faith and helped establish permanent churches in the new lands. The ministers were also willing to interpret biblical scriptures in ways that provided holy approval of the Trekkers' treatment of Africans as inferior "creatures" and their violent seizures of tribal lands.

Thus, during the second half of the nineteenth century, in the context of Afrikaner flight from British rule, followed by Afrikaner seizures of native lands, there came into being a systematic, rigidly dogmatic Calvinistic Afrikaner theology. With its strong emphasis on predestination, the DRC saw itself as ordained by God to lead a united Afrikaner people to the fulfillment of their destiny, which was to take possession of all of southern Africa lands and become the rulers of all the indigenous, inferior African peoples. Thus, armed with the DRC-propagated view of themselves as chosen people on a God-given mission, the Boers could continue doing as they had always done.

In 1857, the DRC authorized "the separation of Coloured and white congregations, which led to the creation of a distinct and subordinate mission church for Coloured people" (Thompson 1995: 66).

Also in 1857, disagreements over matters pertaining to religion and worship had become sufficiently rancorous for there to occur a split among Afrikaner DRC adherents. A group of Transvaal Boers, led by Martinus Wessel, broke from the main branch of the DRC, the *Neder-duitse Gereformeerde Kerk* (NKG), to form their own sect, the *Nederduitse Hervormde Kerk* (NHK). Another religious split within the ranks of the Transvaal Boers occurred in 1859, when Dominus (Reverend) Dirk Postma brought into being another DRC congregation, the *Gereformeerde Kerk* (GK), whose members eventually came to be known as Doppers (Welsh 1999: 224).

The doctrinal differences between the three Afrikaner Dutch Reformed Church congregations—the NGK, the NHK, and the GK—were minimal, according to Dr. Frans O'Brien Geldenhuys, a leading GHK figure during the 1880s. All three have "exactly the same confessions of faith, the same language and the same people, in the same country" (Brink 1996: 96). Nor was it uncommon for ministers and other leaders of the three branches to hold political office, both elected and appointed (Akenson 1992: 87). The Doppers, though, "frowned on such degenerate frivolities as hymn-singing and long coats" (Welsh 1994: 224).

SCHOOLS IN THE BOER REPUBLICS

The first schools in the lands northeastward of the Cape Colony were set up before the arrival of white settlers and the establishment of Boer republics in Natal, the Orange Free State, and the Transvaal. They were mission schools, meant to serve "wandering San (Bushman) and Korana people" (Troup 1976: 12); and since they received no state aid, their numbers increased slowly. But, for the first three decades, the increase in the number of white schools in the territories was even slower.

In fact, up until the 1870s there were very few formally organized schools for white children in these areas, because the Trekker population was at first small and widely dispersed. By 1870, however, populations in some areas had grown and become concentrated to the point where there now existed fledgling towns and villages large enough to support rudimentary schools. Up until that time, most white children in the Orange Free State and the Transvaal received only desultory schooling from parents and teachers at the few church schools in existence or from an occasional itinerant teacher. The education received in the few schools that did exist, however, was "basic . . . with a heavy religious content . . ., the buildings . . . often derelict, teachers . . . poorly qualified, and [student] attendance . . . irregular (Christie 1989: 40).

By 1872, officials in the Orange Free State had finally decided that something had to be done to improve the quality of education for white children. Population growth had created a need for educated people to direct the operations of government and train others who would become the republic's teachers, religious leaders, and medical and legal professionals and the like.

Another reason for the Orange Free State officials' decision to improve the quality of education for white children was the recent (1867) discovery of diamonds on the republic's western border and the subsequent emergence of Kimberly, the city of diamonds, which created opportunities for skilled artisans and other persons with basic reading, writing, and mathematical skills. All of a sudden, education was of great concern to those charged with overseeing the well-being of the Orange Free State and its white inhabitants.

Thus, in 1872, the Orange Free State appointed an inspector general of education, under whose auspices more public schools (i.e., state-financed schools for Whites only) came into existence. "In 1895, the first steps were taken towards compulsory education [for Whites]. All children between 14 and 16, who lived within two miles of a school, had to attend for one year. A system of transit schools was set up in country areas" (Christie 1989: 40).

Opportunities for Orange Free State Blacks to receive formal schooling became virtually nonexistent after the 1865 expulsion of all missionaries; at no time afterward during the nineteenth century did the Orange Free State provide government funds for the education of Blacks.

White education in the Transvaal lagged a few years behind that in the Orange Free State. As late as 1872, "there were four state schools in the whole country"; and in 1877, the year of British annexation and five years after the appointment of an inspector general of education in the Orange Free State, there were in the Transvaal "a mere five pupils in the New High School, only 300 more in all the republic's junior high schools and annual expenditure on education was less than £5,000" (Welsh 1999: 255, 257).

Then, in 1886 came the discovery of gold in the Witwatersrand region of the Transvaal. All of a sudden the Transvaal was no longer a poor, strife-ridden Boer republic tottering on the brink of bankruptcy. As in the Orange Free State after the discovery of diamonds, there was now a need in the Transvaal for more broadly knowledgeable people to conduct and oversee the affairs of state and for more people to train teachers and clerics. Soon there were more state-supported schools in the Transvaal, not only in the towns and villages but also in farm areas, where the government would pay the teachers' salaries if the farmers would supply the classroom buildings.

All in all, though, the Transvaal goverment remained relatively conservative in its approach to education. The 1892 Education Act, for instance, held that the primary responsibility for educating children lay with the children's parents. The responsibilities of government, it proclaimed, were limited to among other things, "the encouragement and support of private schools by giving grants to aid them" and providing "supervision . . . with a view to ensuring that pupils receive the necessary Protestant Christian education" (Behr 1978: 13).

State-aided schools in the Transvaal were, as in the Orange Free State, for Whites only. As a result, not very many Transvaal Africans received any sort of formal education whatsoever. But neither did very many Transvaal Whites. In 1892, for example, "92 percent of [white] scholars in the Transvaal were in primary school; less than 1 percent were above Std 6 (i.e., junior high level)" (Christie 1989: 41).

In Natal, which remained an independent republic for only a brief period and where British-ancestored Whites soon outnumbered Afrikaners, schools of all kinds were more prevalent than in the Orange Free State and the Transvaal. When the British in 1843 took over Natal, they considered education to be a state or government responsibility. Teachers were recruited from England, and there came into existence state schools, state-aided mission and church schools, and private academies. Although, as in the Orange Free State and Transvaal, schools in rural areas in Natal were more scarce and rudimentary than in urban areas.

In theory, government and government-aided schools in Natal were "open to all classes of the Natal population, the non-European children being expected to conform in all respects to European habits and customs" (Troup 1976: 13). But in reality, almost all Africans who went to school in Natal went to exclusively African schools located on native reserves.

In 1875, an Indian Immigrant School Board was established to see to the educational needs of Natal's growing Indian population, the first Indian immigrants having arrived in 1860 to work as indentured labor on the sugar plantations.

By the end of the nineteenth century, however, government and government-aided schools in Natal were not even "in theory" open to all races. Separate and unequal schools for Whites and Nonwhites had become a mandated fact of Natalian life. A special syllabus for native elementary schools was drawn up and implemented in 1886; and during the mid-1890s, the government established an entirely separate system of government schools for Africans. From 1899, "Indians (except for infants and girls, until 1905) were no longer admitted to European schools" (Troup 1976: 13).

By the 1890s, Blacks and Whites in the Cape Colony were also well on their way to receiving legislatively mandated separate and unequal schooling. The racially liberal governors of earlier decades were replaced by men in sympathy with the increasing number of Whites who were opposed to integrated schools where Blacks received the same kinds of schooling as Whites.

Among the major reasons for the intensification of white racism in the Cape Colony were the discovery of diamonds in the Kimberly region and of gold in the Transvaal, which brought about an industrial boom and a greater demand for industrial workers, both skilled and unskilled. If Blacks were educated and trained to the level of Whites and allowed to freely compete for these positions, Whites would be without a competitive advantage. As a result, in 1899

> The Cape superintendent general of education . . . reported . . . that the first duty of the government was . . . to "recognize the position of the European colonists as holding the paramount influence, social and political, and to see that the sons and daughters of the colonists . . . should have at least such an education . . . as will fit them to maintain their unquestioned superiority and supremacy in this land (Wilson and Thompson 1971: 22).

Religion and Schooling
1902–1976

As bearers of a common culture, the Cape Colony, Natal, Orange Free State, and Transvaal Boers shared a common language, a common church affiliation, and a common will to retain unrestrained hegemony over South Africa's Nonwhites and free themselves from British rule. The Boer-Anglo War, which concluded on May 31, 1902, with the signing of the Treaty of Vereeniging, was a setback for them. In signing the treaty they agreed to lay down their arms and that the Orange Free State and the Transvaal were no longer independents; instead, like the Cape Colony and Natal, the two areas would once again be mere colonial appendages of the worldwide British Empire.

Back under British political dominion, the defeated Boers found themselves most directly under the governance of British high commissioner Sir Alfred Milner. He was an avowedly British imperialist bent on bringing lasting stability to the South African colonies by using free, state-supported schools, at which attendance would be compulsory, to impose the English language and British cultural patterns and worldviews on Afrikaner children.

Though the Treaty of Vereeniging had granted Afrikaners the *right* to have their children taught in Dutch, the actual situation during the years immediately following the war was that while education was free and compulsory for all white children between 7 and 14 years of age, Afrikaner students were taught all subjects in English, except English, which was taught in Dutch since Afrikaans was not yet acknowledged as a distinct language.

The British had also, as part of their Anglicizing efforts, begun establishing teacher education and training programs for persons who would teach at the increasing number of lower schools that would be required to teach all Whites of school age.

In response to British attempts to use free, state-supported schools as agents of Anglicization, Afrikaner clergy, teachers, and cultural enthusiasts combined to found the Christian National Commission to bring into existence a system of what in later years would be called **Christian National Education (CNE)** schools. Dutch was the medium of instruction at these schools, which were primarily concerned with the perpetuation of the Afrikaner cultural traditions, the Christian Afrikaner worldview, and the language spoken by the Afrikaner people. At its height, in 1905, the Christian National Commission was operating somewhere between 200 (Troup 1976: 14; Christie 1989: 50) and 300 (Akenson 1992: 87) Christian national schools, with a collective enrollment of 9,000 pupils.

But because they were not free and state schools were, this first group of CNE schools did not last long. They were too expensive to maintain. Plus, the need for them lessened when, after having been granted "responsible government" in, respectively, 1906 and 1907, the provincial legislatures of the Orange Free State and the Transvaal were able to protect the Afrikaner language by passing specific laws (the Hergzog Act and the Smuts Act) holding that "the mother tongue of each child should be the primary language of education through the fourth standard [sixth grade]" and that each white child, English as well as Afrikaner, was to be taught a second European language, either Dutch or English.

Most of the first (Afrikaner) Christian National Education schools thus ended up being assimilated into the Orange Free State and Transvaal provincial school systems. But that did not mean that Afrikaner nationalist-oriented schools were no longer on the agenda of Afrikaner cultural enthusiasts. Influential Afrikaner leaders, secular as well as religious, would continue to advocate Christian National Education until it became a reality across the nation.

In the meantime, in 1909 the British Parliament passed the South Africa Act of Union, making the Cape, Natal, Orange Free State, and Transvaal the four provinces of the Union of South Africa, a self-governing political entity under British dominion, and thereby further easing fears that British annihilation of traditional Afrikaner culture and language was imminent.

"Self-governing" meant that decisions regarding school attendance, school curricula, and the financing of institutions of learning in the various provinces were now solely in the hands of the various Afrikaner-controlled provincial legislatures. There was no longer a British high commissioner or British anything else with the authority to set policies and issue directives concerning the education of Afrikaners, or any other of South Africa's racial groups for that matter. Each provincial legislature could provide or not provide for the education of the members of its various ethnic and racial groups in whatever manner it, and only it, decided.

RACIALLY SEGREGRATED SCHOOLS

Schooling in the Transvaal, Orange Free State, and Natal had been racially segregated before the war and remained so afterward. Even during the years between the end of the war (1902) and the Act of Union (1909), when British administrators were setting educational policy in the former republics, the small minority of Transvaal and Orange Free State Blacks who received any formal schooling of any sort did so at missionary schools. Nowhere in any of four provinces was schooling for Blacks compulsory.

Before the war and the Act of Union, some nonwhite residents of what was then the Cape Colony did, however, as noted previously, attend state-aided racially integrated schools, and there were missionary schools at which some white pupils were educated alongside nonwhite students. Separate and unequal schooling was not yet mandated by Cape law or irresistibly strident white demands. It was not until after the war, with industrialization bringing Blacks and Whites into more direct competition for urban-industrial jobs requiring some degree of skill and literacy, that legislation was enacted making schooling in the Cape racially segregated and unequal. The first legislation, the Cape School Board Act, was enacted in 1905, mandating separate public schools for Whites and Nonwhites.

In Natal, racial segregation in schools became complete in 1905 when Indian girls were no longer allowed to attend European schools (Troup 1976: 13). Bringing its educational systems even more in line with those in Natal and the other provinces, in 1922 the Cape mandated different courses and curricula for African and white students.

> The following year, despite objections from Coloured parents who wanted their children to have the same education as Whites, curricula for Coloured children "adapted to their needs" were introduced. . . . In the Orange Free State in 1924 a special syllabus for Africans was also introduced. . . . [A]lthough at that time the secondary school syllabus remained virtually the same for all races in each province (Troup 1976: 15).

There was no need to introduce separate courses and curricula for African secondary school students, because there weren't enough African secondary-level students to make it worth the effort. In 1905, for instance, only 2.1 percent of the entire African population were in attendance at formally organized schools, and of these, none were in classes above the postprimary level. Nor were there suddenly large increases in the number of African secondary school students during the next couple of decades. "Between 1901 and 1910 only five Africans matriculated; and between 1910 and 1920, 22 Africans matriculated" (Horrell 1963: 29–30).

Prominent among the reasons for education being so much less available to Blacks than to Whites were the different systems of funding for black and white education, which themselves varied from province to province. In 1920, for instance, the Cape abolished all fees for its primary schools. But in the Transvaal, a tax to cover expenditures on black education was imposed on Africans over and above the current poll tax. The Union government stepped in the next year, however, and barred the provinces from directly taxing Africans. The provinces had to spend no less on education from government subsidies than had been spent in the 1921–22 period. In addition, the governor general was empowered to "make grants to any province for the extension of the direct taxes imposed on Africans by Parliament [the national legislature] (Troup 1976: 14–15), which still meant that "[a]ny expansion [of African education] would have to be financed out of taxes paid by Africans themselves" (Christie 1989: 50).

A result of these changes in the financing of African education was that "the provinces thereafter regarded native education as having been taken over by the government and they spent no more on it than the government gave in subsidies" (Troup 1976: 15), which amounted to considerably less than was spent educating Whites.

The state subsidies were also insufficient to make education at black schools totally free for all who attended. Most in attendance paid fees that were too steep for the families of most other Blacks their age. In contrast, since white schools were financed from general tax revenues, white students could attend state-financed schools for free, and the proportion of such funds spent on their education rose as administrators perceived the need.

The amount spent on educating Blacks was not only less than that spent on Whites, it was much less. In 1925, for instance, the average cost per black student in a postprimary class was £2.0.5d, versus £20.4.10d per white student, or 10 times less for blacks (Troup 1976: 15). Figure 8.1 shows a chart of these costs.

The use of different systems and levels of funding for black and white schools was not, however, the fundamental reason so few Blacks were able to attend any school of any sort or why those who did go to school did not receive the same kind and quality of education as Whites. The root cause is reflected in the views expressed in a 1907 article that appeared in the *Christian Express*, a widely read South African newspaper of the time: "The defects of the uneducated [black] man are balanced by the ease with which, owing to his simplicity and ignorance, he can be exploited as an economic asset" (Troup 1976: 14). Of course, the typical South African would have agreed with that statement.

Nor was it only, or even primarily, the employers of labor who were responsible for the low level of economic and educational opportunities available to Blacks. Working-class South African Whites were fiercely determined to maintain their competitive advantage over black workers.

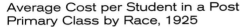

FIGURE 8.1

Average Cost per Student in a Post
Primary Class by Race, 1925

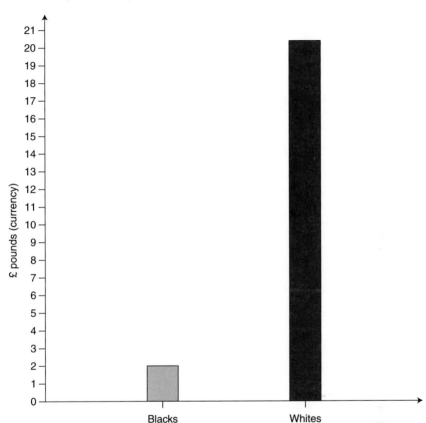

Economic competition between black and white workers was behind the violence that occurred in November 1921, when "the employers
. . . announced their intention of ending the colour bar in semiskilled
work, which had hitherto protected white jobs" (Welsh 1999: 391). In response to this announcement, angry white miners went on strike and,
after failing to persuade their employers to reconsider, organized themselves into armed commando units. In response, in February 1922 former
Anglo-Boer War general and then prime minister Jan Smuts declared
martial law and assumed direct command of government forces.

[A] couple of days' fierce fighting ensued, with the government
forces using machine-guns, tanks and artillery. There were many
casualties, the fighting being widespread; among the dead were
50 from government forces, 138 strikers and bystanders, and

30 "natives." Some of these were "blacklegs" shot by strikers, since black miners and management contrived to keep the coalmines operating. It was hardly a triumph for working-class solidarity—one striker's banner proclaimed: Workers of the World Unite, and Fight for a White South Africa (Welsh 1999: 391).

In the end the white workers won. Smuts's action was loudly condemned by members of the National Party, charging him with killing Afrikaner workers in defense of the interests of Jewish and English businessmen. In capitulation to their demands, government troops were withdrawn and the colorbar in semiskilled work remained.

The following year (1922), Whites gained an even greater advantage in the competition for jobs requiring some degree of skill and literacy. The passage of the Apprenticeship Act of 1922 restricted industrial apprenticeships to persons with eight or more years of schooling. Of course, Blacks, Coloureds, and Indians were less likely to have met the requirement, giving Whites a great advantage; and given the differences in funding for white and nonwhite schools, this advantage was likely to continue.

Some Whites did, however, acknowledge the need for a few Blacks to be educated beyond the primary level all the way up through the college and university levels. There was, after all, a need for some Blacks to serve as teachers in the overcrowded, underfinanced black schools, as well as for a few others to serve their people, on and off the native reserves, as doctors, lawyers, ministers, journalists, interpreters, medical assistants, and low-level clerks and such.

Therefore, in 1916 in the Transkei region of the eastern Cape there came into existence the predominantly black University College of Fort Hare. All South Africa colleges and universities were theoretically open to persons of all races, hence the qualification "predominantly black."

Start-up monies for the operation of Fort Hare came from a variety of sources: missionary groups, private individuals, and the Transkeian Territories General Council, an African governing body of the region. But as result of there being so few African secondary students, the University College of Fort Hare did not immediately begin offering college-level classes. Instead, it began,

> as a senior high school until sufficient students could be enrolled for university courses taking the external examinations of the University of South Africa. Like Lovedale, it drew students from all over Southern and Eastern Africa, a mixing which was valued and sought (Troup 1976: 14).

In 1918, two years after the opening of the University College of Fort Hare, there came into existence the Afrikaner Broederbond, (see Chapter 3), one of whose purposes was propagation of the Afrikaans language and Afrikaner cultural traditions. In 1925, due to the efforts of in-fluential Broederbonders, Afrikaans replaced Dutch as one of the two of-ficial languages of South Africa (Welsh 1999: 400). Afrikaners now had their own officially acknowledged language.

In 1933, the first Afrikaans language Bible was printed and the first Afrikaans sermon was delivered. And by 1944, members of the Broeder-bond were

> roughly 2,500 [in number], carefully selected for their doctrinal pu-rity [and] the depth of their convictions. Roughly one-third of their members were schoolteachers (a critical tactical asset, given the goal of gaining control over education) and approximately one-tenth were civil servants. Significant numbers of clergy (especially Doppers) and academics from the Afrikaans-speaking universities also joined. Large-scale farmers made up most of the remainder (Akenson 1992: 88).

From the ranks of the above Broederbonders would come the archi-tects of Apartheid and the implementators of Christian National Educa-tion in all four of the country's four provinces. By the 1930s, many Broederbonders were, like many high Dutch Reformed Church leaders, openly opposed to bilingualism in European schools. "[I]t is the firm pol-icy of church," the Reverend Willim Nicol wrote in 1941, "reiterated with emphasis at our last synod, that our children must be educated in schools with Afrikaans as the medium. . . . Not only the salvation of our volk [people] but the preservation of our church depends in large measure on separate schools [for Afrikaans-speaking Whites]" (Akenson 1992: 86). Christian National Education would not, however, become a reality until the 1950s.

Despite the opening of the University College of Fort Hare and oc-casional small changes in state and provincial systems and levels of ex-penditures on education, until the 1950s African education had been fo-cused primarily at the elementary school level, received by a minority of school-age Africans, at schools run by missionaries, in classes taught mostly by Africans, most of whom had received no more than an ele-mentary school education.

Regardless of the number of years and overall quality of education they received, though, African children in attendance at mission schools could nonetheless count themselves among the fortunate. In 1939, for in-stance, "fewer than 30 percent of African children were receiving any schooling at all" (Thompson 1995: 164), and most of those received it at mission schools. All in all

> Missionaries presided over "an enormous benevolent empire" that reached into every African reserve community. In 1928, 48 mission-ary organizations were operating in the Union of South Africa.

They employed over 1,700 white missionaries, teachers, doctors, and nurses and over 30,000 African clergy, lay preachers, and teachers. . . . Receiving grants-in-aid from the provincial governments, the missions ran virtually the only institutions where Africans could acquire the literary skills necessary for effective participation in the industrializing economy. In 1935, they registered 342,181 African pupils. Over half were in the elementary Standards [the equivalent of K-2 in the American system], and most of the rest were in Standards 1 to 6 [the U.S. equivalents of grades 3–8]. Only 1,581 Africans were in Standards 7 and 8 [U.S. grades 9 and 10], and a mere 193 were in Standards 9 and 10 [U.S. grades 11 and 12], which culminated in the matriculation, or school-leaving examination (Thompson 1995: 172).

World War II created a need for more Nonwhites in the military and in industrial jobs. All told, South Africa's World War II military forces consisted of approximately 218,000 individuals, of whom 135,171 were white men, 12,818 white women, 27,583 Coloured men, and 42,627 black men. And though Nonwhites were almost entirely relegated to noncombat roles—as laborers, transport drivers, and low-level service and supply personal—"of the 5,500 South Africans killed in World War II, more than a quarter were black" (Thompson 1995: 177).

A positive consequence of the war for Blacks was the lowering of the color bar in industry. Blacks filled previous Whites-only jobs when large numbers of white industrial workers departed for military service. Moreover, those jobs paid higher wages than the Blacks-only jobs. During WWII, the government also tolerated the formation of African labor unions.

Among other positive consequences for Blacks were the abolition of school fees in all government and government-aided primary schools and, in 1943, the granting of one free meal a day for all school children. These measures were aimed at increasing the number of blacks attending school and qualifying them to be trained for the skilled and semiskilled jobs opened up by the war.

Still, when WWII ended in 1945, the ratio of expenditure on white as opposed to black education was as it had been in 1925: 10 to 1. In contrast, the ratio of expenditure on Whites versus Indians and Coloureds stood very close to 4 to 1. So not only was there more spent on white than non-white education; there was also substantially more spent on Coloured and Indian education than on black education. Consequently, there arose a significant income inequality between Blacks and the coloured and indian populations. In 1946, for instance, white per capita income was ten times that of black per capita income, six times that of Asian, and five times that of coloured (Thompson 1995: 156), which means that in 1946, coloured per capita income was twice that of black per capita income.

In 1946, with the war over, conditions for South Africa's Nonwhites began to worsen once again. Deeply aggrieved by the lowering of the color bar in industry that had served to protect them from black competition, white servicemen returned to civilian life determined to rectify the situation. Also, there was widespread fear among Whites of the consequences of the large increases in the populations of the black townships, increases resulting from large numbers of Blacks having left the economically depressed native reserves for wartime employment in the urban industrial areas. By the end of the war there were approximately as many Natives living in urban areas as there were Whites (see Chapter 3).

Headed by D. F. Malan, an ordained minister of the Dutch Reformed Church, the National Party came to power pledging to deal with *die swart gevaar* (the black menace). It enacted legislation and implemented policies that would lead to racial Apartheid, or "separateness" in all areas of life. To refresh the reader's memory:

> Under Apartheid, as it was envisioned by its National Party advocates, Natives—regardless of whether they resided in their designated tribal "reserves" or "homelands" or not, or had ever done so—would no longer be citizens of the Union of South Africa and, therefore, no longer, in any sense, entitled to the same citizenship rights of white South Africans while living, working or journeying through the 87 percent of the country's land mass not designated "tribal homelands." As for economic development of the homelands: the Natives would be encouraged to "develop along their own lines"—whatever that meant. And while Coloureds and Indians would have no designated homelands, their interaction with Whites, Blacks and each other would also be kept to a bare minimum (Gay 1997: 23).

In 1949, National Party leaders appointed the Eiselen Commission to make recommendations for the future education of Natives under conditions of Apartheid. The Committee's final report was submitted in 1952. Among its accepted recommendations was that African students were to be taught in their mother (tribal) tongues, except when learning a foreign language.

The aim of educating African students in their tribal tongues was to reduce contact and communication between members of different tribes and races and to keep black employment prospects far below those of Whites. The commission recommended that no native tribal language be accepted in the White-dominated governmental business or professional worlds. But since the aim was to *reduce*, not totally eliminate, the possibilities of contact and communication between the different tribes and races, African students were to be educated in both official languages, Afrikaans and English. However, they were not to be educated too highly. The black child was to be taught in such a way that [he] will be able to find his way in European communities; to follow oral and written instruction; and to carry on a simple conversation with Europeans about his work and other subjects of common interest. Handiwork taught in the first few years of school should aim at inculcating the "habit of doing manual work" (Troup 1976: 21).

The Eiselen Commission also recommended that the costs of African education should, as soon as possible, be entirely payed for by Africans themselves.

Among the Eiselen Commission's less harsh recommendations were that, within the next 10 years, the number of African primary schools should be increased to accommodate all eight- to eleven-year-olds and that there should be high schools enough "for those who could be absorbed into Bantu Society" (Troup 1976: 21).

In 1953, the year following the release of the Eiselen Commission report, the Bantu Education Act was enacted. Amended in 1954, 1956, 1959, and 1961, the act was a giant step backward for black education. One of its primary objectives was to wrest control of black education from the missionary organizations, very few of which, in the view of prominent National Party leaders, were doing their bit to prepare African students for the decidedly subordinate roles they were destined to occupy in South African society.

"When I have control of Native education," promised Dr. Henrik Verwoerd, then minister of native affairs, during an open parliamentary discussion of the bill,

> I will reform it so that Natives will be taught from childhood to realize that equality with Europeans is not for them. . . . People who believe in equality are not desirable teachers for Natives (Troup 1976: 22).

As was intended, the 1953 Bantu Education Act resulted in control of African education being transferred from the provincial governments to the Union government's Department of Native Affairs, within which was created the Department of Bantu Education. All but a few missionary schools were forced to close as a result of government regulations requiring that all native (Bantu, in government parlance) schools be registered with the Department of Native Affairs. Not to register would be to be in violation of the law. Approval or disapproval of a school's petition to continue operating was contingent on the school's meeting government curriculum requirements.

The 1954 amendment to the act introduced the requirement that the training of teachers for Bantu schools could only take place in Department of Native Affairs training centers. The department would not recognize the qualifications of teachers who trained elsewhere (Christie

1989: 79). This was a huge blow to mission schools, for teacher training had always been one of the most important functions of missionary organizations. And the efforts of the missionaries had borne fruit. By 1951, 59 percent of South Africa's black population and 91 percent of its Coloured were Christians (Thompson 1995: 156)

Seeing the Bantu Education Act for what it was—an attempt to keep them in subservient roles—in December 1954 leaders of the African National Congress called for a boycott of government-controlled schools. But not many people responded to the call. With only one of every two African children able to attend a school of any sort, parents were afraid that children who boycotted classes would be taken off the school rolls and that would be the end of their education.

Then, during the following year, 1955, came the coup de grâce: the government's announcement that all subsidies to mission schools would end by 1960. Furthermore, mission schools would only be registered if they didn't charge tuition fees; the medium (i.e., language) of instruction at mission schools had to be the same as the tribal language of the community it served; and mission schools had to follow course curricula devised by the Department of Native Affairs.

In the end only the Roman Catholics, Seventh Day Adventists, and the Johannesburg Anglican Church were able to maintain schools without benefit of state financial aid, and until the mid-1970s, the schools that those organizations chose to retain were, in keeping with the laws and spirit of Apartheid, racially segregated.

Also in keeping with the dictates of Apartheid was the 1957 Nursing Amendment Act, which established differential training for white and nonwhite prospective nurses and mandated the removal of nonwhite nurses from white hospitals

Before 1959, four English-language universities, four Afrikaans-language universities, one bilingual correspondence university, and the African Native College at Fort Hare existed in South Africa. All four Afrikaans-medium universities and the English-medium Rhodes University admitted only white students, while

> 12 percent of the students at the University of Cape Town and 6 percent of the students at the University of the Witwatersrand were black and were taught in integrated classes; 21 percent of the students in the University of Natal were black and were taught in segregated classes (Thompson 1995: 197).

Then in 1959, the Extension of University Education Act was passed, resulting in the establishment of separate colleges for Coloured and Indian students, as well as one for Zulu students and one for African students in the Transvaal, all under government control. The government also took control of the South African Native College at Fort Hare, making it a college for Xhosa students.

Despite protests by the ANC and a sprinkling of liberal white students and academicians, Blacks were now no longer able to attend white colleges except with the special permission of a cabinet minister, and there was obligatory racial and tribal segregation at all levels of education in South Africa. Though departments for the oversight of the education of South Africa's Coloured and Indian precollege-level student populations were not brought into existence until the 1960s, like black schools, Coloured and Indian schools had to be registered with the government.

During the 1970s and 1980s, school attendance for Indian and Coloured students—like attendance for Whites, but not Blacks—became compulsory. From then on, Coloured and Indian students, also unlike black students, would be taught from the same syllabi as white students.

CHRISTIAN NATIONAL EDUCATION

South African schooling became even more segregated in 1967, when the national legislature passed the National Education Act. With its mandates that the contents of all subjects taught in schools be explicitly both Christian and Afrikaner nationalistic in character, and that pupils from homes where the mother tongue is English be taught in English and pupils from Afrikaans-mother-tongue homes be taught in Afrikaans, the National Education Act set forth the basic principles of Christian National Education that would guide the education of Whites during the Apartheid years.

To ensure equality of white education throughout the four provinces, the National Education Act also mandated that compulsory school attendance requirements and the general contents of the syllabi by which white students were taught be uniform across the provinces. The act also made provisions for white pupils to attend public schools at no charge, not even for books or stationary, and for them to receive as much education as their abilities, interests, and the needs of the country warranted. To ensure that those who taught their children were possessed of the proper Christian National consciousness, the act gave parents a say in the hiring and firing of teachers and in the monitoring of teachers' professional and nonprofessional activities "through parent–teacher associations, school committees, boards of control or school boards or in any other manner" (Christie 1989: 162). Teachers' salaries and all other conditions of employment were also to be uniform throughout the four provinces.

Christian National Education was also meant to constitute the basis of nonwhite education. That was the main reason African education was taken out of the hands of most non-DRC missionary organizations and placed under government control. A 1948 pamphlet set forth the guiding principles and ultimate objectives of Christian National Education: "The

Coloured man . . . must be educated according to National principles. . . . Hence native education must be grounded in the life- and worldview of the Whites, more especially of the Boer nation as the senior white trustee of the native" (Troup 1976: 20; excerpted from Arti- cle 15 of the *Manifesto of the Institute for Christian National Education,* pub- lished in Afrikaans). Stated less obliquely: Teachers of black pupils, most of whom themselves were black, were charged with instilling in their pupils a worldview that would make them acceptant of all the inequities of Apartheid, as well as all of the white supremacist contentions that jus- tified those inequities.

It could not be done, however, even though officials of the Depart- ment of Bantu Education had the final say in the hiring of teachers in black schools and determined the content of the curricula at native schools; even though native teachers at native schools were generally careful not to teach anything overtly counter to what the Department of Bantu Education dictated they teach; and even though there was, as ini- tally envisioned by government leaders, an increase in the total number of African schools. Instilling in South African black children the belief that, by virtue of their skin color, they were inferior to everyone else and therefore *deserved* the worst of everything proved to be an impossible task. It could not be done.

The increase in the number of African schools from 1953 to 1971 was numerically impressive. In 1953, there were approximately 5,000 state-aided mission schools for Africans; by 1971 there were approxi- mately 10,000 such schools for Africans, almost all of which were under the auspices of Department of Bantu Education. The exceptions were the 438 private (i.e., non–state-supported) African elementary and secondary schools, most of which were Roman Catholic schools, the Catholic Church having had the greatest success in raising sufficient funds to allow it to operate schools without government sudsidies.

Although the increase in the number of African schools was im- pressive and resulted in an increase in the number of Africans in schools, there were no matching increases in the number of African school teach- ers or in the percentage of African students being educated beyond the primary grades. As a consequence, during the first two decades of Apartheid, African schools became even more crowded than white, In- dian, and Coloured schools than they had previously been. For the most part, African education remained primary school education; and despite the goals of Christian National Education, African students remained convinced that they deserved better.

In summary of some of the educational equalities of the first two decades of Apartheid, data show that between 1955 and 1971, the over- all number of African students per teacher rose from 45.5 to 57.8, while the ratio for Whites remained approximately 20 to 1. Overall expendi- tures on white education in 1971 were 31 times greater than the overall

TABLE 8.1

1971 Secondary School Enrollment

Racial Group	Percentage of Population
Whites	32.1%
Indians	26.4
Coloureds	12.2
Blacks	4.7

expenditures on black education, even though the black population was then approximately five times greater than the white population. Further, in 1971, the proportion of black students enrolled in secondary schools was 4.7 percent (as opposed to 3.5 percent in 1955), but the percentages of White, Coloured, and Indian pupils in secondary schools were, respectively, 32.1 percent, 12.2 percent, and 26.4 percent, as shown in Table 8.1 (Troup 1976: 30–35). Moreover, until the 1970s, about 70 percent of Africans in school attended for only the first four years (Christie 1989: 56).

Prominent among the reasons for the relatively low black educational attainments was that, as we have noted, black schooling was neither free nor compulsory. It cost. Not only did black students have to pay registration fees and for their own books and stationery, but unlike white, Indian, and Coloured parents, black parents were responsible for bearing the costs of maintaining their children's school buildings, which most often were quite dilapidated.

"Compulsory education," explained Deputy Minister G. F. Malan in a speech before a 1969 gathering of the national legislature, "can be extended to Africans only when they themselves ask for it, when they can finance it themselves, and when their economy can absorb the increased number of educated people" (Wilson and Thompson 1971: 222). The deputy minister must have surely meant that compulsory education for Africans was a long way off.

No wonder then that an analysis of the 1970 census brought forth the estimate that 48 percent of all Africans over 15 years of age were "illiterate in terms of the UN criterion for 'functional literacy' of a minimum of four years schooling" (Troup 1976: 33). No wonder then that it was impossible to convince African students that they were getting the education they deserved. No wonder that during the 1970s and 1980s it was Africans of school age who were most openly and unflinchingly involved in the fight against Apartheid.

CHAPTER 9

Religion and Schooling
1976 to the Present

The era of full-on, all-out student protests against Bantu education and the Apartheid state began with the 1976 Soweto student protests. Soweto, an acronym for Southwestern Township, is a black residential area on the outskirts of Johannesburg (see Chapter 5).

The precipitating cause of the 1976 Soweto student protests was a decree by Dr. Andries Treurnicht, former chairman of the Broederbond and minister of Bantu education, in which he stated that all African students must learn Afrikaans. Part of the logic behind this decree was that the greater the number of literate Africans speaking Afrikaans, the greater the chance of the Afrikaans language surviving throughout the subsequent generations and the easier to impose the Afrikaner worldview on African students. Heretofore, African education had been mostly British missionary education, and educated Africans had been English-speakers, more or less systematically knowledgeable of British culture and ideological systems but not of Afrikaner ones. If Africans became less likely to speak English than Dutch, it was reasoned, they would be less vulnerable to ideas conveyed through the English language, as well as less able to communicate with non–Afrikaans-speakers outside of South Africa.

Fear of Africans' being corrupted by exposure to non-Afrikaner ways of thinking and interrelating with persons of different racial origins had, after all, been why commercial television was not introduced in South Africa until 1976. Commercial TV was mostly American TV. Blacks sometimes appeared on America TV as the social and otherwise equals of Whites. But commercial TV, though heavily censored, came to South Africa anyway. And Soweto students, despite grave admonitions against doing so, took a militant stand against having to learn Afrikaans.

Why should African students have to learn Afrikaans? African students, parents, and political leaders alike asked each other this question. Only about five or so million people in the whole world spoke Afrikaans. It wasn't the dominant language in business, commerce, industry, science, academia, literature, journalism, entertainment, or anything else important or enjoyable, not even in South Africa itself. Besides, if Afrikaans was a useful language to know—which it wasn't—how would learning it help Blacks, who were prohibited by both law and custom from rising to prominence in any of South Africa's major institutions? And most of all, Afrikaans was the language of the police, the courts, the government, the oppressor—people hell bent on continuing to deny Blacks their basic rights as citizens and human beings. Why aid in the survival of the language of the oppressor?

So, on June 16, 1976, 20,000 Soweto schoolchildren marched through their community in protest of having to learn Afrikaans. They didn't want to learn Afrikaans; nor were they going learn Afrikaans, many had decided. When the marchers came upon a police barricade, the police ordered them to halt and turn back. They didn't, and the police opened fire, killing more than 20 students, wounding scores of others, some of the dead and wounded shot in the back as they fled in fright. Video footage of South African police killing and wounding fleeing schoolchildren was shown on TV news programs around the world.

Students responded to the police violence with their own brand of violence, attacking, and in some cases, looting government offices, liquor stores, post offices, a bank, a hotel, cars, and buses. Within days, student violence had spread beyond Soweto, all across the country, even onto the native homelands. Complementing the violent student protests were organized boycotts of classes and exams. Student activists ripped up the exams of those not honoring the boycotts.

The police response was ruthlessly swift and firm. They issued proclamations banning gatherings of even small numbers of people. They broke up banned gatherings, marches, and demonstrations with everything at their disposals: guns, tear gas, "hippos" (i.e., armored tanks), dogs, helicopters, and so on. They used the powers granted to them by the country's legislators to conduct house raids, to set roadblocks for vehicle and personal searches, and to detain without trial those whom they arrested. Of those arrested, some were subjected to such physically torturous interrogation that they died in custody; others were turned into **impimpi,** or police informants.

What were church leaders—or leaders of the "faith communities," as they were referred to in the Truth and Reconciliation Commission reports—doing while all of this was going on? Deciding that it was now time to act on its already vocalized disapproval of Apartheid, the South African Catholic Bishops Conference—in 1976, the year of the outbreak of the Soweto riots—passed a resolution in favor of admitting Nonwhite pupils to the country's white Catholic schools and began doing so on a small scale. Soon thereafter, Anglican and other church schools began doing likewise, also quietly and on a small scale. "In some Catholic schools the percentage of black pupils is as high as 68 percent. But in most other schools it is no more than 5 percent" (Christie 1989: 89).

It was in 1977, with protests following the Soweto massacre having not yet subsided, that Steve Biko, one of the leaders of the **Black Consciousness Movement (BCM),** was arrested. Biko's death of massive head and body wounds while in custody, and the banning of all BCM organizations, only served to bring more students to the streets in another round of school boycotts and protest actions leading to more violent reactions by the police.

It wasn't until 1978 that the police–student violence engendered by the June 16, 1976, Soweto massacre finally subsided. But by then, perhaps as many as a thousand people had been killed, several thousand injured, and the lives of many thousands of black youths disrupted or radically redirected as a result of their having missed a couple of years of classes or having had their schooling officially terminated for participating in the protests.

Also during the latter half of the 1970s, the song "Another Brick in the Wall" by the British rock group Pink Floyd was banned in South African townships because of its refrain "We don't need no education / We don't need no thought control / Hey, teacher, leave them kids alone / All in all, you're just another brick in the wall."

Among the positive results of the Soweto-engendered waves of police–student violence were the withdrawal of the requirement that African students learn the Afrikaans language; the Department of Bantu Education being renamed the Department of Education and Training (DET); more money put into African schooling; and the promise of more attention given to alleviating overcrowding, lack of qualified teachers, and other appalling conditions in African schools.

But still, the country's schools were to remain racially segregated; and per capita spending on the education of white students would continue to be greater than that spent on the education of nonwhite students. Therefore, more student protests would occur.

The next round of widespread school boycotts began in 1980 in Cape Town, with thousands of black students staying out of class in protest against the quality of education they were receiving. As they spread to other regions of the country, these boycotts came to be supported by up to 140,000 students, not all of whom were black. There were also boycotts of Coloured and Indian schools. "Furthermore hundreds of teachers came out in organized public support of the boycott . . . pledg[ing] their solidarity with the students" (Christie 1989: 244).

The underlying causes of the 1980 boycotts were the same as those of the 1976 boycotts: poor equipment, too many students per teacher, too

few qualified teachers, dismissals of teachers who didn't spout the National Party line, corporal punishment, the presence of security personnel at the schools, lack of student input into decisions regarding school
policies and operations, and so forth.

The police responded as they had to the 1976 protests. They banned
political gatherings. They threatened, expelled, and arrested student
leaders. When they thought the situation warranted, they opened fire on
protesters, killing some and wounding others.

By the beginning of 1981 things had quieted down; most of the 1980
protesters had resumed attending classes and the boycott was over.

That the 1980 boycotts caused the government to consider acceding
to some of the demands made by the protesters is evidenced by its 1981
establishment of the de Lange Commission. Peter de Lange was the principal of Rands Afrikaans University in Johannesburg, future head of the
Broederbond, and one of the first Afrikaner leaders to open up the negotiations with members of the ANC leaders in exile that would bring an end
to Apartheid. The commission was charged with investigating the feasi-
bility of providing equal education for all, and it carried out its charge.

One of the recommendations contained in the commission's final
report was that there be a merging of the existent 14 departments of education into one single department responsible for the schooling of all
South Africans of all races and tribes. The government rejected this rec-
ommendation, however, reasoning that if the proposed restructuring of
the education department were acted upon, it would open the door for a
proposal that educational opportunities and resources be equalized
across racial lines. But the government did acquiesce to other de Lange
Commission recommendations, allowing for the provision of more textbooks for African students and for repairs to some of the dilapidated
school buildings in which they were educated.

Also in 1981, the government introduced what was touted as "free
and compulsory schooling" for black students in attendance at
201 schools in 38 different townships. But in actuality, attendance at
these schools was neither altogether free nor compulsory in the sense
that white schools were. Books and stationery (i.e., notebooks and lesson
paper) were free, it was true; but students still had to pay school fees.
Nor did compulsory education mean that the state was compelled to educate all children in these districts. All that compulsory education meant
was that parents who paid the fees to send their children to these schools
had to agree in writing to keep their children in school for a specified
time. This, in turn, meant that it was "up to the parents to make sure
their children [didn't] boycott or miss school. If they [did] then they
[would] have broken a contract and [could] be justifiably expelled"
(Christie 1989: 152).

The government made yet another weak effort in 1981 to make education more accessible to black youngsters. It somewhat reduced the

cost of school attendance by acceding to demands that school uniforms no longer be compulsory for Soweto black school children. There were still, however, too few African schools to educate all African students of school age, severe overcrowding at the African schools that did exist, too many underqualified teachers of African students, and gross inequalities in per capita spending on white and nonwhite school children. Moreover, African students paid school attendance fees while white students didn't.

All in all, then, the state of black education in the 1980s was not vastly different than it had been in the 1970s. For example, during the 1982–83 period per capita expenditure on the education of white children was eight times more than that for black children, and two and a half times more than that for Coloured and Indian children. Other data show that while from 1970 to 1982 there was an almost 100 percent increase (from 2,738,564 to 5,313,016) in the number of African school children, most Africans nonetheless still had less than four years of formal schooling. While most white students made it to standard 10 (12th grade), somewhat less than 2 percent of all African students did (Christie 1989: 100, 104–5).

There had, however, occurred a drop in the percentage of Africans who met the UN criteria for being designated "functionally illiterate." Whereas in 1971, 48 percent of South Africa's African population had met the criteria, as of 1980, 33 percent had—as opposed to 15.5 percent of its Coloured population, 7.6 percent of its Indian population, and .7 percent of its white population. In addition, though lower than they had been in 1971, at 1:43, 1983 teacher–pupil ratios at black schools were still considerably higher than the ratios at Coloured, Indian, and white schools, respectively, 1:27, 1:24, and 1:18 (Christie 1989: 112).

There were also still huge differences in the educational attainments of teachers at black, Coloured, Indian, and white schools. In 1979, for instance, only 2.3 percent of teachers at black schools were holders of college degrees, as opposed to 4.2 percent of teachers at Coloured schools, 19.4 percent at Indian schools, and 32 percent at white schools (see Table 9.1). And while 82.2 percent of teachers at black schools,

TABLE 9.1

Teachers Holding College Degrees,
by Race of Students Taught, 1979

Blacks	2.3%
Coloureds	4.2
Indians	19.4
Whites	32

69.5 percent at Coloured schools, and 15.3 percent at Indian schools had not earned the equivalent of an American high school degree (i.e., completed standard 10), all teachers at white schools had (Christie 1989: 116).

There were also, as many readers have no doubt already surmised, large differences in the salaries of the teachers of black, white, Coloured, and Indian pupils. In 1973, for instance, the starting salaries of black teachers at black schools were one-third as much as those of white teachers. These salary differences, however, did not depend on differences in the qualifications (i.e., educational attainments) of the teachers. In a 1954 speech, Minister of Native Affairs Dr. Henrik Verwoerd explained the disparities as being necessitated by the fact that:

> The European teacher is in the service of the European community and his salary is determined in comparison with the income of the average parent whose children he teaches. . . . In precisely the same way the Bantu teacher serves the Bantu community and his must be fixed accordingly for salary inequalities between black and white teachers (Troup 1976: 40).

MAKING THE COUNTRY UNGOVERNABLE

With still great inequalities in the amount and quality of education received by Blacks and Whites, no wonder that another wave of black student protests and school boycotts began in early 1984, this time spreading out from Atteridge and Saulsville outside of Pretoria and Port Elizabeth in the Eastern Cape to areas throughout the rest of the country.

As before, black students stayed out of school, marched, demonstrated, stoned and set fire to buildings, cars, and buses, and were variously expelled from school, arrested, teargassed, and shot as a result. There were also school boycotts and student protests in response to the 1984 establishment of the tricameral national legislature that included, without substantively empowering, Coloured and Indian components but allowed for no black representation whatsoever.

Such was the situation throughout the remainder of the 1980s, as black youth—students and nonstudents—set about to "make the county ungovernable," in response to exhortation from ANC and leaders of other anti-Apartheid groups.

It was also during these years that "liberation before education" became the slogan of the many thousands of school-age children who had given up attending school to join the fight against the municipal police, the black collaborators and informants, and all manner of other perceived agents of the Apartheid state. Though not all Blacks in all townships completely ceased attending schools, it appears to have been nonetheless true that in most of the country's major urban black townships, school attendance was desultory at best for a great many students.

There was also, as previously noted, chronic fighting between affiliates of the ANC, the PAC, the BCM, and other groups competing for leadership in the black communities. Vigilantist "people's courts" sprung up in the townships, self-empowered to summarily impose and implement death sentences. "Necklacing"—placing a gasoline-soaked rubber tire around a person's neck and setting fire to it—was one of the most brutal means of carrying out these death sentences. Schools, private homes, churches, small township shops, buses, and cars were also set ablaze.

The townships were indeed on their way to becoming ungovernable—by anyone, for years to come. By the mid–1980s, violence was for many people becoming a way of life transcendent of politics and political protest. "Criminals [were] exploit[ing] it to their advantage; clans used it as an excuse to settle old scores; and revenge multiplied its effects manifold" (Waldmeir 1997: 160)

One of the Botha government's responses to increasing defiance of its authority was to unleash the full and furious might of the country's police, intelligence, and military agencies in his declared "total onslaught" against both the internal and external enemies of the Apartheid state.

The boycotts and violent resistance to Apartheid continued and even rose a bit in response to the 1989 Whites-only national parliamentary elections, and they continued on into the 1990s. Even after the formal abolition of Apartheid law, there were still continuous cycles of ever more vehement black student as well as nonstudent protests, violent police responses to the protests, violent responses to the police responses, and intensified Black-on-Black political violence primarily involving student affiliates of the African National Congress, the Pan African Congress, and the Zulu Inkatha Freedom Parrty, the latter often operating with support from the country's police and intelligence agencies.

INEQUALITY IN EDUCATION

In 1990, major changes in the nation's educational policies occurred, but in reality inequalities still existed. With Apartheid laws rescinded and the country on its way to open, all-race elections, all schools were now officially open to all races. By 1991 there were some black students in attendance at some previously Whites-only schools, though not many: "A mere 5,360 . . . or 0.08 percent" of the total number of the country's black students (Mncwabe 1993: xxxiii), which was not nearly enough to alleviate overcrowding in black schools.

Thus, on into the 1990s student boycotts of black township schools were still "more the norm than the exception. . . . There are estimates that on any one school day, approximately 200,000 children scattered throughout the country [were] boycotting classes" (Mncwabe 1993: 27).

The abolition of Apartheid laws and school desegregation did not suddenly bring about an improvement in the conditions under which

TABLE 9.2

Teacher–Pupil Ratios by Race of Students, 1983

Blacks	1:43
Coloureds	1:27
Indians	1:24
Whites	1:18

most Blacks were educated; thus the boycotts didn't end. Even if funding for education had been equalized—and it wasn't—there still would not have been enough classrooms to accommodate all school-age African children. There still would have been too few qualified teachers to teach all school-age African children. The facilities at African schools would still have been woefully inferior to those at white schools.

During the 1980s, for instance, there had been only a small decrease in the teacher–student ratio at black schools. Whereas in 1980 it had been 1:45, in 1990 it was only slightly lower at 1:41. By 1990, the number of black children in South African schools (five million) had risen to the point of being equal to South Africa's total white population. In addition, more black children were entering grade one each year than there were pupils in the entire white school system.

Where was the money going to come from to provide this greatly increased number of black students with the same quality of education as had traditionally been provided to students at white schools? In 1980, the ratio of spending on white education to spending on black education was 10:1. By 1990 it had been halved to 5:1, which had required a great increase in overall expenditures on education in general but still hadn't been nearly enough to provide students in African township schools with the same quality of education as received by students at white or previously all-white schools. It had, however, been enough to raise concerns among white parents that equalization of expenditures on education would result in a drop in the quality of education their children would receive. By 1990 there were also at least as many black university students as there were white university students. Where would the funds come from to accommodate increasingly larger numbers of black university students?

FAITH COMMUNITIES AND APARTHEID

Like black students, black educators, and members of secular black community organizations, black church leaders played prominent roles in the anti-Apartheid struggle. Among the most prominent were Bishop

Desmond Tutu and the Reverends Allen Boesak and Frank Chikane But what about the leaders of the white faith communities, for instance, the English-speaking churches and their leaders? What were their reactions to Apartheid laws and having African education taken out of their hands and placed under government control? How complicit were they in the maintenance of Apartheid? How involved were they in the anti-Apartheid struggle?

Were *all* the various branches of the Dutch Reformed Church and their leaders supportive of Apartheid laws and practices? Were they *all* in agreement that Apartheid was the realization of the will of God? Was DRC support of Apartheid firm and steady right through to the bitter end? How influential are the DRC churches and their leaders in postapartheid South Africa?

Some English-speaking churches and church leaders were complicit in the maintenance of Apartheid. Other leaders became so actively involved in the anti-Apartheid struggle that they ended up being exiled, imprisoned, tortured, or murdered for their efforts. Others simply remained aloof from the struggle.

Nor were all DRC ministers ever in full, unequivocal support of apartheid as the realization of the Will of God. In the wake of the 1948 election and the newly elected government's reaffirmed resolve to carry through its pledges to implement Apartheid, "leaders of all the white South African churches except the Dutch Reformed churches issued statements criticizing Apartheid" (Thompson 1995: 204), but to no avail.

The passage of the 1953 Bantu Education Act and successive legislation leading to the closing of most of South Africa's missionary-run schools also brought forth a storm of protests from leaders of the English-speaking faith communities—also to no avail. The closing of mission schools was all a part of the master plan of Apartheid. The relatively few church schools that did remain in existence (mostly Roman Catholic, Seventh Day Adventist, and Anglican) were initially racially segregated, in conformity with the goals of Apartheid.

Not all English-speaking organizations and their leaders remained silent throughout the 1960s, either. At a 1961 ecumenical conference at Cottesloe in Johannesburg, it was concluded "that almost every aspect of Apartheid was un-scriptual and un-Christian." At first, members of the Dutch churches appeared to be in agreement with this conclusion, until Prime Minister "Verwoerd called his ecclesiastics to order, and [they] duly recanted" (Welsh 1999: 462).

The Dutch churches duly recanted, but not DRC minister Dr. Beyers Naude, then a Broederbonder. By holding fast to the Cottesloe conclusions, and thenceforth living a life compatible with his beliefs, Beyers Naude became the most prominent Afrikaner of the time to actively oppose Apartheid. It is worth nothing that his father was the first to use Afrikaans in a sermon in Graaf Reinert in 1933 (Brink 1998: 96).

The Reverend Naude left the DRC to form and head the interracial Anti-Apartheid Christian Institute, from which was launched the Study Project on Christianity in Apartheid Society (SPOCAS) and calls for more radically defiant responses to the actions of the Apartheid government.

After his break with the DCR, Beyers Naude also became a member of the (black) Dutch Reformed Church in Africa. In 1977, he and the Christian Institute were placed under banning orders for engaging in public criticism of Apartheid policies. By then, though, he was not the only Afrikaner clergyman willing to openly declare Apartheid to be in opposition to Christian principles.

In a 1978 document entitled "The Koinonia Declaration," issued in the *Journal of Theology for Southern Africa,* a group of Afrikaner clergyman voiced their own radical critique of Apartheid, also declaring it to be wrong.

Then there was the Western Synod of the NGK, the largest and original Dutch Reformed Church and in those days sometimes referred to as the "National Party at prayer." In 1984, the year of the beginning of a wave of student boycotts and protests oriented toward making the country ungovernable, the group acknowledged that there was no biblical justification for the evils of Apartheid. Its moderator, Johan Heyns, proclaimed

> there is no such thing as white superiority or black inferiority . . . all people are equal before God. . . . [T]here may not be under any circumstances a [policy] based on oppression, discrimination and exploitation. . . . [T]he task of the Church is to protest unjust laws (O'Meara 1996: 337).

Four other NGK clergymen were among the 20 anonymous Afrikaner dissidents whose responses to questions concerning their backgrounds and motivations formed the substance of Joha Louw-Potgeiter's *Afrikaner Dissidents: A Social Psychological Study of Identity and Dissent.* From them came reports of other anti-Apartheid clergymen meeting surreptitiously in small discussion groups of people of like mind, while at the same time working silently within church structures to bring still other DRC clergymen into the anti-Apartheid fold (Louw-Potgeiter 1988: 90–97).

But it may have been too little, too late for the oldest, largest, and most influential of the Afrikaner churches. By the late 1980s, the power of the traditional DRCs was in serious decline. Some of the younger generation had been turned off by Church racism; others, of all generations, were so turned off by NGK's renunciation of racism that they broke away to form a fourth Afrikaner church body: the Apartheid-affirming, white-supremacist Afrikaner Protestant Church (Brink 1998: 96).

In 1987, Frank Chikane, black minister of the Apostolic Faith Mission, succeeded Beyers Naude as general secretary of the interracial

South African Council of Churches (SACC). Seven years later, Chikane would become director general of the office of deputy president Thabo Mbeki, the man who would succeed Nelson Mandela as president of the Republic of South Africa.

How politically or otherwise influential are South Africa's faith communities in the opening years of the twenty-first century? It is impossible to say. Their influence no doubt varies from individual to individual. All that can be said with certainty is that at present approximately 80 percent of South Africa's 43 million citizens are, at least nominally, Christians of various denominations, and about 8 million of its 35 or so million black citizens (nearly one of every four) follow the "independent African traditions" while interpreting "European values to arrive at an impressive synthesis" (Welsh: 1999: 514).

THE RESTRUCTURED DEPARTMENT OF EDUCATION

When the Mandela government took over in 1994, the 19 separate departments of education that had existed at the height of Apartheid were still in place, despite many previously all-white schools having become racially integrated:

> 5 administering white education, one each for Indians and Coloureds, 11 for black education—in and out of "independent" homelands and "self-governing territories"—and one umbrella department controlling the purse strings and setting different "norms and standards" for the rest (Macware 1993: 34).

Different norms and standards, as well as differences in the levels at which black, white, Coloured, and Indian schools were funded during the years before 1994, are reflected in the following data. When the government of National Unity came into existence, the percentage of South African students taking and passing the school matriculation exam was 48.8 percent for Blacks, 87.5 percent for Coloureds, 97.24 percent for Indians, and 97.3 percent for Whites (see Table 9.3) (Economist Intelligence Unit, 1995: 90)

In an effort to make good its promise of 10 years of free education in first-class schools for everyone, a month after coming to power in April 1994, the Mandela-led ANC government replaced the 19 different, inequitably funded departments of education with a more streamlined system headed by the Ministry of Education, within which was subsumed the national Department of Education. Below and directly linked to the national Department of Education are nine provincial departments of education.

As outlined in the constitution, the national Department of Education is responsible for formulating overall national goals and policies and

TABLE 9.3

Percentage of Students Taking and Passing
Matriculation Exam by Race, 1994

Blacks	48%
Coloureds	87.5
Indians	97.4
Whites	97.3

setting specific national standards for both pupil and teacher training and competence. But the provincial departments of education are each free to "set their own [additional] priorities" and to implement programs to meet national goals and standards in ways of their own choosing (South African Department of Education 1998).

In August 1995, the national Department of Education announced that during the years inclusive of 1998 and 2005 it would be phasing in a new "outcomes-based curriculum" designated Curriculum 2005. By January 1997, desired outcomes of student instruction in each of the eight learning areas that were to form the basis for Curriculum 2005 had been set forth as policy objectives. The implementation of the new curriculum began on schedule in 1998. The eight learning areas are language, literacy, and communications; mathematics and mathematical sciences; human and social sciences; natural sciences; technology; economics; arts and culture; and life orientation.

The South African Qualifications Authority was established in May 1996 "to oversee the development of a National Qualifications Framework (NQF) covering standard setting and quality assurance . . . and move the measurement of achievement in education and training away from inputs and towards outcomes," in other words, to set uniform national standards for teacher training and student instruction, as well as to devise ways of measuring whether those standards are being met.

Soon after the restructuring of the national system of education and the establishment of the above bodies charged with developing national standards for students and teachers, the national legislature passed the South African Schools Act of 1996 (Act 84 of 1996), which became effective on January 1, 1997. Among other things, it

- Mandated compulsory education for all "learners between the ages of 7 and 15 years, or learners reaching the ninth grade, whichever occurs first."
- Sanctioned two categories of schools, "namely public schools and independent schools."

- Set forth conditions of admission of students to public schools.

- Set forth rules and regulations for the "governance and management of public schools, the election of governing bodies and their functions."

- Defined the means by which public schools are to be funded (South African Department of Education 1998).

On July 14, 1997, the Department of Education released a new language policy, according to which students have a right to be taught in a language of their choice; when applying for admission, students must tell the school the language in which they wish to be taught. For their part, schools must take student "requests into account and be seen working towards multilinguism." Multilinguism being one of the stipulated goals of South African education.

Also stipulated in the the current language policy is that students may be taught only in official languages; from the third grade (standard 1) on, pupils have to study the language in which they are instructed and one other language; and failing a language will result in failing an entire grade.

Unfortunately, despite consolidation of the 19 different departments of education and the promulgation of new goals, policies, and operational guidelines, it will nonetheless be a long time before South Africa has either the financial or human resources necessary for delivering on the ANC promise of a first-class education for all. Therein lies the source of many of the country's major problems. Although during its first five years in power, the ANC had built "100,000 new classrooms, and managed to bring 1.5 million learners [at the primary and secondary school levels] and 100,000 higher education students to the system" (Garson 1999), there are still not enough classrooms to accommodate all of South Africa's school-age children.

Evidence of the need for more, and more adequate, schools is contained in data collected during the Department of Education's August 1997 Registry of Need survey. Among other things, the survey showed that there was "no water available within 24 percent of South African schools. Only 43 percent of all schools have electricity; while 79 percent of schools in the Northern Province have none" (South African Department of Education 1998). Of course, the above mentioned schools were for African students.

The still-dismal state of schooling in some black areas was highlighted in an article appearing in the May 30, 1999, electronic edition of *The Mirror*. The subject of the article was a public school in Tshikota, a black residential area on the outskirts of the city of Louis Trichardt, "where [the 500] pupils [in attendance at the school] are compelled to use a local beerhall toilet, because of the lack of this facility at their school." These trips to the beerhall put the students, some of whom are under 10 years old, "in contact with not only drunkards but also with **dagga** [i.e., marijuana] smokers and even glue sniffers who hang around the place." The teachers themselves have to use the facilities at the local men's hostel, a 10-minute walk (Siebane 1999). This evidence makes conceivable a link between the lack of private sanitation facilities in black areas and the the high incidences of rape and drug and alcohol use among black school children, topics to be touched upon shortly. The report also refers to a visit to the school by a local health inspector who found the school building itself to be in dangerous disrepair: most of the classroom "walls had large cracks and the roofing was not anchored to the rafters in some places."

Students in the higher grades at the school had been without teachers for a month. Their previous teachers were "volunteers" paid from the R10 (one rand = $.15) donations of parents. But many of these parents could no longer afford the R10 as a result of the increasing unemployment rate. In addition, none of the eight classrooms in the school has its ceiling intact. Moreover, "the classroom which 57 grade ones and twos share is also used as a library, storeroom, kitchen and office. The administration 'building' is definitely no bigger than two square meters." (Joubert 1999).

How can such conditions exist in black schools in a country that since 1994 has been ruled by a black-majority government committed to wiping out racial inequalities?

Much of the present-day educational inequality is made possible by the provisions of the 1997 Education Act that gave a high degree of autonomy to state schools. With the autonomy granted them, local school committees have the power to set school fees and raise funds in addition to the amounts provided by the state. Consequently, school committees made up of highly educated, affluent persons are better able to raise funds and set educational standards than are committees of poorly educated persons in nonaffluent areas. Thus, schools attended by students of affluent parents have better facilities, higher teacher salaries, and more academically rigorous curricula. In addition, "While the law exempts the poorest parents from paying school fees, parents sending their children to middle-class schools are faced with extra costs, like expensive uniforms," as well as costs for participating in extracurricular activities.

Also, de facto racial segregation exists in some areas: "small towns where most of the white people speak Afrikaans . . . [and] have set up separate English-medium classes, which end up being mostly black" (Pearce 1999).

As a result of the relatively low numbers of black school graduates during the Apartheid era and the relatively low quality of education received by many of those who did matriculate, there are not enough qualified teachers for all the classrooms built to accommodate South Africa's school-age children. Nor are there enough teachers for the country's many functionally illiterate adults desirous of attending literacy classes.

The scope of the educational inequalities that existed during the Apartheid era is suggested by data showing that although the country's 1995 black population was seven times larger than its white population, there were more than twice as many white degree holders (20 years and older) as there were black degree holders (*Statistics South Africa* 1997).

That adult illiteracy is still one of the country's major, but not immediately remediable, problems was brought to public attention in May 1997 with release of a "Project Literacy" announcement that a total of 46 percent of adult South Africans could not read or write (South African Department of Education 1998). Poor facilities and a shortage of qualified teachers at predominantly African schools are conditions that are likely to persist into the immediate future. This is so because although there were no cutbacks on overall spending on education during the 1990s, as the number of pupils attending schools increased, the average amount spent on each pupil has declined (Pearce 1999); thus far the government remains committed to fiscally conservative policies that preclude large increases on the educational expenditures.

An additional reason that South Africa is likely to continue to suffer from a lack of qualified people to teach in the shoddy black schools is that even though the country is currently turning out more black standard 10 (12th grade) and university graduates than ever before, given the wider range of opportunities now available to them, teaching is a less attractive option to black degree-holders than it was when it was one of only a relatively few fields open to them. Attempts to transfer white teachers from middle-class schools in predominantly white areas to schools in high-poverty black areas have resulted in many white teachers leaving the profession.

Apart from having to cope with a shortage of teachers, a shortage of classrooms, classrooms in dilapidated buildings without electricity or central heating, a lack of sanitation facilities on school grounds, and so on, 1990s South African school officials have found themselves having to deal with problems following from widespread drug and alcohol use among South African students.

One report linked increased drug use among students to the lifting of economic sanctions after the nulling and voiding of Apartheid laws, the growth of organized crime syndicates, and South Africa's escalating rape rate. Drugs "exploded onto the school scene" because with the lifting of economic sanctions, South Africa went from being a "drug transit area to a drug destination area." The movement of drugs was "co-ordinated largely by [organized] gangsters." The report also stated that "Of the 16 girls raped every month in Mitchell Plains [located in the Western Cape province], police estimate 70 percent are drunk or high," and some students raise money to support drug habits by "stealing and sometimes prostitution" (Fox 1999).

Exactly how pervasive are drugs in the Western Cape? A Western Cape police officer lamented, "When I ask a class of 30 how many of them are using drugs, more than 20 will put up their hands. . . . Drugs are completely out of control here. From February 1998 to 1999 there were R-3-billion worth of drugs in the Western Cape. The police confiscated only R-33-million" (Fox 1999).

Was there no drug use in the Cape and other parts of South Africa before the end of Apartheid? There was, but according to research findings "the use of cannabis . . . almost doubled for both boys and girls in grade 11 over the last seven years in Cape Town" and there was also increased used of "heavy drugs," inclusive of Mandrax, LSD, and cocaine (O'Connor 1999).

The reasons given by Cape Town students for their drug use are the same as those given by drug users throughout the world: escape from reality and relief of stress; recreation; and rebellion.

Drug use among school children is not, of course, just a Cape Town problem. It is a national problem. Ashley Lynton Houston, a policeman in the KwaZulu-Natal city of Durban, sees drug use in South Africa as being "across the board," among children of various ages, both sexes, and all social class backgrounds. But he sees youngsters of different social classes using drugs for dissimilar reasons: "For the poor, drugs become a means of survival while those who are rich are able to buy the harder substances because they are able to afford them." Thus, in Houston's view, at least part of the student problem is related to changing lifestyles and increased affluence among certain sectors of the population. "Sometimes parents confess to giving their children between R200 and R300 for pocket money." Houston also mentioned rave parties where cocaine and ecstasy are readily available to those with money or something else to offer in return (Bridgraj 1999).

One and one-half million primary and secondary students, 100,000 more classrooms, rooms needed, more college and university students than space to accommodate them, a shortage of teachers at all levels, classrooms in dilapidated buildings without electricity or central heating, and a widespread lack of sanitation facilities on black school grounds and drugs describe the present state of South African education and presents formidable problems for its present-day leaders.

HOPE FOR THE FUTURE?

What of the quality of education being received by those in attendance at South African public schools? Has it risen during the postapartheid years? Has the setting of new standards by NQF in its announced movement away from "the measurement of achievement in education and training from inputs toward outcomes" resulted in the raising of the quality of education received by South African students? At present, it is impossible to determine. The perception of many South African Whites, however, is that the new standards are not as high as the old ones and the overall quality of education in previously all-white schools is lower that it once was.

But because of changes in the contents of matriculation and other standardized exams, no valid comparisons can be made between the achievement levels of Apartheid and postapartheid students of any race. All that can be said with certainty is that as a result of now hundreds of thousands students raised by illiterate or semi-illiterate parents now entering the public education system, within a generation South Africa's illiteracy rate will have been drastically reduced.

The Department of Education's movement away from inputs and toward outcomes may have resulted in some educators giving false reports of student outcomes. An example of this is the 1999 Mpumalanga province matriculation scandal. It became known that the originally announced pass rate (72 percent) for Mpumalanga students taking the matriculation exam had been inflated by unethical, dishonest teachers and administrators wishing to be credited with having achieved outcomes that they had not. The actual pass rate for those taking the 1998 exam was 52 percent. Nonetheless, 52 percent was an improvement over the 1997 pass rate, which was 46 percent (Lubisi 1999). If one wants to find other good news in these figures, it is that while a 48 percent failure rate indicates that large numbers of South African pupils finish the 12th grade not having achieved Department of Education school-leaving standards, at least there are standards that are being maintained.

Despite all the shortcomings of South Africa's system of education, the ANC can take pride in having made education accessible to millions of people who would have been shut out under the Apartheid system. And more educated South Africans means more literate South Africans; more literate South Africans means more South Africans with the potential for being trained as skilled workers and more with the qualifications necessary to enter the economy at middle managerial and professional levels—all of which are preconditions for further economic growth and reductions in the country's unemployment, poverty, and crime rates.

CHAPTER 10

Crime in Postapartheid South Africa

In a 1987 report submitted to the United Nation's Children's Fund, economic historian Francis Wilson and medical doctor Mamphela Ramphele expressed the fear that African children under Apartheid "may be socialized into vandalism or find themselves having to adopt violent measures as a matter of survival and, in the the process, losing any sense of right and wrong. The impact on children's minds and values of the physical violence that they witness and experience, not least at the hands of the police, is a matter of grave concern" (Thompson 1995: 201). Gill Straker in *Faces in the Revolution* (1992) gave empirical support for Wilson and Ramphele's concern that there was indeed arising a deep-seated culture of nonpolitical violence that boded ill for South Africa's future.

By the time of Mandela's release from prison in 1990, nonpolitical criminal violence in the townships had become so rampant that in his first speech to a large township audience, in Soweto, he felt it necessary to express outrage at "criminals masquerading as freedom fighters, harassing innocent people and setting alight vehicles." Mandela warned his audience of 120,000 that "Freedom without civility, freedom without the ability to live in peace, was not true freedom at all . . . [and while] I understand the deprivations our people suffer, I must make it clear that the level of crime in the township is unhealthy and must be eliminated as a matter of urgency" (Mandela 1995: 570).

In 1994, the year the Mandela-led Government of National Unity came to power, South Africa was among the world leaders in incidences of murder, rape, and assault. South Africa's crime rates were still among the world's highest in 1999 when the nation's second multiracial, democratic elections were held and Thebo Mbeki became president of the both the ANC and the South African Republic. And the country's crime rates and incidences of criminal violence remain among the highest in the world today.

PATTERNS OF CRIMINAL BEHAVIOR
IN SOUTH AFRICA

In an attempt to provide a comprehensive overview of patterns of criminal behavior and victimization in South Africa during the 1993–97 period, in 1998 Statistics South Africa (Statssa), the country's leading statistics agency, implemented the country's first *Victims of Crime Survey* (Herschowitz et al. 1998). Data collected were based on self-reports of victimization, whether or not reported to a law enforcement or other official agency, making it the first such nationwide survey ever conducted in South Africa.

Among the survey's general findings was that criminal activity in South Africa tends to closely parallel that in other developing countries, with property crime being the most frequently occurring type. Further, the survey reported that crime is of major concern to almost all South Africans because most have either themselves been victims of criminal acts or know someone who has.

Forty-one percent of the households surveyed claimed to have experienced at least one crime during the 1993–97 period. The most common of all crimes was burglary, experienced by 19 percent of all households (see Table 10.1) Theft of livestock, poultry, and so forth was the second most common crime, experienced by 12 percent of all households. Attempted housebreaking was the third, experienced by 8 percent.

Regarding the most violent of all crimes, "approximately 1 household in 40 (2.5 percent), or 221,000 households, experienced a killing or murder during the five-year period [covered in the survey]." Data from another Statssa report (http://members.tripod.com/311/ten.htm) give the average South African household size as 4.6 people. Thus, during the 1993–97 period, approximately 1,116,000 (4.6 × 221,000) South Africans resided in a household in which a killing or murder occurred. An editorial in South Africa's oldest Afrikaans daily newspaper, gave 65 as the average daily number of South African murder victims, which translates

TABLE 10.1

Most Commonly Reported Crimes in South Africa in 1998

Crime	Percentage of Households
Burglary	19%
Theft of livestock, poultry, and so forth	12
Attempted housebreaking	8
Killing or murder	2.5

into an annual murder rate of approximately 10 times as high as the 1998 U.S. murder rate (*Die Burger* 1998).

According to a 1996 FBI crime report, a forcible rape occurs in the United States every six minutues (Inciardi 1999: 79). But in 1999 one of South Africa's leading daily newspapers reported that "national statistics [show] that a rape occurs every 26 seconds in South Africa" (*DistrictMail & HelderPos* 1999). A 1999 article by *Weekly Mail and Guardian* journalist and rape victim Charlene Smith also gave 1 in every 26 seconds as the frequency of rape occurrence in South Africa (Smith 1999). Another source estimated that "every year 1.3 million [South African] women and children are victims of sexual assault" and that only 1 rape in 36 is reported to the police and only 7 percent of those cases end with the accused perpetrator being prosecuted (Fenster 1999). Further, of 64,000 cases of rape reported between January and November 1998, 14,223 were rapes of females under 18, who are often targeted by HIV-infected men who believe that they will be cured by having sex with a virgin. This belief is not uncommon in South Africa (*Daily Mail and Guardian,* March 19, 1999).

During 1998, 115.8 per 100,000 people were raped in South Africa, versus 34.1 per 100,000 in the United States, making rape more than three times more frequent in South Africa than it was in United States that year (Maykuth, October 30, 1999).

A startling phenomenon of rape as male sport in South Africa received widespread media coverage during the 1990s. **Jack rolling** it is called. Jack rolling is a type of gang rape in "which a mob seals off a street or building and rapes every woman caught in the net" (Maykuth, October 30, 1999). The most common victims of jack rolling are black and poor.

Putting South Africa's rape problem in historical perspective, a source gives 1,263 as the number of its recorded rapes in 1979, versus nearly 50,000 today, and its official 1998 rate as 104.1 rapes per 100,000 people, versus a U.S. rate of 34.4 per 100,000, (see Figure 10.1) (Hawthorne 1999). The same source cites an estimate from South African actress and antirape activist Charize Theron, known to some Americans for her roles in *The Astronaut's Wife, Celebrity,* and *Cider House Rules:* she said that one out of three South African women will be raped in her lifetime.

Data collected during Statssa's 1998 Victims of Crime Survey indicate that during the five years inclusive of 1993 to 1997, 1.4 percent of South Africans over 16 years of age were victims of sexual offenses, of which rape is only one of several. Another finding was that almost half (45 percent) of the 1997 victims of sexual offenses were repeat victims, with 28 percent having been victimized four or more times during that year. This is probably due to the fact that victims of sexual offenses were less likely than victims of other crimes to have been victimized by strangers. More specifically, the survey indicates that half (48 percent) of all sexual offenses occur "inside a private dwelling," with somewhere around 26 percent of sexual assaults occuring at the victim's home.

FIGURE 10.1

1998 Rape Statistics per 100,000 People

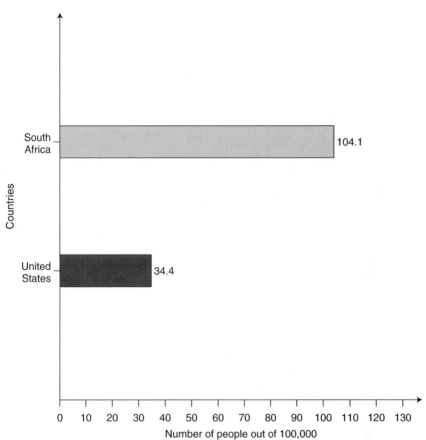

The data also suggest that approximately 76 percent of victims of sexual offenses know their victim by at least name or sight. Of the sexual offense victims, the largest number (26 percent) were victimized by an acquaintance; 15.8 percent by a relative; 10.8 percent by a spouse or partner; another 10.8 percent by a close friend; 9.7 percent by an ex-spouse or partner; 1.6 percent by a boyfriend or girlfriend; and only 23.4 percent by someone who was neither a relative or acquaintance. Thus, criminal sexual offenses in South Africa, of which rape is the most frequent, were not primarily street crimes perpetrated by lurking strangers. Most South African victims of sexual assault, like those in the United States, are victimized by people they know, and sometimes know quite well.

Why such a high frequency of rape in South Africa? One reason is that many South Africans don't consider forcing another person into compliance with their sexual demands to be a serious crime. For instance, 12 percent of the teenage male respondents to a survey of Johannesburg youth admitted to having had sex with a girl without her permission; half expressed the belief that when a girl says no she actually means yes; and 31 percent knew someone who had been raped but felt she had "asked for it" by her dress, carriage, and general mannerisms (Maykuth, October 30, 1999). The survey also revealed that though one in three schoolgirls in Johannesburg had been sexually assaulted, only one in eight knew it was illegal. From this it is easy to conclude that a great deal of rape education is needed among South African teenagers of both sexes.

That rape is not considered a very serious crime even by some middle-aged, highly educated, white South African males is reflected in the sentence handed out by Judge John Foxcroft to a 54-year-old man who in October 1999 was convicted of having raped his 14-year-old daughter. The sentence? Seven years in prison.

Why such a light sentence? Because, in the judge's opinion, since both rapist and victim were members of the same community, little harm was done to the larger community; and by the time the father is released from prison the girl will have moved out of the home they shared and will thus be in no danger from him.

At least, though, the girl reported the rape and the father was prosecuted. In addition, there was widespread public condemnation of both the light sentence imposed on the father and of the judge who imposed it. None of this would have happened before Charlene Smith, Charize Theron, and thousands of other women had begun making efforts to bring other South Africans to an understanding of rape as a serious crime and rapists as serious criminals deserving of serious punishment.

To the above reasons for South Africa's high frequency of rape can be added an additional one: South Africa's high percentage of single-female-headed homes. Forty percent of all South African homes, and an even higher percentage in the poor, black townships, are headed by females (Herschowitz et al. 1998). As a result, many women and young girls live without male protection in communities where, in the absence of strong, efficient law enforcement, male protection is the main female guarantor of physical safety. This is especially so since, in the absence of strong community sanctions, rapists have long been able to consider themselves normal human beings acting in accordance with red-blooded, masculine human nature.

This lack of at least potential adult male protection might be among the reasons that from January to November 1998 there were "3,451 [reported] cases of indecent assault and 3,584 of serious assault" in which children were the victims. It might also be why "more than 1,300 children disappeared from their homes" during those 11 months (*Daily Mail and Guardian* March 19, 1999).

To where did those 1,300 children disappear? Lots of different places, it is probably safe to say. But some, it is no doubt unfortunately true, became frontline workers in South Africa's child-sex tourism industry, which began to develop an increasing large international clientele during the 1990s.

A July 19, 1996 article in the *Weekly Mail and Guardian* told of children abducted and forced into prostitution by organized criminal gangs, or sold or rented out by their parents as a means of increasing family income. Some of these child prostitutes operate from the streets, some from massage parlors, some from brothels, some from taxis, and some in and around migrant labor hostels; others do so between attending classes in pursuit of their matriculation certificates (i.e., high school degrees).

ORGANIZED CRIME AND POLICE CORRUPTION

During the Apartheid years, South Africa's political and diplomatic isolation from the rest of the world, its tight control over movement across and within its borders, and its propensity to keep visiting foreigners under relatively close observation, all served to protect it from the operations of international crime syndicates. All of that changed with the demise of Apartheid. South African Defense Force troops are no longer in constant, intense patrol of the country's borders. There has been a large increase in the number of foreign visitors to the country. People, including freelance criminals and members of organized crime syndicates, are now free to move about the country whenever and wherever they please.

The number of crime syndicates operating in South Africa was estimated to be 238 at the close of 1995 (Thompson 1995: 258). A 1998 *Weekly Mail and Guardian* article gave 190 as the police estimate of the approximate number of crime syndicates then operating in South Africa. This same article quotes a 1997 World Economic Forum report as stating that the sweep of South Africa's organized criminal groups ranks "second only to Colombia's, with its frightening drug cartels, and Russia's, with its omni-present mafia."

The major and most profitable of the organized crime syndicates are international in their scope of operations and have connections with members of the Russia mafia, Chinese triads, or Nigerian organized criminal groups. Many are involved in diamonds and weapons smuggling, the capture and trade of endangered species, the distribution of illegal drugs, and adult and child sex enterprises.

Other more nationally focused South African gangs and crime syndicates concentrate their energies on pulling off highjackings and bank and railroad heists, maintaining profitable extortive relationships with members of their business communities, and running prostitution and national drug, weapons, and stolen car distribution rings.

In South Africa, as in Colombia, Russia, China, and Nigeria, large numbers of police officers and other government officials at all levels are known or suspected to be working in close, and often highly lucrative, complicity with their country's organized crime syndicates. In 1996, for instance, "one in four officers in the greater Johannesburg area were themselves under criminal investigation" (*Weekly Mail and Guardian*, February 13, 1998).

In such low esteem and disrespect were police held during the 1990s that from 1994 to 1998, an average of 240 policemen per year were themselves murder victims (Minnaar 1999). In contrast, in the United States, whose population is approximately seven times that of South Africa's, 65 policemen were killed in 1997 (Reid 2000: 365).

Seventy-five percent of these South African policemen were murdered by gunshot wounds, with 10 percent of these by their own guns. Most were killed while being robbed of their service pistol or rifle, while making an arrest, during an argument with a fellow police officer, while on patrol, or during a fight or argument with a member of the general public. It can't be denied that some were involved in corrupt practices like extortion and bribery and that "they might [have been] killed by elements within organized crime to keep them quiet" (Minnaar 1999).

The existence of at least some organized crime networks of exclusively police officers is often attested to in South African news reports such as one that gave details of the arrests in the Eastern Cape city of Queenstown of 15 White and Coloured policemen and guards involved in a long series of burglaries and the subsequent recovery of appliances, televisions, video machines, clothing, bedding, and electronic equipment stolen during the break-ins (Macgregor 1999).

Like just about everything else in South Africa, the above arrests became, in the minds of at least some people, a racial issue. "'We are all human, we all make mistakes,' a sympathetic white resident said, between deafening cheers and jeers for the accused [as they were led into court to appear before a magistrate]." But a black resident "who danced up a storm in the crowd said he was 'thanking God for the arrests.' " Not so a Coloured woman. In her view, "calls by black residents for justice were in fact defeating the ends of justice and the case had become an issue of racism" (Macgregor 1999).

Of course, South Africa and other developing countries are not the only places where a perusal of newspaper clippings would suggest rampant widespread police corruption. Inciardi, for instance, writes of the 1970s when the Washington, DC–based Police Foundation, "in a period of only 60 days . . . received articles from 30 states . . . report[ing] allegations of graft and corruption in major urban centers, small cities, sheriffs' offices, state police forces, and suburban departments" (1999: 226). Inciardi also writes of the 1994 Mollen Commission's finding of "a 'willful blindness' to corruption throughout the NYPD, which allowed highly organized networks of rogue officers to deal in drugs and prey on citizens in African American and Hispanic neighborhoods" and that "throughout the 1990s the media have reported all types of corruption in most parts of the nation."

Nor did corruption within U.S. police departments end with the 1990s. A June 20, 2000, *San Diego Union Tribune* article, to name just one of many such post-1990s reports of U.S. police corruption, told of the indictment of four Los Angeles County "sheriff's deputies and their accomplices [for] us[ing] stolen credit cards to scam cash from automated teller machines (A1). The article also summarized an ongoing L.A. Police Department scandal involving "up to 40 LAPD officers who falsified reports, planted evidence, perjured themselves in court and sometimes beat or shot suspects. . . . Eighty-four convictions have been overturned as a result of the ongoing investigation, . . ."

Still, and justifiably so, South Africans are more likely to see police corruption in their country as a major problem than are Americans to see police corruption as a major problem in the United States. One of the consequences of these differing perceptions is that South African police are in general less respected by the people they are sworn to protect and more likely to be murdered, on or off duty.

According to Gallup Poll data, 84 percent of U.S. respondents rated the "honesty and ethical standards of police officers" as either average (42 percent), high (34 percent), or very high (8 percent), even though 45 percent of black American respondents and 33 percent of white American repondents anwered yes to the question, Do you think there is any police brutality in your area? (Inciardi 1999: 246).

Thus, while most Americans think there are *some* bad apples among their local police, they nonetheless think that most are honest, ethical, and highly effective in the performance of their duties. South Africans, on the other hand, seem to be less confident in the overall effectiveness of their police officers—with good reason, too. In the United States most homocides are solved, and cop killers are the most likely killers to be arrested and convicted. Not so in South Africa. Only about 3 percent of cop killers in South Africa are arrested and convicted (Minnaar 1999).

One reason for the relatively small likelihood of the murder of a South African police officer resulting in an arrest might be the large number of residents in high-crime areas with grievances against the police. As Amnesty International reported, "Five years after all-race elections ended minority white rule in South Africa . . . [there were still] numerous reports of torture, ill-treatment and suspected unlawful killings by members of the security forces." Also, in 1998 South Africa's Independent Complaints Directorate received reports of 607 deaths of persons in police custody; in 1997 there had been 5,300 complaints of assault by police officers (*Daily Mail and Guardian*, June 16, 1999).

Another reason for the low esteem in which police are held, as well for their relative inefficiency in apprehending and arresting criminals, might be their low levels of education. In 1999, a quarter of all policemen were reported to be functionally illiterate. (*Daily Mail and Guardian*, September 30, 1999).

Data presented in Statistics South Africa's Victims of Crime Survey indicate that the highest rates of dissatisfaction with police conduct and effectiveness are among black South Africans, who typically reside in the country's poorest neighborhoods. Forty-two percent of the black African respondents were dissatisfied with the way police are controlling crime in their neighborhoods. The next highest rates of dissatisfaction were among Indians (36 percent), Coloureds (33 percent), and Whites (30 percent), the latter being, typically residents of the country's most affluent areas. But those in the highest annual household income group (R96,000 or more per annum) were more likely to be dissatisfied (44 percent) than those in other income groups.

Other data presented in the survey suggest that while most contemporary South Africans hold the police in low esteem, the police were not held in very high esteem by Blacks, Coloured, Indians, or Whites before the 1994 elections that brought the ANC to political power. Decidedly less than a majority of all respondents (40 percent), as well as less than a majority of all respondents in each of four racial groups, thought the police had become less effective since the 1994 election. The majority of South Africans think the police are either more, or at least no less, effective than they were before the election. Separating responses by race: practically half (49 percent) of the white respondents, 45 of Indian, 40 percent of Coloured, and somewhat less than 30 percent of African respondents thought the police were less effective than they had been before the 1994 election.

Conversely, 36 percent of Coloured respondents, approximately 30 percent of African, somewhat less than 30 percent of Indian, and 16 percent of white respondents indicated a belief that the police had become more effective since the 1994 election. Whites, then, were far more likely than members of the other three racial groups to see the police as being less effective after than before the 1994 election.

This is understandable. Before the 1994 election, crime occurred less frequently in areas where Whites lived. In addition, more police time and resources were allocated to preventing and solving crimes committed in white areas, as well as crimes committed against Whites, than is now allocated, and police officers responding to crimes in white areas were, during the pre-1994 years, exclusively White. Now South African police are more likely to be nonwhite than white, and some Whites resent them for being so.

The Victims of Crime Survey also reports on individual crimes experienced in 1997. Among other things, these data suggest that 15 per-

cent of the total South African population, or about 6 to 7 million individual South Africans, were victims of at least one crime during 1997.
The most common crime was theft of personal property, experienced by
5 percent of the population, followed by assault (4 percent). About one
person in 200, or .04 percent of all South Africans, were victims of at least
one sexual offense, rape being a sexual offense, but not all sexual offenses being rape.

Coloured and white respondents (16.8 percent and 16.5 percent, respectively) were more likely to be crime victims than were African (14.1
percent) and Indian respondents (11.4 percent). Males (16.4 percent)
were significantly more likely to be crime victims than were females.
Persons in the 16- to 35-year-old age categories were significantly more
likely to be victims than persons in the older age categories.

The survey also reports on the percentage of individuals who had
experienced at least one violent crime or at least one nonviolent crime in
1997. Individual Whites (13.7 percent) were more likely to be victims of
nonviolent crimes that either Coloureds (11.3 percent), Indians (8.6 percent), or Africans (8.3 percent). But Africans and Coloureds (7 percent of
both populations) were more likely to be victims of violent crimes than
Whites (5 percent) or Indians (3.3 percent). Data also show that the
higher a person's income, the more likely that person was to have been a
victim of nonviolent crime. In all, 9.3 percent of all South Africans were
victims of nonviolent crimes in 1997; and 6.5 percent were victims of violent crimes.

When asked where they turned for emotional support at the time of
the crime, most respondents (59.0 percent) indicated that they had
nowhere and no one to turn to. Of the remaining respondents, 17 percent
said they turned to family and friends; 12 percent turned to neighbors;
and 6 percent or less turned to either a church organization, a psy-
chotherapist, traditional healer, or an "armed response [i.e., vigilante]
organization."

That 60 percent of the South African population have no one and
nowhere to turn to for emotional support in times of great need for such
support suggests that most contemporary South Africans live in relative
social isolation devoid of close extended family ties, close neighborhood
friendships, or meaningfully interactive membership in church or other
secondary group organizations. This is surely both a cause and a consequence of South Africa's high crime rates, as is the fact that 40 percent of
all South African homes are headed by females.

So widespread was lack of confidence in the ability of South
African police to meet the challenges of reducing South Africa's high
rates of violent crime against persons and personal property and stopping the spread of organized crime and gang activities that during the
1990s most of South Africa's affluent white, or predominantly white,
suburban residential areas became gated communities, where private

security guards patrol the streets and people live in houses with burglar bars on the windows and guns close at hand.

Crime is also of paramount concern in rural areas, particularly to white farmers, who are frequent victims of criminal acts such as theft of livestock and machinery, burglary, armed robbery, and murder. Such acts are often excused or justified as deserved retribution for past mistreatment of Blacks by white farmers. "More farmers are killed in South Africa than in any other country," bewails one source before concluding that lawlessness in South Africa will be brought under control only when and if the government develops the currently lacking will and ability to bring it under control (*Die Burger*, September 1, 1998).

In the meantime, South African farmers remain one of the most heavily armed groups within the country; and for protection of their lives and property, they are often self-organized into the equivalents of armed neighborhood watch or property patrol groups, some of which have been charged with unjustified shootings of Blacks, thereby providing more justification for black retaliatory violence.

It is not only Whites who live in fear of criminal victimization. Many affluent Blacks feel no more safe than do their white counterparts. For instance, the two-story, middle-class Soweto residence of BMW-owner Frank Chikane was surrounded by iron-barred, "ornately scrolled 12-foot-high security gates" (Goodman 1999: 56). At the time, Chikane was director general of the Office of Deputy President.

By late May 1999, the street on which South Africa's security minister Sydney Mufamadi lived was still in no sense a safe haven from crime. Even with 24-hour police protection of his home, "A third of the 30 homes on [his] upmarket Sandton street [had] in the past seven months [November 1998 to May 1999] been victim to armed robberies, break-ins and an attempted hijacking" (*Daily Mail and Guardian*, May 25, 1999).

Low-income South Africans cannot afford bars on their windows, do not rate around-the-clock state police protection, and cannot afford the services of private security guards. So they rely on dogs, guns, clubs, and other extralegal means to deal with criminal threats to their lives and property. Among these means are vigilante groups and reemergent "people's courts."

One source reports of a fatal mob attack on an elderly woman in revenge for her having posted bail for the release of her son on a rape charge; the castration of a man suspected of having raped an eight-year-old girl; and the necklacing—i.e., placing a gasoline-soaked tire around the neck of a person and then setting it afire—of three residents of an East Rand community suspected of abhorrent criminal activity. "This was the second time she paid bail for him and he went on to commit another crime while he was free," the article quotes one man as having said in justification of the fatal mob attack on the elderly woman. "We can't have one man terrorizing us all the time. The police do nothing" (Williams 1997).

That vigilantism is still a brutal fact of life in nonwhite, nonaffluent South African communities is further evidenced by the strength of Mapogo Matamaga, a vigilante group based in the Northern Province. According to its founder, from 1996 to 1999 Mapogo Matamaga went from being an organization of 100 members to one of 35,000 members.

Though only suspected of involvement in a continuing series of brutal retaliations against criminals and suspected criminals, including the May 1999 throwing of two suspected chainsaw thieves "into a crocodile-infested river, after torturing, beating and incarcerating them," Mapogo Matamaga members are definitely known to be in the business of dispensing public floggings to persons suspected of smaller crimes. Monhle Magolepo, president of Mapogo Matamaga, has been quoted as having said in justification of public floggings, "This is the African way of stopping crime. The criminal must lie on ground, and we must work on his buttocks and put him right" (Soggot and Ngobeni 1999).

Not all vigilante activity is carried on by stable, ongoing, formally organized groups like Mapogo Matamaga. Some is carried on by ad hoc groups, as when a man caught in the act of breaking into a house in Khayelitsha, a Coloured section of Cape Town, "was allegedly dragged into the road by local people and beaten and kicked to death. . . . [Police] were trying to identify those involved in the beating but no one had seen anything" (*Cape Argus,* June 13, 1999).

GOVERNMENT SCANDAL

After the democratic election that elevated their party to the status of governing party, a great many ANC members assumed official office never having had enough of anything—money, material comforts, financial responsibilities, high social status, power over others, responsibility for keeping things running smoothly, or experience in administering large bureaucratic organizations or being being part of an elite group charged with maintaining social order and discipline by personal example.

One day they were banned, hunted, imprisoned, in exile, or restricted to certain areas in certain cities of the country, seemingly forever relegated to lives of material deprivation. The next day, figuratively speaking, they were suddenly on top: running things, wielding power over large masses of people, driving fine cars, living in big houses with electricity, running water, lawns, and swimming pools, in areas they couldn't previously enter without a pass, their kids in attendance at the country's best schools. All kinds of new opportunities and dazzling temptations stood before them.

As a result, from almost day one, ANC leaders have had to deal with a seemingly never-ending series of scandals arising from the inability of high state officials and well-known ANC affiliates to resist succumbing to illicit temptations to advance themselves professionally or otherwise ensure that they will be able to continue to maintain themselves and their families at the level of material existence to which they very quickly became accustomed.

The most shocking of all scandals involving a highly revered ANC-affiliate came to a head in March 1999 when the Reverend Allan Boesak was convicted of four counts of fraud and the theft of $400,000. People of all races were astounded to hear about Boesak, co-founder and one of the most charismatic figures in the 1980s consortium of anti-Apartheid groups calling itself the United Democratic Front, former head of the World Alliance of Reformed Churches, and at one time South Africa's ambassador to the United Nations in Geneva.

Making the Boesak scandal even more newsworthy was that the source of $128,000 of the embezzled money was American singer-songwriter Paul Simon, who had donated $200,000 to Boesak's Foundation for Peace and Justice under the impression that it would be given over to a children's charity. But only $72,000 of it went to the charity. Boesak kept the remaining $128,000 for himself.

The equivalent of $226,000 of the misappropriated money was donated by a Swedish government aid agency and was supposed to have gone to make voter-education videos. Instead, it was used to develop a radio studio for Boesak's wife Elna (*San Diego Union Tribune,* March 18, 1999). Boesak was also convicted of misappropriating $93,000 to an upscale suburban Cape Town home for himself and his white wife Elna and of giving her $4,200 in cash.

A week after Boesak's conviction, and despite pleas for mercy by no less a personage than Archbishop Tutu himself, white judge John Foxcroft sentenced Boesak to six years imprisonment. "Boesak's supporters, including South Africa's finance minister, Trevor Manuel, crowded the court building, some carrying placards saying, 'We won't forget what you did for us' " (*San Diego Union Tribune,* March 25, 1999).

Actual crime and corruption of all sorts and floating suspicions of crime and corruption at all levels were major problems when Mandela assumed leadership of the country in 1994. Under Mbeki's leadership, they still stand as impediments to South Africa's economic growth, as well as threats to its survival as a stable political democracy.

THE FUTURE

What should not be forgotten in discussions of crime and violence in postapartheid South Africa, however, is that they are inherited problems. Violence, as we have seen, has been a constant, pervasive—if not always openly acknowledged—daily fact of South African life since the early years of European settlement. Given all the revelations and confessions of former police officers and members of South Africa's various Apartheid era intelligence agencies that came out of the late-1990s Truth and Reconciliation Commission hearings, it is likely that South Africa was the murder capital of the world long before the 1994 election and the coming to power of a black majority government. The difference between the two eras was that during Apartheid thousands of murders were committed by white police officers and employees of various state security agencies, whereas today most crime is committed by civilian blacks.

What of the future? Did South Africa enter the 2000s showing signs of an increase or a decrease in the overall volume of criminal acts within its borders? Do its various crime rates appear to have stabilized during the final years of the 20th century?

The South African Police Service's Crime Information Analysis Center (CIAC) publishes a *Monthly Bulletin on Reported Crime in South Africa.* The January 1999 *Bulletin* offered crime statistics for the five years inclusive of 1994 and 1998. The data presented show decreases in the commission of certain types of crimes, an increase in the commission of certain types, and stabilizations in the rates of commission of yet other types.

Looking at the rate of commission of violent crimes, exclusive of rape and common assault, good news can be found in CIAC data. Murder declined continuously during the first five years after the coming to power of a black majority government, from 62.1 per 100,000 of the population in 1994 to 52.0 in 1998. Nonetheless, the rate is still among the highest, if not the highest, in the world.

More good news regarding South Africa's murder rate came on October 16, 1999, when President Thabo Mbeki and Inkatha Freedom Party leader Zulu chief Mangosuthu Buthelezi came together in the town of Thokoza to honor the hundreds of ANC and IFP supporters killed during the past years of violent interparty conflict and to pledge to do everything in their power to ensure that the days of such conflicts are over. If those pledges are honored, South Africa will experience even greater declines in the number of murders, assaults, and malicious property destruction, and perhaps rapes, committed within its borders.

The attempted murder rate per 100,000 of the population during the 1994–98 period was a different story. Though somewhat lower in 1998 than 1994, CIAC analysts characterized it as having stabilized rather than decreased. This characterization is justified because from 1994 to 1998 the attempted murder rate per 100,000 of the population went through only slight fluctuations from 64.0 to 60.2 to 63.4 to 60.6 to 62.7.

CIAC analysts also judged the incidence of robbery with aggravating circumstances to have stabilized, because while its occurrence in 1994 was 200 per 100,000, in 1998 it was 188.3 per 100,000.

Regarding social fabric crimes, CIAC data show that the rate of rape per 100,000 fluctuated from 96 in 1994, to 106.6 in 1995, to 111.8 in 1996, to 113.2 in 1997, to 104.1 in 1998. CIAC analysts thus judge that there was a stablization in the occurrence of rape during the first five years of ANC government. The data also, however, allow for the conclusion that during the first five years of ANC rule there was both an increase and a decrease in the incidence of rape. The most dramatic increase occurred during the second year. The most dramatic decrease occurred during the fifth year, which might or might not mean attempts to reduce the incidence of rape through media campaigns and other efforts to mobilize the public against its perpetrators had, by the late-1990s, finally begun to pay off. In any case, rape remains a more common crime in South Africa than in any place else in the world.

Regarding the commission of property-related crimes during the 1994–98 period, CIAC data show clear, continuous decreases only in stock theft and shoplifting. Otherwise, there were what CIAC analysts justifiably concluded to be increases in the rates of housebreaking, both residential and business, other robbery, theft of and out of motor vehicles, and other thefts.

All in all, then, it is with justification that crime is still of great concern to almost all South Africans. It occurs more frequently in their country than in almost any other country in the world. It does appear, however, that South Africa entered the twenty-first century experiencing declines in the incidences of violent crimes such as murder, robbery involving the use or threat of violence, rape, and common assault. But there were no declines in the high rates of property-related or economic crimes, such as burglary, carjackings and truckjackings, and bank and other robberies. This was to be expected since South Africa is still a nation of primarily poor people. Poverty fosters property-related crimes even more than it fosters violence.

Thus, one of the most daunting, immediately pressing challenges facing South Africa's leaders in the twenty-first century is the reduction of their country's poverty population.

CHAPTER 11

The South African Economy

South Africa's high crime rate is buoyed by its high rates of unemployment and poverty. Its high rates of unemployment and poverty are sustained not only by the low levels of education and job skills that prevail among the country's majority black population but also by an economy that has expanded too slowly to bring government revenues up to levels necessary for the fulfillment of the ANC promise of a significantly better material standard of life for all.

The racial inequalities of material life conditions and life chances that existed at the time of the coming to power of the ANC are reflected in a 1995 Central Statistical Services (CSS) report giving South Africa's official black unemployment rate as more than six times that of the white unemployment rate and almost twice as high as that of the Coloured unemployment rate.

Of the black unemployed in 1995, 50 percent were under 30; almost 70 percent had been unemployed for more than a year; and almost 90 percent had "no training or skills at all" (Economist Intelligence Unit, 2nd Quarter 1995: 12–13). From these data alone one could have predicted high poverty rates and continued low levels of material existence for large numbers of blacks for many years to come.

Regarding the actual, concrete material conditions of life for the majority of South Africa's black population, a 1997 Statistics South Africa report presented data showing that at the time of coming to power of the ANC, Blacks were without what practically all of the country's white population would consider the most basic amenities of life (see Figure 11.1). As the data show, in October 1995 the percentage of Blacks whose main source of energy for cooking was other than electricity or gas as 54 percent versus 2 percent for Whites. The percentage of Blacks whose main source of domestic water was other than running tap water

FIGURE 11.1

1996 Statistics South Africa Report
Basic Ameneties of Life, 1995

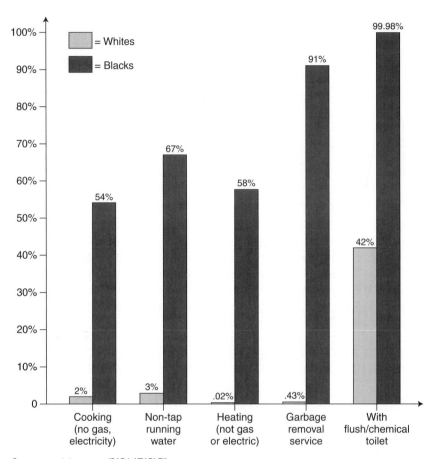

Source: www.statssa.gov.za/SABrief/TABLE5.

in the dwelling was 67 percent versus 3 percent for Whites. The percentage of Blacks whose main source for heating was other than electricity or gas was 58 percent versus 1 percent for Whites. The percentage of Blacks without regular access to a flush or chemical toilet was 58 percent versus .02 percent for Whites. The percentage of Blacks receiving garbage removal service from a local (i.e., public) authority was 43 percent versus 91 percent for Whites.

Given the above differences in unemployment rates and life conditions of black and white South Africans, it is not surprising that Blacks are also less likely to be in good health than are Whites. Blacks are, for instance, more likely to have a serious sight defect (2.5 percent of the popu-

FIGURE 11.2

Likelihood of Having a Disability
in South Africa by Race, 1995

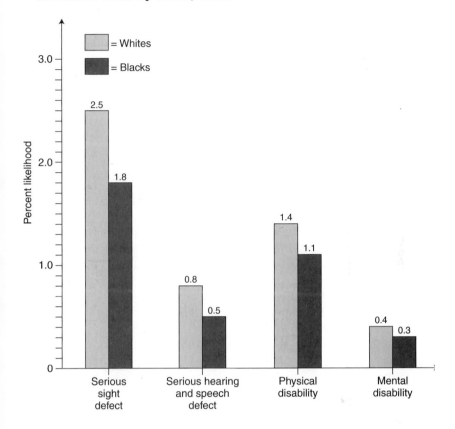

lation versus 1.8 percent of the white population), a serious hearing and
speech defect (.8 percent versus .5 percent), a physical disability (1.4 percent versus 1.1 percent), and a mental disability (.4 percent versus .3 percent) (see Figure 11.2).

Though the ANC won the April 1994 general election partly on the
promise to build one million houses within the next five years, by early
1998 only 200,000 of the promised houses had been built. Housing Minister Sankie Mthembi-Mahanyele was constrained to announce that the
goal of one million new homes by 1999 would not be met until "a later
date, subject to the availability of resources" (Goodman 1999: 349).

South Africa entered the year 2000 a half million or so homes short
of the goal announced six years previously; and even though the nearly
300,000 newly built homes have electricity and running water, they are
not what a great many people who now live in them expected. They are

small, not at all what Americans and Europeans would envision low-income or any other type of new housing to be. Nor are they the type of middle- and upper-class Western-style homes lived in by South Africa's new black political and economic elites.

One source described a presumably typical home in a new housing development in Cape Town as a "one-room, galvanized corrugated metal structure shaped like a small Quonset hut [that] has more in common with the portable tool sheds dotting back yards in America. Inside the walls are uninsulated from the cool, rainy Cape Town winters." And atop it all is a roof that leaks (Perkins 1997). Another report described a typical home in a new settlement in the Weltevreden Valley as "a tiny, whitewashed cinder-block room with a roof," one family on the very day they moved in already "busy nailing up another room made of wooden pallets and corrugated steel" (Goodman 1999: 229).

Disappointed though many may be, the residents of these recently built homes with electricity and indoor plumbing are nonetheless more fortunate than the seven or so million South Africans living in what during Apartheid were called *squatters' camps,* now more euphemistically called *informal settlements.* Residents of the informal settlements live in makeshift dwellings of wood, corrugated steel, aluminum, fiberglass, canvas, cardboard, or whatever else might give privacy and serve, even if only for a while, as shelter from the elements.

These informal settlements are located on public, and sometimes privately owned, lands, without gas and electricity hookups or running water and sanitation services. The best thing that can be said about life in such housing is that it is rent free. Of course, since they exist without official authorization, informal settlements may at any time be razed to the ground, leaving masses of people homeless, which occasionally happened during Apartheid. No such thing is likely to happen in present-day South Africa, though. Where would the people go? What would would they do? Plus, the overwhelming majority of the residents of the informal settlements are ANC supporters; and the ANC wishes for them to continue to be ANC supporters.

If the government needs the support of the masses of homeless and semihomeless, then why no mass outcry or antigovernment demonstrations by people living in those conditions in the midst of such a great housing crisis? Because that is the way it has always been in South Africa. Millions and millions of people lived in squatters' camps and the majority of Africans lived in homes without electricity and running water for decades before ANC came to power. Since then, however, fewer and fewer do. New housing is being built, just not as rapidly and of the quality as first envisioned. Still, life in the informal settlements of the late 1990s was "just plain depressing," as described by one observer. He was "struck by the disunity of the place. No one knows where anyone lives, and there is no apparent order to where people settle. . . . It is

TABLE 11.1

Life Expectancy in 1991

Race	Years
Africans	60.3
Coloureds	66.5
Indians	68.89
Whites	73.1

a fractured, squalid place united only by the fact that everyone there hates it" (Goodman 1999: 223). As we have seen, there is indeed much to hate: crime, violence, corruption, stench, poverty, few people to be trusted and turned to in times of need, emotional or otherwise.

Different likelihoods of being employed, different likelihoods of living in homes with electricity, flush toilets, and running water, and therefore, different likelihoods of being in good health were reflected in the different life expectancies of South Africa's four population groups on the eve of the coming to power of the black majority government. The life expectancy for an African born in 1991 was 60.3 years, as opposed to 66.5 for Coloureds, 68.89 for Indians, and 73.1 for Whites, as shown in Table 11.1 (Statistics South Africa 1996).

Statssa has also developed what it calls its "Human Development Index," a measure of people's ability to live a long and healthy life, to be able to communicate, to participate in the life of the community, and to have sufficient means to obtain a decent living.

Statssa calculations of the Human Development Index of South Africa's 1991 population by race, not surprisingly, showed great differences in the overall abilities of members of its four racial groups to live a long, healthy life as an active, socially esteemed, self-respecting participant in community affairs living at a decent material level of subsistence. Whites having the greatest likelihood of living such a life, Blacks the least. Specifically, the 1991 index was .500 for Africans, .663 for Coloureds, .836 for Indians, and .901 for Whites (see Table 11.2).

Differences in the conditions of life experienced by typical members of the four population groups persisted throughout the 1990s. Part of the reason for this was that there was not much economic growth in the latter half of the 1990s. In fact, during the first four years of black majority rule (1994–97) South Africa was deep in the throes of an economic recession, reflected in data showing an overall decrease in South Africa's absorption of labor rate, that is, the percentage of persons between the ages of 15 and 65 who were employed, from 48 percent in 1994 to 44 percent in 1997.

TABLE 11.2

Human Development Index, 1991

Race	Measures
Africans	.500
Indians	.863
Coloureds	.663
Whites	.901

Specifically, the data show substantially lower labor absorption rates for African men (35 percent) than for white men (68 percent) and substantially lower labor absorption rates for African women (22 percent) than for white women (44 percent). In other words, African men and women of working age were only approximately half as likely to be employed as were, respectively, white men and women.

The labor absorption rate gives the percentage of all persons of working age who are employed, regardless of whether or not they are able or willing to work or in active pursuit of work. The unemployment rate, on the other hand, gives the percentage of persons of working age without a job who have taken active steps to find one and are available to start work within a week.

Statistics South Africa data also, and quite predictably, show an increase in South Africa's official unemployment rate from 20 percent in 1994, to 17 percent in 1995, to 21 percent in 1996, and 22.9 percent in 1997. In addition, the 1997 official unemployment rate for Africans, who constituted approximately 77 percent of the country's population, was 29 percent, making it close to twice as high as the rate for Coloureds (16 percent), almost three times as high as for Indians (10 percent), and more than seven times as for Whites (4 percent).

A further breakdown of the 1997 unemployment figures shows that African women were more likely to be unemployed (35 percent) than men or women in any of the four official population groups, whereas white men, with an unemployment rate of 3 percent, are the least likely to be unemployed (see Figure 11.3).

Why a rise in the number and percentages of unemployed? Why such high rates of unemployment among blacks? A decrease in the number of nonagricultural jobs is one reason. Statistics South Africa estimates that the number of jobs in the formal nonagriculture . . . gradually decreased from approximately 5.3 million in December 1994 to approximately 5.1 million in 1997. In other words, from 1994 to 1997 the South African economy lost of 200,000 nonagricultural jobs.

FIGURE   11.3

South Africa's Official Unemployment Rate
During the 1994–1997 Recession

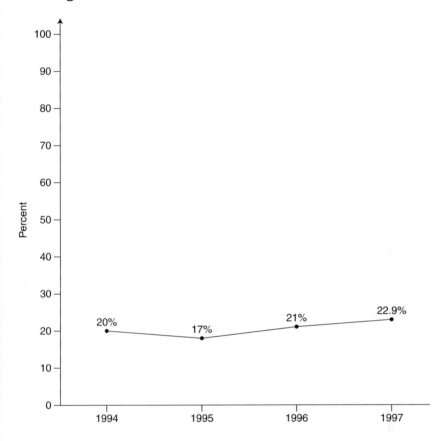

Nor did the loss of jobs in the formal nonagricultural sector of the South African economy end in 1997. A source gave around 400,000 as the the number of jobs lost in the formal sector during the previous four years, adding that "Some critics [of the government's economic policies] have even put the losses at twice that level" (Walker 1999). Another report gave the country's 1999 unemployment rate as 37 percent and number of jobs lost since 1994 as 500,000, this "during an era when the economy needed to generate 350,000 jobs for young people entering the work force" (Maykuth, July 11, 1999).

The inability of South Africa to produce jobs for young people entering the labor market is reflected in data showing the 1997 employment rate for males in the 15–30 age category to have been 27 percent, as opposed to 66 percent for males in the 31–45 age category.

All in all, then, since the coming to power of the ANC, the South African economy has lost hundreds of thousands of jobs, thus helping to keep the country's official overall unemployment rate at no less than 30 percent and its unemployment rate among persons 30 and younger higher than that of persons older than 30. Or, put differently, during the late 1990s was going through a deep economic recession—resulting in high unemployment—which among other things, contributed to stabilization of its crime rates at high levels.

RECESSION

The reasons for South Africa going through the late 1990s in a state of economic recession are many and mostly interrelated. Apartheid is one of the major reasons.

As a result of foreign boycotts of its products and the withdrawal of foreign investment capital from the country during the latter years of Apartheid, the South African economy had been in decline long before the 1994 all-race elections and the coming to power of a black majority government. The international economic sanctions imposed against the Apartheid state resulted in the curtailments of the exhange of products between South Africa and anti-Apartheid nations.

By the 1980s, the boycotts of South African products, the closing of foreign-owned plants and factories, and the continuing loss of foreign investment capital had already resulted in the country becoming more economically isolated and thus forced to rely less on imports to satisfy both its industrial and consumer needs. As a consequence, South Africa was forced to produce many products (e.g., chemicals, steel, automobiles, and a wide variety of domestic consumer goods) that, if not for the economic sanctions, could have been more cheaply imported from other nations. The domestic manufacturers of those products enjoyed virtual monopolies and were thus under no immediate pressure to operate as efficiently as possible; so they didn't. Nor did they reinvest in their businesses to any great extent, given the uncertainty about the future political stability of the Apartheid state coupled with fears that if the ANC came to power it would nationalize businesses.

Therefore, when Apartheid ended and international sanctions were lifted, many South African manufacturing enterprises were forced to go under as a result of their inability to successfully compete in the global marketplace. Many of those that survived have been able to do so through mechanization, which of course leads to a loss of jobs. Take clothing and other textile manufacturers, for example. As a result of mechanization, "Thousands of jobs were lost. The South African Clothing and Textile Workers Union had 200,000 members when it was formed in 1989; but by July 1999 [it] had only 130,000 members (Maykuth, July 11, 1999).

What also kept business profits high and made the employment of wage labor more economical during the years of Apartheid than it now is were the low wages paid to nonwhite workers. The ANC, however, came to power with massive support from black unions and low-wage workers from all sectors of the economy; and it has maintained that support by, among other things, establishing minimum wage rates for workers and requiring employers to "commit to affirmative action plans" and "pay 1 percent of payroll into a skills-development fund . . . [in order to] 'progressively reduce' the wage gaps between workers and bosses." A result of the ANC's commitment to championing the interests of labor was that, despite the country's high rate of unemployment, during the 1990s the wages of South African workers increased by almost 4 percent a year. (Maykuth, July 11, 1999).

This contradiction between the demand for labor and demands of labor are further evidenced by two late 1990s news reports. One told of a peaceful march by South African miners seeking a 13 percent boost in pay (*San Diego Union Tribune,* August 18, 1999). The other reported that "about 103,000 South Africans have lost their jobs since 1997, and 80,000 more job losses are anticipated" (*San Diego Union Tribune,* July 18, 1999).

The government's commitment to raising wage levels plays well with workers, and increasing the buying power of workers creates a greater demand for consumer goods produced or distributed by South African businesspeople, thus stimulating overall economic growth. But owners of South African manufacturing enterprises and other employers of labor complain that by raising the cost of employing workers, the government thereby offers strong disincentives to investment in labor-intensive enterprises.

The only incentive offered to them by the government, the employers' position holds, is to mechanize the production of goods and services, thereby cutting labor costs by reducing the number of wage employees. Therefore, present government economic policies, employers have argued, only serve to maintain high unemployment.

Another reason South Africa entered into an economic recession was a decline in precious metal prices during the 1990s. This decline had a particularly strong impact on the South African economy because revenue from its previously extremely profitable gold mines had before the demise of Apartheid served to subsidize other nonrevenue government-subsidized industries.

POSTAPARTHEID FOREIGN INVESTMENT AND OPTIMISM FOR GROWTH

Though many of the country's economic problems were natural outcomes of Apartheid, the end of Apartheid did not result in the immediate resolution of all of those problems. People throughout the international community expressed great joy and relief that Apartheid was finally a thing of the past, but foreign investment capital returned to the country at a much slower rate than South Africa's leaders had anticipated.

South Africa's high rates of crime and violence during the early 1990s, widespread nonpayment of township rents and service fees, labor strikes resulting in escalating wage rates for skilled and unskilled workers alike, and fears of the occurrence of the all-out race war that never quite happened all served to make foreign investors much more cautious than they might otherwise have been.

In the beginning, investors most typically "bought shares in long-established companies, reacquired control of sudsidiaries from which they had withdrawn during the era of sanctions, and arranged to market goods that had been manufactured in their home countries, but they did not invest in much new construction or create many new jobs" (Thompson 1995: 263).

There was some new investment in the South African economy and there were new jobs created during the early years of black majority rule. U.S. Department of Commerce figures show that from 1993 to 1997 approximately 300 U.S. companies invested in the South African economy (Perkins 1997). The problem was that that wasn't enough new investment. The South African economy lost old jobs faster than new investments created new jobs.

Not all black South Africans, however, experienced the 1990s as years of economic recession. Many had it better than perhaps they had ever dreamed. Apart from those who came to occupy positions within government, police, military, state security, and other publicly financed agencies, some blacks attained positions within the private economic sector that would have been unthinkable just a few years before.

In addition, black entrepreneurship increased at an impressive rate. From 1995 to 1999, black entrepreneurs took control of companies listed on the stock exchange 10 times faster than did Afrikaners 50 years ago. Or stated somewhat differently: "It took Afrikaner capital 10 times longer to achieve the level of listed corporate ownership than the new [black] dealmakers have notched up in the past four years" (Haffajee 1999).

There also arose a sizable new black middle class whose members now ride around in luxury cars; shop at expensive boutiques; live in expensive, formerly all-white suburbs; send their children to private schools; and belong to exclusive, once whites-only country clubs and are part of informal, mutually assisting and reinforcing networks of interlocked top black executives and political elites. Many of the black corporate elites have benefited from formerly holding top government positions or from government procurement policies whereby black-owned businesses get 10 extra points in the competition for government contracts to build roads, buildings, install computers, and provide a whole host of other goods and services to government agencies (Haffajee 1999).

Also contributing to the growth and stabilization of a black middle class are, for example, the National Empowerment Fund, created to provide financial backing for aspiring black entrepreneurs and small business owners with expansion potential, and affirmative action legislation enacted to increase the number of Blacks employed as skilled workers and managerial-level employees.

But though the government's black empowerment and other affirmative action policies helped many individual Blacks, economists such as Hermann van Pappendorp, chief of BOE securities, and Dennis Dykes, chief economist of the banking group Nedcor, have argued that these policies tend to make South African companies both less competitive and less efficient. They cite these policies as reasons why the ANC hasn't managed to increase the productive capacity of the economy during the 1990s and why foreign investment in the South African economy didn't proceed at the rate it was hoped, foreign investors being concerned with labor costs and efficiency (Pearson 1999).

In the long run, though, as the ANC leaders know, a prosperous, growing black middle class is one of the major prerequisites for political stability in South Africa and continuation of ANC political hegemony. And the black middle class is growing. Data show that by 1998 new black investments in listed and unlisted companies totaled approximately four billion dollars, up more than fourfold from the previous year's total (Haffajee 1999). Financial services, telecommunications, and mass media are just three of blue-chip sectors of the economy into which black investment capital is reportedly going.

Despite the existence of a rapidly growing and ever more influential black entrepreneurial class, Whites are nonetheless still far and away South Africa's dominant economic group. In an assessment of the state of South Africa on the eve of its second all-race election, a source reckoned that "Whites . . . hold nine out of ten of the top jobs: they live in big houses, pack the best restaurants, dominate Prizegiving Day at the best schools" (Vine 1999).

With Whites still holding the dominant positions in its economy, but Blacks making inroads, South Africa as a whole has entered the 2000s in what appears to be a slow emergence from the economic recession of the 1990s.

According to the above-mentioned South African economists van Pappendorp and Dykes, advanced economics degree-holder and Mandela's successor Thabo Mbeki is viewed more favorably by both foreign and domestic investors than was Mandela. Investors are aware that it was Mbeki who had, in effect, run the country during Mandela's final 18 months in office, during which greater fiscal prudence—that is, less government expenditures on social service programs and less capitulation to labor demands—was instituted, resulting in a reduction of the budget deficit and a curbing of inflation. "In fact," Dykes proclaimed, "the financial sector is sound and well regulated. The policies are [now] pretty much what the IMF [International Monetary Fuind] would prescribe in these circumstances" (Pearson 1999).

Another reason for investor confidence in the Mbeki government came on August 7, 1999, when Tito Bboweni, a black African, became governor of the South Africa's Reserve Bank. Bboweni promised not to do anything "earth-shattering" but instead to continue to pursue conservative economic policies, despite pressures to stimulate economic growth by printing more money and giving out more loans to small businesses, both of which would be inflationary but not counter to the interests of the African masses. "The role of the bank," Bboweni stated, "is to create a climate of financial stability in which economic growth and wealth creation will be sustainable" (*San Diego Union Tribune,* August 8, 1999).

Still one more cause for optimism that the South African economy was entering the 2000s in a state of overall growth was the rapid postapartheid growth of its tourism-related industries. High rates of crime and reports of widespread political violence notwithstanding, during the five years after the coming to power of the black majority ANC government, foreign visitors to South Africa increased by more than 50 percent, to more than 5 million a year, and "Tourism and related industries, which contributed an estimated $11 billion to the country's gross domestic product last year [1998], expect to quadruple that figure in the next decade" (Hawthorne 1999).

Seeing tourism as an important source of revenue, since 1998 the South African government has annually pumped millions into campaigns to attract tourists from affluent Western countries such as the United States, Britain, Germany, France, and Italy. By mid-1999, each of those countries was the source of more than 2,000 tourists a month (Hawthorne 1999).

Where do the tourists go and what do they see? Some tour packages include tours of urban townships and bed and breakfast with an indigenous family. Rural tribal villages and homelands are included in other tour packages, as are visits to South Africa's wilderness areas and wild game parks, its wineries, its beaches, its gambling resorts, and to any other place else foreigners are willing to pay to go and experience.

Jobs created as a result of the increase in tourism and the growth of tourism-related industries are not for the most part, however, high paying. They tend to be low-level service jobs in hotels and at resorts, jobs that will pull relatively few of their occupants into the ranks of the middle-income skilled and white-collar workers.

But there is hope for growth of better jobs in South Africa. For instance, during an early August 1999 visit to South Africa, British prime minister Tony Blair signed an agreement that "could mean $6.6 billion in British investment when the government buys military equipment" from South Africa (*San Diego Union Tribune,* August 1, 1999). If this happens there will then surely be an increase in the demand for unionized un-skilled, semiskilled, and skilled workers at wage levels considerably above the bare margins of subsistence.

President Mbeki had further cause for optimism after a September 21, 1999, breakfast meeting with American industrialist David Rocke-feller, Peggy Dulaney (Rockefeller's daughter), and CEOs of companies such as Xerox, Shell, JP Morgan, Merrill Lynch, Chase Manhattan, Citibank, Coca-Cola, and Goldman Sachs, and investment guru George Soros. So impressed were the American business leaders with the stable political situation in South Africa that Rockefeller expressed certitude that "investment funds would continue to flow into the country" (*Johannesburg Star*, September 22, 1999).

As for South Africa's infamously high rates of crime and incidences of official corruption, Rockefeller didn't appear to see them as cause for any great concern. "Obviously there are problems about crime and cor-ruption," he is reported to have said, "but these will be found not only in South Africa. In general, the [American] business community has a very favorable attitude [concerning the profitability of investments in the South African economy]."

Mbeki emerged from the meeting with Rockefeller and other Amer-ican investors reportedly "believ[ing they] would spread the word about South Africa in the wider business community."

The unanswered question though is will American investments flow into sectors of the economy that will result in a significant increase in gov-ernment revenues and a lowering of the black unemployment rate?

One piece of good news was that in late 1999 the price of gold had risen to a 30-year high, with no reason to expect a precipitious drop in the near future. The South African economy had for many years been propped up by the proceeds from the country's gold mines.

Although black entrepreneurship has grown tremendously and blacks are now represented at all levels in all sectors of the economy, eco-nomic power at the highest and most influential level still remains firmly in the hands of Whites, and it will continue to remain so for the forsee-able future. Also, as reflected in the still overall high black unemploy-ment rate and low levels of material existence at which most Blacks live, black economic inroads have been made by mostly middle-class, rela-tively educated blacks, whose economic gains have not been shared by the masses of unemployed, unskilled blacks.

It is also mostly high ANC officials and a handful of relatively highly educated and prosperous blacks who have benefited from the metamor-phosis of the civil service elite from being all white to majority black. And though the ANC received most of the black votes cast in the June 1999 election, there is widespread dissatisfaction with the speed at which the ANC-led government has moved to make good the election promises to upgrade the life conditions of all blacks rather than just the black elite.

Some of this dissatisfaction with the rate at which their material lives have been improving is reflected in the continuation of traditions developed during the Apartheid era. One of these traditions is the non-payment of rents and public service fees by township residents, which in turn deprives local governments of some of the money needed to make good on ANC promises to build more and better housing and increase the overall level of services to black township residents. But how can people without the means make the payments?

In the spring of 1995, President Mandela attempted to put an end to the widespread nonpayment of rents and public service fees by announcing that communities that do pay them will have their services upgraded before those that don't. But it didn't work. The rates of nonpayment held no less steady than did the poverty and unemployment rates. Early 1996 government estimates were that approximately 65 percent of South Africa's township residents still were not paying the fees.

During successive years, municipalities began disconnecting electricity services to nonpaying individuals and communities. So now, illegal reconnections of electricity and other services have become rampant. To combat such illegal practices, some municipal authorities have taken to removing electricity meters that have been tampered with and charging large fees to have them reinstalled. The result? Still large numbers of people live unhappily without electricity.

Another source of black dissatisfaction is the ANC's failure to live up to its 1994 election promise to redistribute 30 percent of the country's land back to blacks. It has not happened, and Mbeki has revealed no plans to make it happen. To dispossess Whites of large amounts of land would not only result in massive white flight from the country, it would scare off both present and potential investors, making them once again fearful that political and economic conditions in South Africa are too uncertain to risk further infusions of capital.

White flight and foreign investors are not, however, the immediate concerns of the black masses. They are concerned that the government may never make good on its promise of land redistribution, full employment, and the like for all. White flight and foreign investors are the concern of the elite blacks, the ones who have profited most from the revolution.

High crime rates, high unemployment rates, the typically low educational attainments of its black constituents, the possibility of increasing dissatisfaction with the rate at which the ANC is going about fulfilling its promises are not the only problems facing South Africa's current political leaders. If South Africa is to experience increased economic prosperity and continue to exist as a stable political democracy, its government will also have to lower the levels of dissatisfaction among its nonblack citizenry, many of whom see the ANC governing in the interests of the country's Blacks and only the country's Blacks.

Contemporary South Africa

Its Discontents and Future Prospects

WHITE FLIGHT

There are many reasons for white dissatifaction with the current state of affairs in contemporary South Africa. One of the results of this dissatisfaction has been white flight: thousands of white South African emigrants to Australia, New Zealand, Europe, and North America.

One of the reasons for white flight is, of course, white racism. White racist attitudes did not suddenly dissolve with the dissolution of the Apartheid state. Born in a world organized and governed in strict conformity to white supremacist principles, raised in families that lived in accordance with white supremacist principles, educated in schools where the primary commitment was to instilling white supremacist principles in the minds of their charges, many white South Africans found repugnant the thought of living in a racially desegregated society in which political power was wielded by a black majority government; and so they left South Africa, emigrating to countries with sizable white majorities.

Some white racists remain in hopes of securing a politically independent white homeland, somewhere or another within the country's present political boundaries, where only Whites are allowed to live. Or short of acquiring a politically independent white homeland, some remain in hopes of at least being able to live in all-white areas of the country where contact with Nonwhites would be as uncommon and nonegalitarian as it was during the Apartheid era.

One such place is Orania, an all-white, Afrikaans-speaking community of approximately 600 people, established in 1991, just after Mandela's release from prison. One of Orania's most energetic residents is Anje Boshoff, the granddaughter of former South African prime minister and minister of Bantu Education Hendrik Verwoerd. Some Orania residents, Boshoff is reported to have said, would be "strongly opposed to having black people living in our town." Claiming not to be a racist, Boshoff said she and others moved to Orania in 1997 "to practice our own [Afrikaner] traditions without coming into conflict with other cultures." Their ultimate goal is to create a population and economic base sufficient to "be acknowledged as a Volkstaat (Afrikaner nation-state) by both the South African government and the international community" (Fenster 1999: 70).

Another reason for white flight was, and still is, fear of black political, economic, and physical reprisals against Whites. These fears were heightened during the late 1990s with the Truth and Reconciliation Commission hearings, which brought to light many Apartheid era atrocities committed against Blacks by members of the Apartheid state's police, security, and national defense forces.

The TRC hearings also created bitterness and gave rise to sharp divisions and hostilities within Afrikanerdom. Persons appearing before the TRC in confession of their deeds had to necessarily name others involved in either the commission or the commissioning of these deeds. Many of those implicated then felt constrained or were subpoenaed to come before the TRC to either deny or confess to their involvements. Those confessions often led to still others appearing before the TRC. Some of those whose confessions led to their former colleagues and supervisors having to appear before the commission were shunned, ostracized, or, in some instances, threatened by fellow Whites. Thus, many who had means left South Africa during the 1990s; others are contemplating doing so as soon as they are able.

But white racism, fear of black reprisals for atrocities committed as servants of the Apartheid state, and fear of white reprisals for having implicated former colleagues and bureaucratic supervisors in these atrocities have never been the only reasons for white flight. Another cause is South Africa's high crime rate.

Though racists often point to South Africa's high rates of crime and violence as justification for their racist beliefs and practices and as evidence of the folly of having let blacks take over, one *does not have to be* racist to not want to live in constant fear for the physical safety of oneself and one's family and other loved ones. The internecine Black-on-Black political violence of the 1980s and 1990s was real and often spilled over into areas frequented by Whites. Innocent people were indeed sometimes killed in the crossfire. Also real were the rise in the homocide rate; the increases in the numbers of rapes and other sexual assaults; the increases in armed robberies, nonsexual assaults, carjackings, burglaries, and thefts of livestock and farm implements; and the spread of other kinds of life- and property-threatening activities.

There is also widespread concern among Whites, Coloureds, and Indians that the government's affirmative action, or "job reservation," and college and university admission policies have made them victims of racial discrimination of the same types that Blacks had to endure before the end of Apartheid. Under the previous whites-only governments, virtually all of the jobs in all sectors of the economy affording a middle-class or above standard of living went to Whites and only Whites. Implementation of affirmative action hiring policies has, however, resulted in a smaller percentage such jobs going to Whites. One of the results of this is that white job prospects are not what they once were.

A similar situation exists as a result of affirmative action policies regarding admissions to college and universities. Given limited space and resources, more black students means relatively fewer students of other races. White protests against such policies have fallen mostly on deaf ears. Job reservation policies favoring one racial group over all others was firmly instituted in South Africa a century and a half ago, by Whites for the benefit of Whites. Many Blacks feel that it is now their turn to benefit from policies that favor them over other racial groups. What can Whites say now? Nothing, except that such policies are unfair and lead to inefficiencies. Many argue that in a truly nonracist society, people would be hired, promoted, and admitted to colleges because of their abilities not because of their race. The most just and efficient societies are those in which people rise only on the basis of their abilities. Yes, right, just, and efficient, many Blacks might say in sarcastic reply, just like in South Africa before the coming to power of a black majority government.

The ANC was so committed to attaining black representation in all sectors of South African society that in 1998 its leaders announced they were dissatisfied with the lack of black players on the nation's top rugby and cricket teams and were thus considering forcing teams to introduce race quotas. Though they ultimately did not, the mere threat of doing so was sufficient to prompt the South African Rugby Football Union and the United Cricket Board of South Africa, much to the dismay of sports fans and athletes across the country, to produce their own affirmative action plans, outlining the specific steps they intended to take to ensure more black participation on rugby and cricket teams at all levels.

Unhappiness with the idea of sports team quotas is not exclusive to Whites. According to an article in 1999, for example, two of the cricket's relatively few top-level non-white players, mixed-race batsman Herschelle Gibbs and black bowler Makhaya Ntini, argued for selection based strictly on merit: "Players of colour who have made it so far have earned it," said Ntini. "But it seems that they could be going to select those who are not quite ready. That would be wrong." The article, however, notes that "despite the best intentions of sports governing bodies," and presumably the best intentions of those who feel as Ntini does, "many white players are resistant to change and racism still blights the sports field." As evidence the article cites the forced apology of well-known all-rounder Brian McMillan for a racially offensive remark during a local match; an Eastern Province player who was banned for two years after being found guilty of calling a black opponent "a half-breed kaffir"; and a Springbok player who used the very "same insult in addressing a black South African woman in a New Zealand bar (Thomasson 1999).

The Springboks are South Africa's world-class national rugby team and a source of great pride and joy for the Afrikaner populace. In fact, as a gesture of interracial unity, a year after becoming South Africa's first black president, Nelson Mandela, attired in a Springbok jersey, attended a ceremony at which he personally handed the World (Rugby) cup to the leaders of the 1995 world champion all-white team. Two years later, though, the South African Rugby Football Union "dragged Mandela to court over a government probe into racism in the sport" (Thomasson 1999). Then in May 1999 a parliamentary report charged that racism is still prevalent in rugby—"white teams refusing to go into black townships to play . . . , selectors choosing all-white teams and black clubs being neglected by development programmes" (Bernes-Lasserre, 1999).

Racism was once again an issue on June 24, 1999, when a *Daily Mail and Guardian* article carried a report of an apology made by Springbok coach Nick Mallet for having asserted, on the eve of the team's first match in defense of the World Cup, that "he would not be pushed with his selection choices, or ever take part in anything that can be construed as window dressing." In apology for the above statement, Mallet explained that he was referring specifically to "the Springbok [i.e., national] level, where I am required to select the best team." Otherwise, he assured that he was committed to "creating opportunities for players of colour at all levels," as evidenced by his record of selecting players of color to play on teams he has coached at lower levels (Shapshak 1999).

And such is how things stand today: pressure from the black minister of sport has led to affirmative action in rugby and cricket team selection at the provincial and lower levels of participation, and Whites fear that there will soon be no place for them—even in sports. One of the reasons for the relative paucity of top-level black rugby and cricket players is that, like everything else in South Africa, sports participation has long correlated with race: soccer being the sport with the greatest black involvement; rugby and cricket always having been predominantly white sports.

The coming to power of the ANC also resulted in deep resentments among residents of affluent white areas suddenly joined together into municipal units inclusive of poor black township areas. With governments at all levels charged with using tax revenues to first improve conditions in the black areas—where nonpayment of rents and public service fees are still common—Whites complain of paying higher taxes for the upgrading of services for people who pay little or no taxes. Fearful of ever-increasing reductions in their overall standard of living in the years to come, some Whites have either already left the country or are seriously comtemplating doing so. There have even been short-lived tax boycotts by white residents of certain communities.

That there was some white resistance to school and residential integration is evidenced by increases in the late 1990s in the number of exclusive (i.e., prohibitively expensive for only but a few blacks) private all-white schools and all-white communities such as the aforementioned Orania. Such resistance still exists. Why should we send our children to school with less academically prepared children from the poorer areas? goes the white justification for private schools. Would not being in classes with less academically prepared children result in our children learning less than they otherwise would? Would not leaving South Africa be the best way to ensure that they receive the quality of education necessary for success in the modern world?

All in all, though, the overriding cause of white dissatisfaction with life in the "new" South Africa is that it is not what it was before. The new political dispensation hasn't brought many Whites anything tangible that they didn't already have; rather, it has taken things away from them, intangible as well as tangible things. No doubt about it, Whites have lost some important things. They have lost their monopolies on political power; on middle- and high-income jobs; and on economic power, social status, personal dignity, and the full enjoyment of the full range of human rights.

This sense of loss is evidenced in survey data indicating that fully 90 percent do indeed "believe they are the country's losers," even though they—numbering approximately 4.4 million and constituting somewhere between 10 and 12 percent of the country's total population—remain in possession of the largest share of the country's economic resources, live in the nicest homes in the nicest areas, and send their children to the best pubic and private schools. Furthermore, the report continues, "Only 4 percent of white respondents [to] a recent opinion poll thought the ANC cared for them; 70 percent of blacks did" (Roberts 1999).

Since people often leave South Africa to take up permanent residence elsewhere without giving official notice of their intention, it is impossible to know exactly how many thousands of people have left. Government statistics indicate that about 8,000 South Africans emigrated in 1997 after a peak of 10,235 in 1994. However, emigration lawyer Colin Adno has stated that government statistics tend to understate the number of people taking permanent leave of the country, for the reason given above (Roberts 1999).

Three days after the above data appeared in the *Daily Mail and Guardian,* the paper carried an article in which it was proclaimed that "while newspaper headlines threaten an imminent exodus, official figures show a 7 percent drop in the numbers leaving the country in 1998 compared with 1997" (Younge 1999). Whatever the exact numbers and percentages of Whites who have left the country since the coming to power of the ANC, the cause for concern lies not in the fact that thousands have left but that "more than half of those who left [during the 1990s were] economically active and more than half of those . . . professional, semiprofessional or managerial. Their departure not only depletes the pool of skilled labor but forces up the wages of those who stay, thus adding to already existing inequalities" (Younge 1999). In addition, the departure of such people resulted in a shrinkage of the country's tax base at a time when it was desperately seeking ways to expand that base as a means of reducing the unemployment rate and generating funds to provide more and better schools and electricity and sanitation facilities to more homes.

A PEACEFUL COEXISTENCE

Another source of present-day white dissatisfaction follows from the fact that the Afrikaners who negotiated the transfer of political power to the black majority did so with the openly expressed expectation that they would be able to maintain their positions of economic dominance and be allowed the freedoms and given the resources necessary to ensure the propagation of the Afrikaans language and Afrikaner culture. Although it would no longer be a racially segregated society, the Afrikaners would nonetheless be living essentially apart from other racial groups in a racially desegregated rather than racially integrated society.

What are the differences between racial segregation, racial desegregation, and racial integregation? In its most complete form, **racial segregation** involves the kind of social, physical, economic, and political separation of people of different races as existed in South Africa during Apartheid. Total or complete **racial integration** stands in opposition to racial segregation. It exists as a result of members of two or more previously distinct racial groups having merged into one indivisible group and, in the process, wiping out all social, cultural, and biological differences that existed between them before the merger.

Desegregation, on the other hand, is a term sometimes used by scholars and social activists to make the point that while segregated and integrated constitute the extreme states of interracial relations in a multiracial society, there also exists middle ground. Desegregation involves, as happened in South Africa during the 1990s, "the removal from the social structure of legal and social barriers based on racial and ethnic discrimination against a group" (Blackwell 1985: 161). The term *desegregation* does not, however, carry the same meaning as does *integration*. A racially desegregated society is one in which racial integration could, in the absence of legal barriers, exist but does not, for whatever reason.

Desegregation is not the only middle ground. There is also **cultural pluralism.** The term *cultural pluralism* was coined in 1915 by Horace

Kallen, a Harvard-educated Jewish philosopher. Expressing the sentiments of other ethnic group leaders who feared that total integration would result in the cultural extinctions of their groups, Kallen argued against the total "Americanization" of immigrants and all other efforts to create a "cultural melting pot" in which all the various ethnic cultures would have merged together to create a larger culture in which the old ethnic differences no longer existed. For Kallen and other cultural pluralists, many of the traditional ethnic group differences were well worth preserving, for their own sake and because they provide historical continuity and linkages between individuals and their ancestors (Gordon 1964: 132–59). Cultural pluralists, then, given their goals, stand in opposition to efforts to fully integrate the societies in which they live.

Therefore, speaking in accordance with the definitions given above, it can be said that the Afrikaners who negotiated the transfer of political power to the country's black majority had the creation of a culturally and racially pluralistic, rather than a racially and culturally integrated, South African nation as their ultimate objective. And by giving official recognition to four distinct racial or population groups and 11 different languages, the South African Constitution, in effect, provided the means for the maintenance of racial and cultural pluralism. Or so it may have at first seemed.

But with the demise of Apartheid, once-taboo interracial marriages became possible. Friendships and sexual unions across racial lines became common. Increasingly more members of the country's black majority came to occupy positions in the economy and live in homes in neighborhoods that were once open to Whites only. Black children now sit next to white children at previously whites-only schools. Black representation in the police, state security, and defense forces now threatens to overwhelm Afrikaner representation. And all of this appears to be causing large numbers of Afrikaners to doubt whether cultural pluralism is, in the long run, possible in the new South Africa.

Increasingly more Afrikaners seem to see themselves and their fellow Afrikaners as under seige: their culture, their language, their once-dominant social status, their economic dominance, their whole way of life, their very identity as a people under threat of rapid extinction if they do not maintain the same degree of personal, social, and cultural distance from Nonwhites as was mandated during the days of Apartheid. For that, after all, is what Apartheid was all about: cultural pluralism with each racial, ethnic, and tribal group having a social, political, occupational, and territorial existence *apart* from all the others.

Desegregated schools at which Afrikaner students attend classes taught in Afrikaans, while Blacks attend classes taught in English and other languages, are examples of ways in which Afrikaners resistant to interacting with Blacks as equals have avoided doing so. The aforementioned all-white community of Orania—located "a five-hour drive from major cities . . . in a harsh terrain where the summers are fiercely hot and the winters are bitterly cold" (Fenster 1999: 70)—is another example.

Other examples are given by Krog, who tells of small towns where during the late 1990s Blacks were still refused service in local bars and restaurants and "chased out into the street" for requesting it (1998: 275). Although Krog does not offer it as such, this may be at least a partial explanation for the killing of 19 farmers in a period of three months during which she was traveling around the country as a radio journalist reporting on the deliberations of the TRC (356).

Wilhelm Verwoerd Jr.—the former prime minister's grandson, a former researcher for the TRC, a member of the Stellenbosch University faculty, and husband of Melanie Verwoerd, who in 1998 was herself an ANC member of parliament—has expressed what represents the disillusioned Afrikaner liberal view, seeing "peaceful coexistence (i.e., pluralism rather than interracial unity or integration) as all that can be hoped for in his lifetime—and even that might not be possible" (Goodman 1999: 175).

Verwoerd may be right. Any uneasy but peaceful coexistence may be all that can realistically be hoped for in his lifetime. Racial Apartheid is the goal of more Afrikaners than just the residents of the town of Orania or the "overweight men . . . drinking brandy and Coke and talking about rugby" in the small town Afrikaner bars from which Blacks are chased out into the street for requesting service. This was evidenced in May 1999 when a group of Afrikaner leaders submitted to President Mandela what has been described as "research backing their demand for some form of self-determination, either local self-government or a separate homeland" (Roberts 1999).

None of this is surprising. Never have large numbers of Afrikaners been in advocacy of cultural or racial integration with English, African, or any other people. Afrikaners have long saw isolation from other peoples as the most effective means of ensuring their survival as a people. Their way of surviving has been to remain separate and distinct from, as well as politically dominant over, members of other South African racial and ethnic groups. That is why South Africa experienced the Anglo-Boer War, Christian National Education, the Broederbond, all the years and years of affirmative action for Afrikaners, Afrikaans-medium schools for Afrikaners and English-median schools for white English-speakers, and Apartheid.

Not everyone who thinks they were, or would be, better off under the governance of a predominantly white political party is an Afrikaner or even white, for that matter. There are also large numbers of Coloureds who apparently think so too. This is clearly reflected in both the 1994 and 1999 election results. Only in the Western Cape—where the majority (55 percent) are classified as Coloured, as opposed to 25 percent white and 19 percent African—did candidates put forth by the white-dominant parties win a majority of the popular vote and thus a majority of seats in the provincial legislature.

Mike Nicol has written of a March 2, 1994, conversation in which a young, Coloured, Western Cape resident explained why he was going to vote for the National Party. "I mean what have they done to me? This country wouldn't be like this today without them. Just look at [the rest of] Africa, it's a mess. The ANC's going to take all our houses away, Mister Mike. All we've worked for they're going to take. The Blacks don't like the Coloureds, it's a fact" (1995: 36).

Goodman (1999) wrote that during his 1998 travels through South Africa he was "continually struck—horrified, actually—by the attitudes many Coloureds hold toward Africans" (225). He noted that while during his travels through South Africa in the 1980s, the most racist comments he heard were invariably uttered by Boers, but by the late 1990s they invariably came from Coloureds.

As an example of a malcontented Coloured and some of the reasons for Coloured discontentment, Goodman described a young Coloured hitchhiker he picked up during his travels across the Cape. "[T]he *bleks* are *lazy*," said the youth, who had recently quit his job laying bricks. "This whole country is going to *kak* [feces] under Mandela. He's giving this whole country to the Kaffirs. This place will go the same way as the rest of Africa, with Blacks killing each other. I'm not a racist, man, but I think it was better before." The hitchhiker then went on to state what Goodman perceives to be a widespread Coloured lament: "Under Apartheid, we weren't white enough. Under the ANC we aren't black enough" (225).

As we have seen, under Apartheid Coloureds *were* better off—than Blacks, that is. They were generally accorded a higher social status than Blacks, more was spent on their education than on black education, and their educational attainments were generally higher than those of Blacks. Coloureds also had access to a wider range of jobs than did Blacks, their incomes were generally higher than Blacks, and their residential areas were generally not so bleak as black areas. Most Coloured, approximately 80 percent, spoke Afrikaans and adhered to the same religious faith as did members of the dominant white group. As a result of all of the above, a great many Coloureds felt, and still do feel, justified in looking down on Blacks and perceiving that they have nothing in common with them.

During his observations of the way Coloured students treated and interacted with African students at a previously Coloured-only secondary school in Cape Town, Crain Soudien (1998) found signs of "a deep and often crass racial antipathy" toward African students, manifested in the frequent and open use of the racially derogatory term *Kaffir* when speaking about and in the presence of Blacks; a widespread unwillingness to relate to African students as their either intellectual or social equals; and openly expressed contempt for African traditions and beliefs and for African political leaders.

Did the treatment they received from the Coloured students cause the black students to hate school? No, is the answer given by Soudien. African students disliked the racism they encountered at the school but not attendance at the school per se. School was a means to achieving a better life in a better world. They liked being able to attend the school. They just didn't like some of the people they encountered and some of the treatment they received while being educated for entry into the better world awaiting them if they were successful in their studies. Nor did they, in general, remain humbly passive in the face of racist atttitudes and behaviors. Monde, for example, said:

> there are things that I do, personally [when someone comes up to me] with a racist attitude. I'll tell that person from A to Z, if I manage to come to Z. But I do tell that person. And even speak so that the whole class hears that I'm telling this person this and that. Not to be ignorant, not to be this and that (Soudien 1998: 25).

The African students at the above school (Second Suburbs Secondary) are, after all, members the country's numerically and politically dominant population group. With the full range of educational opportunities now opened up to them and the full range of professional-occupational opportunities open to those who acquire the requisite education, why would they feel inferior to Coloureds or need to act as if they did? The Coloured racism they experience is, in the new South Africa, empty, toothless, and of no long-term consequence. The old racial hierarchy that placed Coloureds above Blacks is no longer operational; for though the majority of Blacks still live on the margins of subsistence, many nonetheless now occupy positions, in all sectors of the society and economy, that place them well above the positions now or ever occupied by the overwhelming majority of Coloureds.

Coloureds as a group are, therefore, in a bind. Their traditionally intermediate status between Blacks and Whites on the various stratification hierarchies followed from the racist belief that Whites were in all important ways superior to Blacks and thus more deserving of all the things the world has to offer; therefore, persons with some white ancestors were superior to and more deserving than persons with no white ancestors.

But now that decisions regarding the distribution of wealth, political power, and social status are no longer being guided by the racist belief in white superiority, even if it's just some white ancestry involved, the status of Coloureds relative to Blacks has dropped. As Blacks have gained status, Coloureds have lost status. And it is not just status that they have lost. Affirmative action policies, implemented by the ruling black majority political party, has given Blacks preferential access to job and educational opportunities that they, Coloureds, never had.

But unlike Whites dissatisfied with the state of race relations in present-day South Africa, very few Coloureds have the money or the money-earning skills or professional qualifications to leave South Africa and make better material lives for themselves and their families elsewhere. Moreover, where else but in South Africa would they be Coloureds? In the United States and other places there is no such thing; they would be Blacks.

Where but in South Africa would fluency in Afrikaans be an asset? It is spoken only in South Africa and only by approximately 20 percent of the population. Since it is unlikely that Coloureds would be accepted into emigrant Afrikaner communities in the United States, Canada, Australia, New Zealand, and Europe, where would they go? What would they be, and what would they do when they arrived there? With whom would they affiliate? The blacks in those countries?

Thus, despite their discontentment with the new sociopolitical dispensation, there will not be, in the foreseeable future, a mass exodus of Coloureds from South Africa. Most have no choice but to remain—as Afrikaans-speaking, Dutch Reformed Church adherents, the majority of whom support the mostly white political parties.

How likely is an eventual Coloured biological assimilation with South Africa's Afrikaner population? Anje Boshoff, discussed earlier, has said that Blacks would not be welcome in her all-white Afrikaans-speaking community of Orania; but she also said she "wouldn't be upset if [her] son came home with a Mulatto as long as she spoke Afrikaans and shared [Afrikaner] values. But it would be terrible if he came home with an English-speaking woman" (Fenster 1999: 7). However, I do not think widespread intermarriage between Coloureds and Afrikaners is likely in the near future.

Although occurring more frequently today than in previous times, Coloured–Afrikaner marriages are still quite rare. Boshoff's expressed sentiments notwithstanding, it is still the case that Afrikaners who marry Nonwhites thereby marry themselves right out of Afrikanerdom. That's why Afrikaners have established isolated all-white communities, demanded a separate white homeland, and maintained great social distance from other races during their day-to-day activities in desegregated South Africa. Widespread intermarriage with Coloureds or other Nonwhites would be the end of Afrikaners as they know themselves; their descendants would ultimately be Coloureds, mixed-race, rather than Afrikaner, for Afrikaners are by definition white.

Racial divisions, racial antipathies, rampant crime, corrupt police, corrupt politicians, unwise judges, dishonest educators who inflate their students' scores on standardized tests, clamorings for a separate white homeland, all-white residential areas, public places in certain parts of the country where Blacks and other Nonwhites are not welcome—can South America survive it all? Or do these problems place the country in danger of imminent social, political, and economic collapse?

Yes, South Africa can indeed survive all of the above. Witness the economically prosperous, politically stable, and democratic United States of America. It too has experienced racial divisions and animosities; high crime rates; corrupt police, politicians, and other public officials; dishonest educators who inflate student scores on standardized tests; armed and dangerous groups clamoring for separate black and white homelands; and neighborhoods and public places all over America where persons of one race or another dare not go for fear of their life.

AIDS

So yes, perhaps South Africa can overcome the myriad of problems discussed so far. But a deadly, more recent threat has arisen: the HIV virus.

Of all the threats to South African economic prosperity and political stability, the one that looms as the largest and most potentially devastating is the HIV virus. So rapid was the spread of the HIV virus during the 1990s that unless drastically reduced, South Africa will most assuredly be unable to achieve the economic growth necessary to build all the needed houses and schools, train all the needed professionals and skilled workers, or even reduce its crime rates in anything close to the near future.

Why the rapid spread of the HIV virus after the coming to power of the ANC? One reason is that after the demise of Apartheid and the subsequent lifting of international economic sanctions against South Africa, the country was no longer isolated from the rest of the world. All of a sudden it was wide open. There were suddenly many more foreign airplanes and ships with foreign crews and passengers landing at South African airports and docking at its seaports, some disembarking people who carried the HIV virus.

There was also, as previously mentioned, an end to the tight control of movement across South Africa's borders from contiguous African countries where the AIDS virus had been relatively widespread. One result of this has been an influx of many thousands of unauthorized immigrants from African countries to the north who are now taking some of the blame for South Africa's high unemployment rate as well as the spread of AIDS (Hussein 1998). In addition, the end of hostilities between the ANC and the South Africa Defense Force resulted in the return home of ANC guerrilla troops operating from bases inside these neighboring countries, all of whom were heroes but some of whom were also HIV carriers.

The spread of the HIV virus has also been aided by attitudes held by large numbers of South Africans regarding HIV carriers and their beliefs regarding the manner in which the virus is spread, ways to avoid contacting the virus, and ways of killing the virus once it has been contacted. According to recent data, in 1998, South Africa had "the world's fastest growing AIDS epidemic," up to 30 percent of its adult population being carriers of the HIV virus. Moreover, in many South African communities attitudes toward carriers remained severely unsympathetic, as evidenced by the report of a woman being beaten to death by her neighbors for shaming their community by revealing her HIV infection on Zulu language radio and TV (*San Diego Union Tribune,* December 28, 1998). Another report in which it was stated that one in five South African women is HIV-positive, gave further anecdotal evidence in the form of an account of the scorn and degradation heaped upon a black female student and other South African female carriers of the HIV virus (Fenster 1999).

Among the consequences of these severely unsympathetic attitudes toward HIV carriers are that relatively few people submit to being tested for the virus; those who do and find out that they are carriers often keep it to themselves for fear of violent community sanctions; more and more people are becoming infected, many by people who didn't even know they are at risk; and by mid-2000, the HIV-infection rate of South Africans will have risen to 1 in 10, or 10 percent of the country's total population (*San Diego Union Tribune,* May 21, 2000).

Due to the high rate of HIV infection in the Eastern Cape, "The provincial government says its already embattled health services will collapse under the subsequent financial pressure within the next five years." In the Eastern Cape, as elsewhere, the rate of infection was high and still rising within the 20 to 24 age group, having gone from 12.6 percent in 1997, to 15.9 percent in 1998, to 18 percent or more in 1999 (*Daily Mail and Guardian,* May 31, 1999).

A national government source predicted that "within a few years AIDS will slash the average life expectancy from 60 years to 40, and leave one million orphans." The single largest group of HIV carriers reported were young black women, most of whom live at the poverty level. Many of these women continue to have sex out of the desire to have children, to whom they are likely to pass on the virus. But not all female carriers are poor and uneducated. "At one university, 80 percent of the female students proved HIV-positive in a recent test" (McGreal, August 1, 1999).

Other attitudes are aiding in the spread of the HIV virus. There is, first of all, the widespread belief that HIV virus can be killed by having sex with a virgin, which is a contributor to the increasing number of young female rape victims.

Another is the belief in some African communities that virginity testing is necessary to ensure the "purity of prospective brides and the honor of their families." Unfortunately, one of the results of virginity testing has been the substitution of anal for vaginal intercourse by those wishing to be able to pass the test (*The Natal Witness,* June 14, 1999; McGreal, September 29, 1999).

There are also attitudes such as those held by a Mr. Sipho Malinga, deputy headmaster of a school in KwaZulu-Natal. In Malinga's view, condom use should not be condoned. "We are against the use of condoms," he is reported to have said. "We think condoms promote lust for sex. If a person has condoms he can go to another man's wife knowing he will not get her pregnant. . . . I don't think we should teach children about such things" (McGreal, September 29, 1999).

But the attitudes that help perpetuate the problem aside, the reality of the HIV crisis in South Africa is startling. There was an increase in the number of HIV-infected South Africans from 2,448,239 in 1996 to three million by the end of 1998. Ten percent of the total South African population is HIV-infected; upward of 30 percent of the adult South African population HIV-infected. One of every five South African women is a carrier of the virus. Persons in their 20s are more likely to be carriers than older persons. Blacks are more likely to be carriers than Whites. As a result, South African public health and social welfare systems are moving closer to collapsing under the strain.

In the fall of 1999, President Mbeki stated that the drug AZT, which had been proven to be effective in eliminating mother-to-unborn-child transmission, was too dangerous to give to pregnant, HIV-infected South African women or to South African rape victims and would, thus, not be distributed among them. As might be expected, this decision resulted in widespread protests from both AIDS activists and medical professionals.

Controversy over the South African government's AIDS policies continued on into the year 2000 and heated up when it was revealed in March that $6.2 million of the country's $17 million 1999 AIDS budget went unspent. Further, in May President Mbeki appointed American scientists Peter Duesberg and David Rasnick, both of whom deny a causal relationship between HIV and AIDS, to his 33-member AIDS advisory panel. Many contended that the effects of these government actions was to further rather than thwart the spread of AIDS. As of this writing, within South Africa the debate over the specific causes of AIDS continues to rage and the HIV virus continues to spread rapidly, especially among South Africans in their 20s, which bodes especially ill for the country's young people.

The spread of AIDS, of course, has dire economic consequences. Most adults who die of complications from AIDS usually do so during what would otherwise be their most economically productive and influential parenting years, leaving behind aging parents and orphans for the already financially strapped government to maintain. Thus, since the number and percentage of HIV carriers has been increasing rather than decreasing, it is probable that so will the number of AIDS orphans and economically dependent elderly black parents and relatives of persons dead of AIDS complications. A likely result will be increased poverty and joblessness in the next generation.

According to a report presented to the South African Parliament's Committee on Welfare and Population Development, as of September 1999 approximately 120,000 South African children were HIV carriers and "one in seven children under the age of five [are] expected to be orphaned by the year 2005 as a result of HIV/AIDS" (Segar, 1999). Another report gives two million as the number of South African AIDS orphans expected by the year 2010 (Collins 2000).

Hope that more will be done to stop the spread of the HIV virus was given in October 2000 by Mbeki spokesperson Joel Netschitenzhe, who was reported to have said "Mbeki has decided to curb his own comments on the cause [i.e., source] of the AIDS virus." (*SanDiego Union Tribune*, October 17, 2000).

Curbing one's comments on the cause of the virus is not, of course, the same as taking broader, more concerted measures to halt or retard its spread. But Mbeki's decision to do so does suggest that his views concerning the cause of AIDS and the most effective ways to stop its spread may not be as firmly held as they once were, and, over time, might move even closer to the views held by most AIDS researchers. If such a change in thinking has occurred, then perhaps the Mbeki-led South African government will open itself to taking broader multi-pronged efforts to stop the spread of AIDS.

In any event, the AIDS epidemic will soon overshadow and exacerbate all the country's other problems unless something more is done to stop or at least drastically retard its spread.

GLOSSARY

African National Congress (ANC)   See *South African Native National Congress.*

Africans   The darkest skinned or more purely negroid South African population group; sometimes referred to as either blacks (as they would be in the United States and elsewhere) or natives. They constitute approximately 77 percent of South Africa's current population.

Afrikaans   A Dutch-derived language spoken by approximately 60 percent of South Africa's current white population.

Afrikaners   White South African speakers of the Afrikaans language who are, in general, affiliated with the Dutch Reformed Church and, up until the 1990s, occupied the top positions in South Africa's governing bodies, as well as its military, state security, and police agencies.

Afrikaner Weerstandsbeweging (AWB)   Meaning the Afrikaner Resistance Movement. A white, right-wing, Afrikaner vigilantist group formed during the 1980s by ex-policeman Eugene Terreblanche. The AWB insignia contains three sevens arranged to resemble a swastika. During the Apartheid years one of its goals was to counter black guerrilla attacks on state facilities and white-owned farms and businesses. During the postapartheid years it became an advocate of the creation of a separate whites-only homeland within the territorial confines of present-day South Africa.

Anglo-Boer War   See *Second Freedom War.*

Apartheid   Means "separateness." Instituted after the coming to power of the National Party in 1948, Apartheid was an attempt to divide South Africa's racial groups into separate socioeconomic units based in different parts of the country, where, and only where, they enjoyed full citizenship rights. Under Apartheid, for instance, Africans were no longer citizens of the Union of South Africa and, therefore, no longer entitled to the same citizenship rights as white South Africans when living, working, or traveling through the 87 percent of the country's landmass not designated "tribal homelands."

assegai   Spear.

assimilation   "A one-way process in which an individual or group takes on the culture and identity of another group and becomes part of that group" (Theodorson and Theodorson 1970: 17).

banned   To be banned was, during the Apartheid era, to be prohibited from making speeches and from being in the simultaneous company of two or more persons. It was illegal to publicly quote a banned person and illegal for a banned person's picture to appear in public.

Battle of Blood River   The battle on December 16, 1838, at which Boer forces defeated Zulu forces in revenge of the massacre of a group of Boers led by Piet Retief, who had come to the camp of the Zulu king Dingaan in the expectation of formalizing a peace agreement.

bitter-enders   Members of Afrikaner commando units in the Anglo-Boer War who pledged to never surrender to the British, no matter what or how hopeless their situation seemed.

Black Circuit of 1812   Court proceedings created to hear Khoikhoi allegations of mistreatment by their white masters in the districts of George, Uitenhenge, and Graaf-Reinet, resulting in massive, not always peaceful, Boer protests.

Black Consciousness Movement (BCM)   Evolving during the 1970s, it encompassed groups and individuals advocating the rejection of values and ideologies derived from Whites. The BCM emphasis, like the emphasis of U.S. black power advocates, was on black self-reliance and independence from Whites. Steve Biko was one of the recognized leaders of South Africa's BCM.

Black Flag Rebellion   Staged in Kimberly in January 1875 in protest of the British government's proclaimed intention of extending full political and economic rights to Blacks in the diamond mining and other South African territories under British dominion. Though the rebellion was quashed, in the end Blacks did not enjoy the same rights as Whites.

Black Sash   An all-female, mostly English-speaking group committed to passive resistance to Apartheid.

Boers   In Dutch it means "farmers." The term came into South African usage during the seventeenth century to differentiate white farmers from white urban dwellers; by the nineteenth century the term had become synonymous with *Afrikaners,* that is, Dutch- or Afrikaans-speaking, Dutch Reform Church–affiliated South African whites.

Boer War   See *Second Freedom War.*

Broederbond   Means "brotherhood." Established in 1918 with the goals of propagating Afrikaner culture and furthering the advancement of Afrikaners in all areas of South African life, the Broederbond went partially underground in 1923 and remains influential until the present day.

Bushmen   A light-brown-complexioned, steatopygic hunter-gatherer people living in what would become the Cape Colony after the arrival of the first European settlers. Their descendants would be included among the Cape Coloured.

Christian National Education (CNE)   Education oriented toward imparting an Afrikaner Christian worldview, preserving the Afrikaans language and Afrikaner cultural traditions, and maintaining Afrikaner supremacy in all areas of South African life.

civilized labor policy   Instituted in 1924, it ratified the practice of paying white workers more than black workers even when they were engaged in the same work. Its purpose was to maintain Afrikaner solidarity across social class lines.

Coloureds   One of South Africa's four officially recognized population groups, Coloureds are persons of mixed racial ancestry and constitute approximately 9 percent of South Africa's current population. Up until the 1990s, Coloureds in general occupied a higher social status than Blacks and at various times possessed political and economic rights and privileges not possessed by Blacks.

commandos   The more or less ad hoc, informally organized voluntary militia units that waged war against native tribes as well as British military units and still exist in some conservative pockets of white settlement in contemporary

South Africa. Present-day commando units are usually concerned with protecting white communities from hostile as well as nonhostile actions by and interactions with blacks; they are also used to secure independent whites-only homelands within the territorial confines of the Republic of South Africa.

Congress of South African Trade Unions (COSATU)   Formed in 1984 with a commitment to the use of nonviolent means to end Apartheid.

Conservative Party   Formed during the 1980s by House of Assembly member Andries Treurnicht after being expelled from the National Party for his virulent rejection of the concept of power sharing with Nonwhites.

Convention for a Democratic South Africa (CODESA)   Convened at the end of 1991 by the National Party to write a new constitution and to bring about an agreement on the structure of the government that would come into existence after the first all-race elections.

culture   A group's culture includes all the means by which that group adapts to its environment in order to meet its members' needs for food, shelter, intergroup communication, intergroup solidarity, protection from enemies, recreation, and other things necessary for survival.

cultural pluralism   A state of social being within which racial, ethnic, or cultural groups maintain their distinct identities and cultural patterns while, at the same time, being integrated within common, overriding economic, political, and legal structures.

dagga   Marijuana.

Day of the Vow   December 16, the day on which Boer fighters purportedly made a covenant with God in return for Him giving them victory over the Zulus in what would become known as the Battle of Blood River.

desegregation, racial   A social condition within which there exist no legal barriers to racial integration.

Dingaan's Day   December 16, 1938, the day a Boer military force, under the command of Andries Pretorius, invaded Zulu land and defeated the forces of the Zulu king Dingaan in the Battle of Blood River in revenge of Dingaan's massacre of a contingent of Voortrekkers who came to his camp in the expectation of formalizing a peace agreement.

Dutch East India Company   Most often referred to in this book as simply the Company. It was on its ships and in its employ that the first contingent of European settlers arrived in what is now the Republic of South Africa.

Dutch Reformed Church (DRC)   The church with which most Afrikaners are affiliated. Its three main branches are the *Nederduitse Gereformeerde Kerk* (NKG), the *Nederduitse Hervordme Kerk* (NHK), and the *Gereformeerde Kerk* (GK).

English Labour Party   Came into existence after the Anglo-Boer War advocating an all-white socialism and immediate self-government.

ethnic group   Used in this book to denote a group with a distinct self and social identity based on cultural characteristics, for example, Afrikaner, English, Indian, and so on.

First Freedom War   A series of battles in 1880–81 involving British regiments and Transvaal Boer commando units seeking to win complete freedom from British political oversight. In 1881, Britain withdrew its troops and gave the

Transvaal complete self-government subject to the suzerainty of the British queen. Transvaal political independence was to be relatively short lived, though.

franchise   The right to participate and vote in the South African political system.

Freedom Charter   The product of a 1955 interracial meeting of the Congress of the People, this document called for the abolition of all forms of Apartheid, universal suffrage, land redistribution, and the nationalization of South African private sector industries.

Freedom Day   May 1, 1950. The day of the first protest of Apartheid laws and policies jointly organized by black, Indian, Coloured, and communist-affiliated groups.

Government of National Unity (GNU)   Formed after the 1994 elections as a coalition government, with Nelson Mandela as president and Frederick de Klerk of the National Party as one of its two deputy presidents. One of its main objectives was to bring into being a new constitution heralding a new, more just political order.

Great Trek   The exodus of thousands of Afrikaners out of the Cape Colony to places northward. It was in response to, among other things, the British government's issuance of Ordinance 50 and the outlawing of slavery in British possessions.

hands-uppers   Boers who during the Anglo-Boer War laid down their arms in surrender to their British foes. Many of these hands-uppers were subsequently placed in what the British euphemistically called camps of refuge.

Het Volk   Means "the people." It was an Afrikaner political organization formed in the aftermath of the Anglo-Boer War (before the granting of representative government by the South Africa Act of Union) to bring bitter-enders, hands-uppers, and national scouts back together as a united political force.

Hottentot   A derogatory term for a Khoikhoi.

Huguenots   Calvinist Protestants who, before their arrival in the Cape Colony, had fled to the Netherlands to escape violent persecution in predominantly Catholic France. After their arrival in the Cape Colony they took on the cultural characteristics of the already-settled, predominantly Protestant Calvinist, Dutch-speaking population, and within a generation or two their descendants were culturally indistinguishable from other Dutch-speaking Afrikaners.

impi   A Zulu warrior unit.

impimpi   Black police informants of the Apartheid era.

integration, racial   Exists as the result of members of two or more previous separated or distinct racial groups merging into one indivisible group.

jack rolling   A type of gang rape in which a mob seals off a street or building and rapes every woman caught in the net.

Jameson raid   In January 1896, a force led by Dr. Leander Jameson and backed financially by Cecil B. Rhodes attempted to bring about an uprising of English-speaking miners in South Africa that would force the British government to send troops to their rescue and thereby bring about a declared Boer-Anglo war that would result in the South African Republic being annexed to the British Empire. Though the raid did not come off as planned, it did lead to Boer preparations for a war that resulted in the annexation of the Orange Free State and the South African Republic.

Kaffir A word of Arabic derivation that means "nonbeliever," but in South Africa, the term has long carried the same contemptuous connotation as *nigger*.

Khoikhoi A light-brown-complexioned pastoral people living on the Cape at the time of arrival of the first European settlers. Their descendants combined with other groups to constitute the Cape Coloureds.

knobkerrie A wooden stick with a heavy wooden head, used as a weapon; during the early 1990s, Zulu members of the IFP carried knobkerries to political rallies and meetings.

manumit To free from slavery.

mfecane The early nineteenth century period of rapacious Zulu conquest and assimilation of other black African tribal groups into the Zulu fold under the leadership of the dreaded Zulu king Shaka.

miscegenation Race-mixing; commonly used to denote interracial sex.

national scouts Afrikaners who, during the Anglo-Boer War, fought on the side of the British against their fellow Afrikaners.

National Party Formed at the outbreak of World War II when Prime Minister Hertzog quit the United Party over its decision to go to war against Germany. Hertzog together with D. F. Malan of the Purified National Party formed what was actually called the Reunited National Party. In 1984, the National Party became South Africa's ruling party and gave the world Apartheid.

necklacing The act of placing a gasoline-soaked rubber tire around a person's neck and setting fire to it.

Ordinance 50 Issued in 1828, giving "Hottentots and other free people of colour" the same legal rights as Whites.

Ossewa-Brandwag An Afrikaner nationalist group formed during the centennial celebrations of the Boer victory in the Battle of Blood River (1838). During World War II, the group came out in militant opposition to the South African government's decision to go to war against Germany.

Pan Africanist Congress (PAC) Formed in 1959 in rejection of multiracial cooperation, it labeled both Whites and Indians as "foreign minority groups" with no "natural" or "earned" place in South Africa. Later, however, it accepted Nonblacks into its membership.

population groups The Republic of South Africa gives official recognition to four racial groups: black, white, Coloured, and Asian. In official discussions and documents, these racial groups are often referred to as population groups.

Plaas Boers Settled, primarily wine, fruit, grain, and vegetable farmers of the seventeenth and eighteenth centuries.

predestination The belief that individuals are put on this earth for specific God-ordained purposes. Thus, all that is done by human beings is done in fulfillment of their God-given destiny. The concept is also extended to nations.

Progressives An English political group formed in the immediate aftermath of the Anglo-Boer War, before the granting of representative government. They were British, wished to remain British, and were in no hurry for representative government to come to the South African provinces.

Purified National Party   Formed in December 1933 by defectors from the South African Party, under the leadership of Broederbonder D. F. Malan. The Purified Nation Party became the most vehemently nationalist of the Afrikaner parties in the 1930s.

reference books   A euphemism for the pass books, giving name, tribal affiliation, and other life and work history, that Blacks were required to always have on their person during the years of Apartheid.

Responsibles   An English group formed in the immediate aftermath of the Anglo-Boer War, before the granting of representative government. Its members were primarily working class and, confident that Afrikaners could be trusted to accord them equal political rights, were for immediate self-government.

San   See *Bushmen.*

Second Freedom War   Called the Boer War by those sympathetic to the British aims; the Anglo-Boer War or the Boer-Anglo War by those wishing to be seen as taking a more neutral stance. It began with the Boer republics' fight to maintain their independence from Britain and ended with the signing of the Treaty of Vereeniging, bringing the Boer republics back under British control.

segregation, racial   The social, political, economic, or other separation of groups or individuals by race.

sharecropping   An agreement whereby a nonlandowner agrees to cultivate land in return for a share in the profits of the cultivated land with its owner.

Sharpeville massacre   Occurred on March 21, 1960, when police fired into a crowd of unarmed Africans marching through the township of Sharpeville, located near the Transvaal town of Vereeniging, in protest of the country's pass laws. The results were 69 Africans killed and hundreds wounded; massive protest demonstrations in townships all throughout the country; thousands of people of all races arrested; and the ANC and PAC declared illegal organizations.

shebeen   A small, illegally operated bar or beer joint located in a black township.

sjambok   A short whip made by either rubber or rawhide. Used by South African police during political demonstrations to quell or subdue protestors or others resisting their authority in the same way U.S. police might use what Americans would call a blackjack.

Slagters Nek Rebellion of 1815   A Boer revolt precipitated by British attempts to arrest a Boer (F. Bezuidenhout) for not living up to the terms of his employment contract with a Khoikhoi.

South Africa Act of Union   Passed in 1909 by the British Parliament, this act made the Transvaal, the Orange Free State, Natal, and the Cape Colony the four provinces of the Union of South Africa, a self-governing dominion.

South African Defense Force   The agency or department overseeing all of South Africa's military forces.

South African Native National Congress (SANNC)   Came into existence in 1912; renamed the African National Congress (ANC) in 1923. Its stated purpose was to bring South Africans of various clans, tribes, and races into one political organization in pursuit of the extension of full citizenship rights to all. Under the leadership of Nelson Mandela, it become the Republic of South Africa's ruling party in 1994.

South African Party The party that assumed power after the passage of the South Africa Act of Union granting self-government to the four South African provinces. Headed by Louis Botha, the SAP was overwhelmingly Afrikaner but had substantial English support.

South African National Party Formed in 1914 by a group of vehemently nationalistic Afrikaners who, under the leadership of J. B. M. Hertzog, quit the Botha-led South African Party. Their aims were the preservation of white supremacy and the Afrikaner language and culture and total independence from Great Britain.

Soweto massacre On June 16, 1976, police fired into a mass of African students marching through Soweto Township (Johannesburg) in protest of a government mandate that they learn Afrikaans. Many students were shot in the back while fleeing the charging police. The result was a nationwide mobilization of African students resulting in student boycotts and sometimes violent anti-Apartheid activities that lasted off and on through the 1980s.

steatopygic Possessed of unusually large buttocks.

Third Force Members of Apartheid police and government agencies who surreptitiously encouraged violence between ANC, PAC, and IFC activists; they themselves sometimes carried out assassinations of ANC and PAC activists as means of abetting the Zulu cause.

Torch Commando Formed by white World War II veterans, the group held and participated in peaceful, small-scale parades and demonstrations in opposition to Apartheid.

total onslaught President Botha's late 1980s response to increasing defiance of the authority of the Apartheid state, consisting of the unleashing of the full might of the country's police, intelligence, and military agencies against the enemies of Apartheid.

township A densely populated black ghetto located on the outskirts of whites-only towns and residential areas.

Treaty of Vereeniging Signed on May 31, 1902, it brought an end to the Boer War and returned the Orange Free State and South African Republic to British political dominion. It also left natives in the formerly independent republics still without economic and political rights.

trekboers Seminomadic, white farmers-herdsmen-hunters-traders of the seventeenth, eighteenth, and early nineteenth centuries who survived by supplying the Company and independent urban dwellers with meat, ostrich feathers, ivory, horns, fat, and other pastoral products.

Truth and Reconciliation Commission (TRC) Formed in 1996 to determine the content and extent of political crimes against Nonwhites by Apartheid state military personnel, civil servants, and other defenders of Apartheid. Persons determined to be guilty of such crimes, but who confessed to them, would not be prosecuted. Persons who did not confess to all of their crimes would be prosecuted.

Uitlanders "Outsiders," or non-Afrikaner residents of the nineteenth century Boer republics.

Umkhonto we Sizwe (MK) Means "Spear of the Nation." It was the military arm of the African National Congress. Its mission was to engage in the sabotage of government buildings and facilities.

United Defiance Campaign   Launched on April 6, 1952, the 300th anniversary of the arrival of the first contingent of white settlers at Table Bay in the Cape Province, the United Defiance Campaign consisted of nationwide strikes in protest of Apartheid. Among the results were scores of deaths and thousands of people arrested and incarcerated.

Unionist Party   The main opposition party during the 1910 election and the years immediately following the Act of Union granting self-government to the four South African provinces. Led by Dr. Leander Jameson, of the aborted Jameson raid, the Unionist Party was primarily English.

United Democratic Front (UDM)   An interracial organization formed in 1984 as the representative of 575 separate anti-Apartheid groups ranging from trade unions to social clubs, all committed to ending Apartheid through nonviolent means.

United South African National Party   Came into existence as a result of the merger of the South African Party and the South African National Party, both of which were afraid of losing strength as a result of the formation of the Purified National Party.

Vlakplaas   A special counterinsurgency unit formed by the Apartheid government to neutralize black political opposition. Its agents were revealed to have trained hit or assassination squads.

volk   Means "people." But it also carries a connotation of special or chosen people.

Voortrekkers   Means "pioneers." The thousands of Afrikaners whose flight during the 1830s from the Cape constituted the Great Trek in response to, among other things, the British government's issuance of Ordinance 50 and the outlawing of slavery on British-ruled territory.

Xhosa   Black African tribal peoples who, by the time of the arrival of the first European settlers, had long lived in communities of mixed farmers—settled agriculturists who also tended herds of cattle—in and around communities located north and east of the Khoikhoi and Bushmen areas. Though their ways of life were similar, different Xhosa tribes spoke a wide variety of Bantu languages.

Zulu Inkatha Freedom Party (IFP)   Formed during the early 1970s as the Zulu nationalist party. Based in present-day KwaZulu-Natal, it is headed by Zulu chief Māngosuthu Buthelezi.

REFERENCES

Akenson, Donald. *God's Peoples*. Ithaca, NY: Cornell University, 1992.

Behr, A. L. *New Perspectives in South African Education*. Durban: Butterworth, 1978. Cited in Christie 1985, p. 40.

Benson, Mary. *A Far Cry*. Pretoria: Raven Writers Series, 1996.

Bernes-Lasserre, Phillippe. "SA's Sporting Success Racial Bickering." *Daily Guardian and Mail*, May 28, 1999, wysiwyg://53/http://www.mg.co.za/mg/news/99may2/28may-sport_racism.html.

Blackwell, James E. *The Black Community: Diversity and Unity*. New York: Harper and Row, 1985.

Bridgraj, Ajith. "A Cop Who Really Cares." *The Teacher*, June 1999, wysiwyg://70/http://www.teacher.co.za/9906/cop.html.

Brink, André. *Reinventing a Continent*. Cambridge, Mass: Zoland Books, 1998.

Burns, Robert. "Cohen Visits South Africa, Is Cautious on Closer Military Ties." *San Diego Union Tribune*. February 10, 1999, p. A19.

Cape Argus. "Mob Lynches Burglar." June 13, 1999, www.inc.co.za./online/news2/south-africa/crime/housebreaker0906.html.

Christie, Pam. *The Right to Learn*. Johannesburg: Raven Press, 1989.

Cohen, Louis. *Reminiscences*. London: Bennett & Company, 1911. Summarized in Thomas 1996, pp. 96–98.

Collins, Huntley. "AZT Provides Glimmer of Hope in Africa's AIDS Epidemic." *San Diego Union Tribune*, May 28, 2000, p. A37.

Daily Mail and Guardian. "Mufamadi's Neighbors Beset by Crime." May 25, 1999, wysiwyg://10/http://www.mg.co.za/mg/za/news.html.

Daily Mail and Guardian. "100,000 Police, Soldiers, Deployed for Polls." May 31, 1999, wysiwyg://21http://www.mg.co.za/mg/za/news.html.

Daily Mail and Guardian. "Human Rights Abuses Continue in SA." June 16, 1999, wysiwyg://26/http://www.mg.co.za/mg/za/news.html.

Daily Mail and Guardian. "Killer Soldier." September 17, 1999. wysiwyg:// 26/ http://www.mg.co.za/mg/za/news.html.

Daily Mail and Guardian. "Election Results 1999." September 27, 1999, www.gov.za/elections/results99.html.

Daily Mail and Guardian. "HIV Wracks Eastern Cape." September 27, 1999, wysiwyg://37/http://www.mg.co.za/news.html.

Die Burger. "Manhunt Continues in Eastern Cape." September 1, 1998, www.naspers.co.za/dieburger/english/news1.html.

Dispatch Online. "SA's Democratic Maturity Praised." Osner Reports, June 6, 1999, www.dispatch.co.za./1999/06/03/southafrica/maturity.html.

DistrictMail & HelderPos. "Rape Alert." April 16, 1999, www.helderberg.com./
current1.html.

Economist Intelligence Unit. *County Report: South Africa.* London: *The Economist,*
1995, 1996.

Edwards, I. E. *The 1820 Settlers in Southern Africa.* London:, 1934. Cited in Welsh
1999, p. 128.

Eybers, G. W. *Select Constitutional Documents Illustrating South African History,
1795–1910.* London:, 1918. Quoted in Thompson 1995, p. 69.

Fenster, Pnina. "The Women of South Africa." *Marie Claire,* September 1999,
pp. 61–72.

Fetter, Bruce. "South Africa." In *World Book Encyclopedia.* Chicago: World Book,
Inc., 1992, pp. 608–21.

Fox, Debbie. "Drugs and Drink at the Heart of the Cape." *The Teacher,* June 1999,
wysiwyg://66/http://www.teacher.co.za/9906/drugs1.html.

Garrett, E. and E. J. Edwards. *The Story of an African Crisis.* London:, 1897. Quoted
in Thomas 1996, p. 301.

Garson, Philippa. "The Unaddressed Election Issues." *Daily Guardian and Mail,*
May 26, 1999, wysiwyg://12/http://www.mg.co.za/mg/news/99may2/
26may-elections.html.

Gay, Phillip T. "Out of the Darkness into the Rainbow?" In *Race, Ethnicity and
Gender: A Global Perspective,* eds. Samuel P. Oliner and Phillip T. Gay.
Dubuque, IA: Kendall/Hunt, 1997, pp. 225–52.

Gerzina, Gretchen. *Black London.* New Brunswick, NJ: Rutgers, 1995.

Goodman, David. "Cape Town's District Six Rises Again." In *Race and Ethnic Relations 98/99,* ed., John Kromkowski. Guilford CT: Dushkin/McGraw-Hill,
1998, pp. 73–76.

Goodman, David. *Fault Lines.* Berkeley: University of California, 1999.

Gossett, Thomas F. *Race: The History of an Idea in America.* New York: Oxford,
1997.

Haffajee, Ferial. "The Meteoric Rise of the Black Middle Class." *Daily Mail and
Guardian,* April 6, 1999, wysiwyg://35/http://www.mg.co.za/mg/news/
99aprl/6apr-buppies.html.

Hammond, John Hays. *The Transvaal Trouble.* London:, 1900. Quoted in Le May
1995, p. 97.

Hawthorne, Peter. "Victim of His Own Reforms." *Time,* September 8, 1997, p. 67.

——. "South Africa's Makeover." *Time,* July 12, 1999.

——. "An Epidemic of Rapes." *Time,* November 1, 1999, p. 59.

Heese, J. A. *Die herkoms van die Afrikaner, 1657–1867.* Cape Town: 1971. Cited in
Thompson 1995, p. 45.

Herschowitz, Ros; et al. *Victims of Crime Survey 1993–97.* Pretoria: Statistics South
Africa, 1998, www.statssa.gov.za/Victims-of-crime/prelim.html.

Horrell, M. *African Education: Some Origins and Development until 1953.* Johannesburg: South African Institute of Race Relations, 1963. Cited in Troup 1976,
p. 14.

———. *The Education of the Coloured Community in South Africa: 1652–1970.* Johannesburg: South African Institute of Race Relations, 1970.

Hussein, Solomon. "From Accommodation and Control to Control and Intervention." In *War and Peace in Southern Africa,* Washington, D.C.: Brookings Institute Press, 1998. eds. Rotberg et al. 1998, pp. 122–49.

Inciardi, James. *Criminal Justice.* New York: Harcourt Brace, 1999.

Johannesburg Star. "PAC Plan Military Burial for Killer," Sept. 22, 1999. www.io/co.za./news/newsview.

———. *Johannesburg Star.* "U.S. Business Leaders Impressed with SA." September 22, 1999.

Joubert, Dorothy. "The Sad Story of a Struggling School." *The Mirror,* May 30, 1999, www.emirror.co.za/news/communz.html#daba.

Koch, E. "Without Visible Means of Subsistence: Slumyard Culture in Johannesburg 1918–1940." In *Town and Countryside in the Transvaal: Capitalist Penetration and Popular Response,* ed. B. Bozzoli. Johannesburg: Ravan, 1983. Quoted in Worden 1995, p. 43.

Krog, Antjie. *Country of My Skull.* New York: Random House, 1998.

Le May, G. H. L. *The Afrikaners.* Cambridge: Blackwell, 1995.

Los Angeles Times. "Mandela Offers Words of Hope in Last Address." February 6, 1999, p. A4.

Louw-Potgeiter, Joha. *Afrikaner Dissidents: A Social Psychological Study of Identity and Dissent.* Philadelphia: Multilingual Matters Ltd., 1988.

Lubisi, Dumisane. "Failed Mpuma Matrics to Rewrite Exams." *Daily Mail and Guardian,* June 1, 1999, wysiwyg://21/http://www.mg.co.za/ mg/za/ news.html.

MacCrone, I. D. *Race Attitudes in South Africa.* Oxford:, 1937. Quoted in Le May 1995, pp. 16–17.

Macgregor, David. "Dirty Cops Help Themselves in Fake Burglaries." *Saturday Argus,* June 13, 1999, www.inc.co.za/online/news2/south-africa/crime/dirtycop1206.html.

Malherbe, E. G. *Education in South Africa,* Vol. 2. Cape Town: 1977, Vol. 2 (2 vols), p. 101.

Mandela, Nelson. *The Long Walk to Freedom.* Boston: Little, Brown, 1995.

Marais, J. S. *The Cape Coloured People.* London:, 1939. Quoted in Le May 1995, p. 36.

Mathabane, Mark. *Kaffir Boy.* New York: New American Library, 1986.

Maykuth, Andrew. "South Africa Labor Reaps Bitter Harvest From Democracy." *San Diego Union Tribune,* July 11: 1999, p. A25.

———. "Rampant Assaults Spur South Firm to Offer Rape Insurance." *San Diego Union Tribune,* October 10, 1999, p. A21.

McGreal, Chris. "SA Faces Spectre of a Million AIDS Orphans." *Daily Mail and Guardian,* August 1999, wysiwyg://25/http://www.mg.co.za/mg/news/99aug1/3aug-aids.html.

————. "Race Tension Leads to Funeral Dispute." *San Diego Union Tribune*, September 22, 1999, p. A15.

————. "Virgin Tests Make a Comeback." *Daily Mail and Guardian*, September 29, 1999, wysiwyg://23/http://www.mg.co.za./mg/news/99sep2/ 29sep-aids_virgin.html.

McNeil, Donald G., Jr., "Botha Cleared of Contempt on Technicality." June 2, 1999, p. A2.

Macgregor, David. "Dirty Cops Help Themselves in Fake Burglaries, *Saturday Argus*, June 13, 1999, www.inc.co.za/online/news2/south-africa/crime/dirtycop1206.html.

Minnaar, Anthony. "One Policeman Killed a Day." *Daily Guardian and Mail*, May 26, 1999, wysiwyg://20/http://www.mg.co.za/mg/news/99may26may-police3.html.

Mncwabe, Mandla. *Post-Apartheid Education*. Lanham: University Press of America, 1993.

Murphy, Dean. "Former President's Book Revisits Apartheid Years." *Los Angeles Times*, February 6, 1999, p. A2.

Natal Witness. "Women's Group Opposes Virginity Tests." June 14, 1999, wysiwyg://main.28/http://www.witness.co.za/story19990614009.html.

Nicol, Mike. *The Waiting Country*. London: Gollancz, 1995.

O'Connor, Sean. "A World Full of Difficult Choices." *The Teacher*, June 1999, wysiwyg://68/http://www.teacher.co.za/9906/drugs.html.

Office of the President. "Speech by President Nelson Mandela at the Final Sitting of the First Democratically Elected President." 1999, www.polity.org.za/govdocs/speeches/1999/sp0326a.html.

O'Meara, W. A. J. *Kekewich in Kimberly*. London: Medici Society, 1926. Quoted in Thomas 1996, p. 340.

Pakenham, Thomas. *The Boer War*. New York: Avon Books, 1979.

Patterson, Sheila. *The Last Trek*. Westport, CT: Greenwood Press, 1981.

Payton, Charles A. *The Diamond Diggings of South Africa*. London:, 1872. Quoted in Thomas 1996, p. 84.

Pearce, Justin. "Education: A Promise Hard to Keep." BBC Online Network, May 26, 1999, news.bbc.co.uk'hi/english'special-r-elections/newsid-352000/352189.stm.

Pearson, Bryan. "Mbeki Has Confidence of Business Community: Economists." *Daily Mail and Guardian*, May 26, 1999, wysiwyg:://23/http://www.mg.co.za/mg/news/99may2/26may-biz-confidence.html.

Perkins, Olivera. "Apartheid Has Ended, But . . ." December 14, 1997, p. G5.

Reid, Sue Titus. *Crime and Criminology*. New York: McGraw-Hill, 2000.

Roberts, Bronwen. "ANC Rule Leaves White South Africans Pessimistic." *Daily Mail and Guardian*, May 28, 1999, wysiwyg://55/http://www.mg.co.za/mg/news/99may2/28may-election_whites.html.

Rose, Brian, ed. *Department of Bantu Education Annual Report*. 1971. Cited in Troup 1976, p. 11.

Rose, B. and Tunmer, R. *Documents in South African History.* Johannesburg: Ad. Dunker, 1975. Adapted in Christie 1985, p. 37.

Ross, R. *Cape of Torments: Slavery and Resistance in South Africa.* London:, 1983. Cited in Thompson 1995, p. 58.

San Diego Union Tribune. "Tutu Reportedly Reportedly Target of Threat." June 3, 1996, p. A17.

———. "In Final Sermon, Tutu Warns South Africa of Corruption." July 4, 1996. p. A7.

———. "High Level Official Is Forced from ANC for Embarrassing Mandela." September 2, 1996.

———. "Mandela Lashes Out at Critics in Farewell." December 17, 1997, p. A2.

———. " 'Blooming' Mandela admits His Love Life Causing Trouble." February 9, 1998.

———. "South Africa's Army Chief Quits over False Report." April 7, 1998.

———. "Trial of Apartheid Leader Botha Proceeds after Talks Break Down." April 16, 1998, p. A14.

———. "South African Rights Panel Will Study Press Racism." November 17, 1998, p. A11.

———. "Official of South Africa Party Slain." January 24, 1999.

———. "Slaying of ANC Foe Alarms South Africa." January 25, 1999, p. A8.

———. "Resignation Deals Blow to South African Election Preparations." January 27, 1999, p. A13.

———. "Ex-Cops Denied Amnesty in Biko Deaths." February 17, 1999.

———. "Ex-ANC Leader Guilty of Stealing Aid Funds in South Africa." March 18, 1999, p. A21.

———. "Anti-Apartheid Hero Boesak Sentenced to Prison for Theft." March 25, 1999, p. A14.

———. "South African Leader's AIDS Stance Causing Alarm." May 21, 2000, p. A32.

———. "Huge Arms Cache Found in South Africa." May 22, 1999, p. A12.

———. "Mandela Asks Whites to Back ANC Candidates." June 1, 1999.

———. "South African Miners Protest Gold Sales." July 18, 1999, p. A20.

———. "African Black Runs Key Bank: Reserve Governor Puts Stability First." August 8, 1999.

———. "Blair Signs Deal with South Africa." August 8, 1999, p. A21.

———. "South African Miners March for Pay Boost." August 18, 1999, p. A29.

———. "South Africa to Trim Military Ranks." November 13, 1999.

———. "Woman Beaten to Death by South African Neighbors for Admitting HIV." December 28, 1999, p. A10.

———. "L.A. Scandals May Make for Media Fodder." June 20, 2000, p. A1.

———. "South African Leader Alters AIDS Stance." October 17, 2000, p. A10.

Segar, Susan. "AIDS Means Children Will Head Homes." *Natal Witness,* September 22, 1999, wysiwyg://17/http://www.witness.co.za/wit_aids990923.html.

Shapshak, David. "Mallet: Misunderstood in Race Selection Row." *Daily Mail and Guardian,* June 24, 1999, wysiwyg://12/http://www.mg.co.za/mg/za/sports.html.

Siebane, Alpheus. "Pupils Share Toilets with Beer Hall Drunkard." *The Mirror,* May 30, 1999, www.emirror.co.za/news/communz.html#daba.

Smith, Charlene. "Rape Victims Are Not Statistics. . . . We Are People." *Weekly Guardian and Mail,* April 9, 1999, wysiwyg://24/http://www.sn.apc.org/wmail/issues/990409/NEWS27.html.

Soggot, Mungo, and Evidence Wa Ka Ngobeni. "We Must Work on Their Buttocks." *Daily Mail and Guardian,* May 14, 1999, wysiwyg://57/http://www.mg.co.za/mg/news/99may1/14may-vigilante.html.

———. *Weekly Mail and Guardian,* Feb. 13, 1990

———. *Daily Mail and Guardian,* June 16, 1999

Soudien, Crain. " 'We Know Why We're Here': The Experience of African Children in a 'Coloured' School in Cape Town, South Africa." *Race, Ethnicity and Education* 1, no. 1 (March 1998), pp. 7–31.

South African Department of Education. *South Africa: An Overview.* 1998, www.gov.za/yearbook/education.html.

South African Police Service. *The Monthly Bulletin on Reported Crime in South Africa.* January 1999, www.saps.co.za/8_crimeinfo/bulletin/1999(1).html.

Sparks, Allister. *Tommorrow Is Another Country.* New York: Hill and Wang, 1995.

Statistics South Africa. 1997, www.statssa.gov.za/SABrief/table5.htm.

———. 1997, www.statssa.gov.za/SABrief/table6.htm.

———. "Geography and Climate."www.statssa.gov.za/ASBrief/table1.htm.

———. "South Africa."members.tripod.com/311/ten.htm.

Straker, Gill. *Faces in the Revolution: The Psychological Effects of Violence on Township Youth in South Africa.* Athens, OH: Ohio University Press, 1992.

Theodorson, George A., and Achilles G. Theodorson. *A Modern Dictionary of Sociology.* New York: Crowell, 1969.

Thomas, Anthony. *Rhodes.* New York: St. Martin's Press, 1996.

Thomasson, Emma. "South African Sports Bodies Address 'Lily White' Criticisms." *Daily Mail and Guardian,* April 5, 1999, wysiwyg://62h/http://www.mg.co.za/mg/news/99apr1/5apr-sport_race.html.

Thompson, Leonard. *A History of South Africa.* New Haven: Yale University Press, 1995.

Troup, Freda. *Forbidden Pastures.* London: International Defence & Aid Fund, 1976.

Vine, Jeremy. "The Rainbow Nation Takes Stock." May 26, 1999, news.bb.co.uk/hi/english/special_r. . ._africa_elections/newsid_349000/349722.stm.

Wakin, Daniel J. "Mandela Era Ends with Peaceful Vote." *San Diego Union Tribune,* June, 3, 1999, p. A15.

Waldmeir, Patty. *Anatomy of a Miracle.* New Brunswick, NJ: Rutgers University Press 1998.

Walker, James. "South Africa's Economy: Much to Be Done." BBC Online Network, May 26, 1999, news.bbc.co.uk/hi/english/special_r-elections/newsid_352000/352596.stm.

Weekly Mail and Guardian. "Child-Sex Industry Booms in South Africa." July 19, 1996, wysiwyg://39/http://web.sn.apc.org/wmail/issues/960719/NEWS41.html.

———. "Cause for National Shame." March 19, 1999, wysiwyg://29/http://www.sn.apc.org/wmail/issues/990319/NEWS58.html.

Welsh, Frank. *South Africa: A Narrative History.* New York: Kodansha International, 1999.

Wheatcroft, Geoffrey. *The Randlords.* London: Weidenfeld and Nicolson, 1985. Quoted in Thomas 1996, p. 83.

Williams, Tag. "Vigilantes Spread across the Country." *Electron Mail and Guardian,* March 1997, www.mg.co.za./mg/news/97mar1/11mar-vigilante.html.

Wilson, Francis and Ramphele Mamphela. "Children in South Africa." *In Children on the Front Line,* New York, United Nations, 1987.

Wilson, M., and L. Thompson. *The Oxford History of South Africa.* Vol. 11. Oxford: Oxford University Press, 1971. Cited in Troup 1976, pp. 1, 6, 11, and 34.

Worden, Nigel. *The Making of Modern South Africa.* Cambridge: Blackwell, 1995.

Younge, Gary. "Ducking as the Pawpaw Hits the Fan." *Daily Mail and Guardian,* May 31, 1999, wysiwyg://53http://www.mg.co.za./mg/news/ 99may2/3may-emigration.html.

INDEX

DATE DUE

Demco, inc. 38-293